The Rainbow Book

A Collection of Facebook Devotionals

John H. Voss

Parson's Porch Books

The Rainbow Book
ISBN: Softcover 978-1-955581-91-2
Copyright © 2022 by John H. Voss

Parson's Porch Books is an imprint of Parson's Porch *&* Company (PP*&*C) in Cleveland, Tennessee. PP*&*C is a self-funded charity which earns money by publishing books of noted authors, representing all genres. Its face and voice is **David Russell Tullock** (dtullock@parsonsporch.com).

Parson's Porch *&* Company *turns books into bread & milk* by sharing its profits with the poor.

www.parsonsporch.com

The Rainbow Book

Contents

6

Preface

For the past few years, I have been writing weekly devotionals and posting them on Facebook. Usually, they are based on a Bible passage, but many focus on an event or observation that I've noticed and I use as the basis for comment. This book is a compilation of many of the devotionals. Each is rather brief and provides space at the conclusion for your own notes and thoughts.

My desire is that the book would be used as a daily devotional providing spiritual insight and encouragement. Each devotional is brief, yet spiritually substantive. I am thankful for the encouragement of those who have read the devotionals and commented on them, and I am also thankful for the editing skills of Jeffery McClendon, who helped compile these in meaningful order. I am also grateful for Tony and Casey Schwingle taking the beautiful rainbow photograph that became the book's cover picture.

Often in the hectic pace of life, a brief reminder of God's love is what we need most. I hope The Rainbow Book is both a blessing to you and a reminder of how much God loves you.

The Rainbow

I was asked several times why I sold the home and farm where I had lived for many years, and the best answer I could give was, "It was the rainbow picture." Over the years, there have been several occasions when I felt deeply motivated spiritually to take certain actions, and this was one of them.

My grandfather moved here in 1932, and this house has been the focal point of my family's presence in this community for nearly a century. Following a thunderstorm one summer afternoon, this beautiful rainbow appeared to perfectly surround the old house. When I first saw the picture, I knew that it was my turn to live here.

Years ago, I became intrigued by the spiritual meaning of a rainbow. Its origin is described in the Bible when God set His "rainbow in the cloud" to assure faithful Noah that never again would the world be destroyed by a flood. But a rainbow is more than just a beautiful phenomenon of nature, and it surely doesn't lead one to a pot of gold.

Every rainbow is a divine reminder that faith overcomes floods; that on the other side of every dark cloud is beautiful sunshine; and that God's promise of protection is greater than any peril we face. As long as there is a rainbow of divine assurance, we are not going to be drowned by the circumstances of life.

My family has had its ups and downs, as I am sure yours has, and each of us has also had our private moments of physical and spiritual struggle. But, when I look at the picture of the rainbow over our old home, I realize anew how God has blessed me and my family, just as He has yours. Sure, there have been many days when each of us had no idea when the flood of fear, fatigue, and frustration would subside, but God knew all along where our ark would safely land, and He gave us His rainbow to remind us of just how totally His love envelops us.

But a rainbow is physical, and it is only a symbol. The greatest reminder of God's love is Jesus and His love for all people of every race, creed, and color. The redeemed of Christ make up His radiant church that glorifies His love to the world, just like that first rainbow did.

Next time you see a rainbow, don't think of a pot of gold. Instead, think of yourself and question whether you are part of His radiant promise of redeeming love for all people and a glorious part of His divine promise that, through faith in Christ, we have no reason to fear the future.

The Old Rose Bush

Alone and neglected, the rose bush stood in the side of the yard by the pasture fence, still struggling to live in the soil where it was planted many years ago. No one knew much about it, because it bloomed so little and so infrequently that it was hard to know its true color. Honestly, it was difficult to tell if it was even a rose bush, and I came very close to digging it up and throwing it away.

But, for some strange reason, I began to identify personally with the old rose and see my own life captured in its tangled branches, along with the lives of many others, and it became a living picture of what so many people face in life. It was not from lack of effort that the rose did not bloom with all the youth and vigor of its bygone days. It was still where it had always been, but life had somehow moved on. All of the beauty and vitality of life and the lovely landscape that had once defined its purpose and meaning had moved to the other side of the yard and left it alone and virtually abandoned.

The old rose was not the eye catcher it used to be. Its youth and beauty had been drained away by the unrelenting demands of living and trying to bring joy and happiness to others. Now, the rose was faded, frail, and facing its final days, or so it seemed. And so, it stood there, doing its best to still bloom, but knowing that all eyes now focused on the beauty of life elsewhere. All of us who have more years behind us than in front of us know that feeling.

But the closer I looked, the more I realized the similarity of our existence. The old rose had branches that were useless and had not borne a rose in years. There were significant parts of its life that were a burden, a hindrance, and lifeless dead weight. I could identify with that. With a bad heart, vision in only one eye, increasing hearing loss, and body parts that frequently do not want to all go in the same direction at the same time, I may think that I can still crow like a young rooster, but the truth is, the bright red comb on the top of my rooster head flopped over long ago. Like the old rose, the vitality of life has moved and left me where I was planted.

But, when I pondered its struggle for life, I discovered something very revealing about the rose. It was still bound up in a wire support—like a tomato cage—that had been there since it was planted. Here it was, trying its best to bloom, and yet still struggling against binding shackles that had been there for years. Yep, that is me, and it

14

may be you, too. Things that happened over sixty years ago still haunt me today, and I know those memories will be there until I die. Call it post-traumatic stress from a terribly unhappy childhood that left me filled with insecurity and feelings of inferiority, a fear of rejection, and a lack of comfort in close personal relationships—just an old bush out by the side of the yard still bound up after all these years.

And so, I removed the steel cage imprisoning the rose and cut away the dead, unproductive branches. I placed new flower beds nearby, and once again the old rose was surrounded by the beauty and vitality of life. Guess what happened?

After all those years of just existing and trying to survive tangled up in forces that bound it, strangled it, and were an unceasing burden, it found a new life. Just like Jesus said He would do with our lives when the lifeless, fruitless, and useless branches were pruned away and the shackles of the past were removed, the old rose bush fully bloomed out with the most radiant red flowers one could desire. The transformation was both shocking and inspiring.

Be honest with yourself. All of us have days when we feel alone, neglected, and overwhelmed with burdens. Life has moved on, family and friends do not call or visit very often, and the beauty and exuberance of youth and good health have moved. We sit alone in the porch rocker and wonder if this is all that's left.

It can be, unless want to be like the old rose bush and get rid of useless burdens and baggage in your life that hold you back and make you miserable. It is not too late to break free from the shackles of insecurity and uncertainty that have long bound you. With firm resolve, cast aside that which limits you, and for the first time in years—BLOOM—and release the radiant, Christian spirit within you! With Jesus' help, you will be amazed at how beautiful your life can still be—just like the old rose bush.

A Father's Amazing Love

The parable of the prodigal son is deeply challenging, even radical for its day. Its greatest meaning is not about a rebellious young man, but rather about a total transformation in the social and religious concept of "father."

Israel was a patriarchal society, and a man retained control and influence over each successive generation of his descendants for the duration of his life. The religious law gave a father virtual life and death control over his children, and a defiant, rebellious son could be stoned to death, apparently with the belief that God would be pleased by such a harsh, cold-blooded act.

Further, no provision of the law or the traditions of the elders of Israel allowed anyone to refer to God as father, and, in fact, that was one of the acts of blasphemy leveled against Jesus by His accusers, or as one of them snorted, "at least we know who our father is."

Jesus taught His followers a radical new concept. He began the Lord's Prayer with two words that transform our relationship with God: "Our Father." In the Sermon on the Mount, He referred to God as "your heavenly Father," or a similar phrase, at least sixteen times. Jesus' desire was to transform our concept of father from an earthly individual to a greater belief in a heavenly father from whom all blessings flow.

The prodigal son learned an entirely new understanding about the role of a loving and merciful father. Just as it changed his life, it will change your life, too.

II

Deuteronomy 21: 8-21 required the father of a stubborn and rebellious son to stone his child to death. Although it is uncertain how often this was done, it nevertheless was the religious law of Israel and could be carried out without punishment for the father. When the prodigal son impudently demanded his inheritance share, he was taking his life into his own hands, knowing his father could kill him at any time.

This austere, cold, legalistic view of a father's power and authority influenced how people viewed the power and authority of God, and it certainly shaped my life. But Jesus changed that through this amazing parable. The best way I can explain the impact of the parable of the prodigal son on my life is by sharing not only a portion of my spiritual journey with you, but also my ultimate discovery of my Father's amazing love.

The first nine years of my life were fearfully lived under the domination of a father who, for the slightest reason, would beat me with a hedge limb on my legs, back, and my little rear until I could hardly stand. He left me screaming in pain, and he usually did this outside so that, as he said, the neighbors could see him correcting his children in a godly manner. His brutality emotionally scarred me for life.

Also, I was raised in a strict Southern Baptist environment where God was viewed in the same way that I viewed my father. If I sinned, God's punishment and vengeance would be severe. I cannot count the times that, in reference to someone's sinful deed, I heard the statement, "God Almighty ought to strike them dead for that."

I grew up being completely afraid of God, just as I had been afraid of my father. In my young mind, there was no difference in their power over me. If I strayed, I just fearfully assumed God would beat me down as my father had done many times.

One of the greatest spiritual changes that I made as a maturing Christian was learning to view God in the way that Jesus described the mercy and love of the prodigal son's father. I had no personal concept of a loving father who reached out to me with mercy and compassion. In all honesty, I was afraid to believe that was true about God. For a long time, I was afraid to come to my heavenly Father out of fear He would yet strike me down, just as I was taught as a little boy.

How Jesus described the amazing love of the father toward his prodigal son in this parable profoundly changed me, and it still brings me to tears often. I simply never knew such love from my father, and for a long time, I doubted such love was possible from my heavenly Father. I was a miserable, struggling young Christian, engaged in daily warfare with emotional forces beyond my control, who expected God to punish me at any moment for just being me.

But, when I climbed out of my pig pen of fear, and I went home to my heavenly Father's open arms, everything changed. For the first time in my life, I experienced a father's amazing love and mercy.

17

Many of you struggle with wanting a deeper understanding of the love of your Father in heaven. Many of you grew up in the same conservative religious environment I did, and I suspect that many of you are more afraid of God than you have love for Him. It is my prayer that this devotional will help you more fully experience your Father's amazing love.

III

Through the power of verbal imagery, let's journey to a place you've probably not been to before, but until you go there, you will not truly appreciate the power and divine holiness of the parable of the prodigal son. The parable's narrative covers a broad period of time, but its life-transforming spiritual impact covers a time span of less than five minutes. It occurs along a dusty road outside an unnamed city and involves only two people, a father and his long-lost son. Quietly and reverently go there with me in your mind so that you can personally experience what happened.

The young man is walking slowly and hesitatingly, his head bowed and his shoulders stooped, as if he is physically forcing his hot, dusty feet to take each step. He is walking toward his father's house, and it is a journey he does not want to make—a journey he never intended to make in the earlier days of his rebellious youth when he seemed so certain about the defiant course he had chosen in life.

But his circumstances had radically changed for the worse, and he found himself emotionally consumed by nightmarish despair he never envisioned. He had wasted the inheritance demanded from his father, he had abandoned his native land and moved to a foreign country, and he became so desperate and hungry that he ate the food of unclean swine. He had destroyed his relationship with his father, his country, and his God.

Now he was a broken young man slowly walking toward the fatal fate that awaited him. He knew that his father had the legal right and authority to stone him to death, and that's what he expected. But he had reached such a low point of despair that he had rather die than continue living with the shame of his actions. He just wanted it to be over.

So, as he slowly trudged along this dusty road toward the fate of death by stoning at the hands of his father, his weary eyes saw something that stopped him cold in his tracks, frozen with fear. He saw the figure of a man walking rapidly toward him. It was his father, and the moment he had so deeply dreaded was near...only moments away.

His father then started running toward him. The young man was tempted to run in the opposite direction and forever avoid this fatherly encounter. He thought about fighting his father in continued defiance and prolonging his life as much as possible. Every human emotion of fear and apprehension gripped his body and immobilized him on the side of that dusty road.

Now his father was running toward him almost breathlessly, and he couldn't imagine why. Was he filled with that much anger and rage? Then, as his father got closer, the young man saw something he could not believe: His father was weeping and joyously shouting praises of thanksgiving. A broad smile of indescribable joy covered his face rather than a scowl of bitterness.

He ran to his son, threw his arms around him, and repeatedly kissed and hugged him. "I've never stopped hoping you would come home, and I looked for you every day, not knowing if you were dead or alive. I saw you when you were a long way off, and I started toward you as fast as I could to meet you and welcome you home." Suddenly that lifeless, dusty roadside erupted in shouts of joy, love, and reconciliation.

In that moment, through the power of this parable, Jesus told us that a father's power no longer focuses on a legal right to punish, but rather on his loving desire to redeem and restore what was lost through sinful defiance and rebellion. The writer of First John does not say that "God is law"; rather, he states that "God is love."

I have no way of knowing what condition your life is in, but if you find yourself wallowing in a pig pen of disillusionment and despair because of mistakes you have made and the painful consequences of poor choices, do not be afraid to go home to your loving heavenly Father. Right now, get up, stop being afraid of God, and go home to Him. His love and His grace are greater than all your sins! You, too, can experience your Father's amazing love.

IV

When the prodigal son returned home, his father joyously had a ring placed on his son's finger, his robe draped around the young man's shoulders, and sandals placed on his feet. In terms of size, the ring was the least significant, but it represented an unmerited gift of grace larger than the younger son could have imagined.

As a symbol of the father's unrestrained joy and unconditional love, the ring was surely the father's signet ring. Ordinarily, a signet ring contained a small personal seal engraved with one's initials or other identifying mark. It could be pressed into a drop of hot wax on a legal document to validate a personal transaction.

The prodigal had already demanded and wasted his share of his father's estate. Now, because of the consequences of his sin, he was willing to become just a slave for his father in order to survive. He had destroyed all rights of inheritance, and he was entitled to nothing more. Sadly, he no longer saw himself as his father's son.

The law gave the older son a double portion of the father's inheritance, and he took control of the father's estate. But the ring radically changed that. The father's mercy and grace compelled him to place his signet ring on the younger son's finger, which not only granted him authority to act for his father, but it in effect transferred control of all that the father had to this returning sinful child.

Through the ring, this forgiven sinner, once worthy of death, was graciously given power to both act and speak on behalf of his father, and he became his father's representative and ambassador. The entirety of the father's estate was given to this redeemed sinful son, including the portion deemed by law to be the older son's inheritance. Love, mercy, and grace took priority over the constraints of law.

In the parable, the ring changed the entire concept of inheritance so that the one who was least entitled to inherit his father's estate and kingdom would receive all of it. Why? Because the prodigal son truly understood his father's mercy and grace. Thus, Jesus said, "Blessed are the poor in spirit, for theirs is the kingdom of heaven."

Don't forget to spiritually place your Father's signet ring on your finger today. It does not matter what the world throws at you. When you are down and struggling with the burdens of life, just think of the ring: You are a joint heir with Jesus to the entirety of your Father's heavenly kingdom. Oh, the amazing blessings of grace!

Our Heavenly Father

Jesus taught His followers a radical new concept. He began the Lord's Prayer with two words that will transform our relationship with God and with each other if we will truly believe this truth—"Our Father." In the Sermon on the Mount, Jesus referred to God as "your heavenly Father," or a similar phrase, at least sixteen times. His desire was to transform our concept of father from an earthly individual to a greater belief in a heavenly Father from whom all blessings flow.

Israel was a patriarchal society, and a man retained control and influence over each successive generation of his descendants for the duration of his life. The religious law gave a father virtual life and death control over his children, and a defiant, rebellious son could be stoned to death, apparently with the belief that God would be pleased by such a harsh, cold-blooded act.

Further, no provision of the law or the traditions of the elders of Israel allowed anyone to refer to God as father, and, in fact, that was one of the acts of blasphemy levelled against Jesus by His accusers, or as one of them snorted, "at least we know who our father is."

"Our Heavenly Father" introduced a radical and spiritually transforming concept—the fatherhood of God and the brotherhood of believers. God was not some austere judge holding a code of cold, merciless law over our head, but rather a merciful, loving Father who would lovingly forgive our sins and grant us the blessings of His heavenly kingdom. Life was transformed from bearing the burdens of an earthly life to rejoicing in the blessings of an eternal life that began here on earth by faith in Christ.

"Our Heavenly Father" transformed the callus exclusion of those not covered by the ancient covenant of law to the inclusion of all who would believe in Jesus, not just in Israel, but anywhere in the world. People of every known race, creed, and color could become an adopted child of God through faith. That was inconceivable under the ancient law of Israel. The "family of God" became world-wide and not limited to one middle-east nation. God's redeeming love extended to every man, woman, boy, and girl on earth without partiality.

If we dare to pray "Our Heavenly Father" on this Father's Day, then we must be willing to experience the radical spiritual and emotional transformation these words demand. Life moves from an earthly to a heavenly realm; our values change; our political and social views change; all other Christians anywhere in the world become our brothers and sisters; we love and include people of every color and character into our bond of love; and we love our brothers and sisters as Christ first loved us. Our attitude and opinions on human rights change; prejudice and racism disappear; our commitment to supporting and caring for one another is heightened; and our understanding of and compassion for the human struggles of others who are different from us becomes deeper and more meaningful. Condemnation is removed from our vocabulary and from our heart.

"Our Heavenly Father" can empower and establish Christianity as the single greatest force transforming America and the world for good—if we are truly willing to pray, "Our Heavenly Father." But if we could be so bold as to truly pray these words, wouldn't that make today our Father's Day!

The Wisdom of Aging

I

I'm attending the celebration of a long life this afternoon. It is my Aunt Irene Thompson's 100th birthday, and family and friends are gathering to celebrate the life of this Christian servant, who is the only member of my family to attain this longevity milestone. The idea of living one hundred years intrigues me, and it is something I personally want to do. I think it would be fascinating to measure God's blessings over a century of life.

In many ways, Aunt Irene's life and mine find commonality in this old house. She and the family moved here in 1932 when the house was only seven years old, and Aunt Irene was about eleven years old. The house was relatively new, large, impressive, and had all the amenities common for that time in a fine country home—no indoor plumbing, no bathroom, no cooling, no electricity, heated by several fireplaces, no running water in the kitchen, water pulled up by a well-bucket from a backyard well, food cooked on a wood burning stove, and clothes for a family of nine hand-washed on a scrub board with water heated in a black wash pot over an open fire.

But it was a beautiful home nearly a hundred years ago, with pine boards on the floor, walls, and ceiling. Aunt Irene and two sisters had an upstairs room all to themselves—in summer attic heat under a tin roof with one window for ventilation. But they thought it was the grandest place they had ever lived.

Today, it is renovated and transformed—nothing at all like it was when Aunt Irene moved in. And we complain about inconveniences. Shame on us: We ought to thank God every day for the blessings of comfort and ease.

If I should be blessed to live for a century, I wonder what I will see and experience in 2048? So much change is occurring. It's impossible for my old brain to take it all in. I'm still trying to figure out how a color television works.

But change is inevitable, and all we can do is buy a ticket and take a ride into tomorrow. The plodding mule pulling the creaking old wagon in which Aunt Irene slowly rode up to this house has now morphed into a jet hurling me down the express lane of life with constantly increasing rapidity, or so it seems.

"Tempus Fugit," time flies, becomes more real every day. Maybe that's why I find more beauty these days in sunsets rather than sunrises. The lyrics to September Song ring increasingly and hauntingly true: "Oh, it's a long, long while from May until December, but the days grow short when you reach September....Oh the days dwindle down to a precious few, September, November...and these few precious days I'll spend with you."

I simply want to spend the rest of my precious days writing and telling you about Jesus and His love for you. And I plan to spend these last days and years in this same old house where Aunt Irene began her life of service a century ago. And when I do move for the last time, it will be to my eternal home in heaven and, as the old hymn says, to "a land where I'll never grow old."

I want to share some thoughts with you about the blessings and wisdom of aging. So, find your reading glasses (if you can remember where you put them), get in your favorite rocker with a cup of hot chocolate, and gratefully reflect on the blessings of age.

II

The old hymn well captured the midnight moment broadcast by a stately grandfather clock: "The chimes of time ring out the news...another day is done." I have an old chiming clock, too, and often at the midnight hour, when restful sleep scampers all around me like a playful puppy that won't settle down, I hear it melodiously reminding me of the same sobering truth...another day is gone. In the middle of the dark night, today became yesterday, and I took one more step down the driveway of destiny.

But at this pivotal point in my life, that point where the road forks between what was and what will be, age has strangely become a friend and not a foe. Age, not age defined by the chronology of time, but age defined as the treasury of life, has rather quietly walked up beside me, placed a steadying hand on my shoulder, and softly said, "I'll walk with you the rest of the way."

Like a much-needed consoling companion, age is always recalling and reminiscing with me about the exuberant days of youth, the bygone dreams of decades ago that have slowly turned into the memories of yesterday, and the fleeting faces of friends that suddenly and vividly appear and then just as quickly fade into the fog of memory.

The more I have pondered age and the inescapable limitations of time, the more I am reminded of how the Bible uses age to give us enormous spiritual comfort, as if it were a heavenly balm of reassurance prescribed to bring peace and quiet to an old soul rocked by the uncertainty of modern-day life.

The ancient scriptures even describe the aging process. Ecclesiastes, a masterpiece of biblical wisdom literature, states:

> "Remember now your Creator in the days of your youth, before the difficult days come, and the years draw near when you say, 'I have no pleasure in them'... In the day when the keepers of the house tremble, and the strong men bow down; when the grinders cease because they are few, and those that look through the windows grow dim; when the doors are shut in the streets, and the sound of grinding is low; when one rises up at the sound of a bird, and all the daughters of music are brought low. Also they are afraid of height, and of terrors in the way; when the almond tree blossoms, the grasshopper is a burden, before the silver cord is loosed, or the golden bowl is broken, or the pitcher shattered at the fountain, or the wheel broken at the well. Then the dust will return to the earth as it was, and the spirit will return to God who gave it" (Ecc. 12:1-7).

Indeed, inevitably it happens to each of us: Our teeth become fewer, our hearing fails, our arms and legs weaken, our vision becomes dimmer, we awaken at the slightest sound, our hair turns gray, and our desire fails. But, that's no reason for despair. That's when age, our constant companion, gently whispers: "Be at peace. You have been blessed with a long, abundant life. Your journey is not yet over." And you will be strengthened by a simple poetic promise, which is a personal favorite that I often quote to myself: "The woods are lovely, dark and deep. But I have promises to keep, and miles to go before I sleep." Keep walking the path of aging with wisdom and discernment, and you will be amazed at the pearls of great price you will discover.

The ancient Jewish religion placed such emphasis on wisdom that it became personified in their faith, as if wisdom were a person. Wisdom was elevated to the highest level of religious observances by designating a separate section of the scriptures as the Books of Wisdom (Proverbs, Ecclesiastes, Job, Psalms, and Song of Solomon) and by considering wisdom of greater value than rubies and pearls.

Wisdom is biblically described in various meaningful ways: She was there in the beginning of creation; she prepares a sumptuous feast for those who hear her instruction; and she is a gifted and wise teacher. Through the power of wisdom, those of average mental ability can become a wise sage, those in leadership positions can rule judiciously and wisely, and anyone earnestly seeking greater wisdom will be rewarded. Proverbs states that the purpose of divine wisdom is to "...receive the instruction of...justice, judgment, and equity. "

Ponder those words for a moment: As we age, our concept of justice for all people becomes more like the mercy of God, regardless of racial, ethnic, or physical differences. Our sense of judgment between the words, promises, and principles of both people and government becomes more pronounced, and we more quickly see the difference between truth and the fakery of fools and charlatans.

The wisdom of old age blows a wind of change on the smoldering embers of our conscience that enflames a burning desire for equity and fairness for all. Our physical eyesight may dim, but the eyes of our moral and spiritual being focus with righteous indignation on the unfairness, discrimination, and hostility poured out by economic, political, and even spiritual leaders on those less fortunate, those who are physically different, and those unable to defend and protect themselves. When we see the most basic promise of America—liberty and justice for all—ripped from the hands, hearts, and lives of those simply desiring to be a part of the American dream, we see the gross unfairness of demagoguery.

Ancient Israel had a social and religious system that revered the wisdom of the older generation. "The traditions of the elders" was given the highest priority in determining social and religious ideas. That respect for the wisdom of age is sadly missing in our country today, and we suffer because of it.

But, regardless of how old you are or your physical condition, you can still exert the wisdom of your age. If you see injustice, do something! Become the champion of those who have no champion. Use your judgment that you have sharpened through the years to point out truth from untruth. Don't worry about offending someone. You have earned the right through a long life to speak the thoughts of your wise, old mind. Demand fairness for all around you. Do not sit idle and watch the poor and innocent victimized. Find the strength to grab your crutches, or your walking cane, and rise up with all the power of age and wisdom and say, "Enough of this! For Christ's sake, stop it!"

I don't care how old you are or how frail you may feel, you are never too old to use your age and wisdom to serve Jesus and make a difference in the lives of others.

IV

What is wisdom? Many define it as knowledge, insight, intuitive understanding, and sage advice. However, ancient Jewish theology defined wisdom as incorporating a broad understanding of the relationship between physical life and spiritual life and recognizing the control over everyday forces in physical life by the mind, will, and purpose of God. Ultimate wisdom yielded full control of one's life to God through a life of divine righteousness.

Thus, in both the Old and New Testaments, wisdom is revealed and personified as a "life" that has been present with God since the beginning of time that unifies God and man. Jesus described this life as "eternal life" that He would give to covenant Christians as a free gift because of their faith in Him.

Can this spiritual treasure be described in meaningful physical terms? Proverbs 8:11 states, "For wisdom is better than rubies, and all the things one may desire cannot be compared with her." What an amazing statement! Everything you have ever wanted or dreamed about doesn't compare with the wisdom of age that is yours as a free gift in Christ.

"Rubies" can also mean jewels or pearls. From these ancient writings, the concept of a "pearl of wisdom" is derived, and wisdom of the greatest and most life-transforming value was referred to as a "pearl of great price."

Jesus used this ancient truth to describe a person who discovered a pearl of great price, and because of the unending joy he knew that it would bring him, he sold everything he had to acquire this priceless treasure. Just as Proverbs stated, nothing he had ever owned or wanted remotely compared to this treasure. Jesus said the spiritual treasure of the kingdom of heaven was the same.

So, does the wisdom of age give us an ever-increasing ability to see the pearl of great price as a spiritual treasure we have in our heart by faith that can never be lost, rather than some physical treasure we hold in our hand that can be easily taken from us?

The writer of Ecclesiastes spoke of a wide range of things he had fruitlessly pursued in life hoping to find joy and meaning. It was all "vanity of vanities," he concluded—like chasing after soap bubbles in the March wind. Just when you think you have it, the bubble pops and evaporates in your hand.

You may have had similar experiences in life. You labored long and hard to own something that ended up owning you; friendships with those you admired ended in disappointment; greater income only put you deeper in debt; and the big home of your dreams now echoes with only your voice talking to yourself. In all honesty, how much of your life have you spent vainly chasing after the soap bubble of happiness in the constantly shifting winds of change in your life? Do you ever look back on portions of your life and whisper, "vanity of vanities...what was I thinking?"

The wisdom of age can indeed become a pearl of great wisdom and insight for you today. When you look back over the years of your physical life, and then clearly see the promise of eternal life with Jesus in heaven, nothing on this earth matters much in comparison. You are more than willing to lay aside all earthly treasures in order to possess this pearl of great price—the joy of an eternal life in heaven with Jesus. You can possess this priceless pearl today by your faith in Him.

V

Age has changed me. I don't look like I once did, and I don't act like I did in the days of my youth. But, most interestingly, I don't think like I did when I thought I had decades of life beckoning me to explore them. Fate turned on the timer of life, and the clicking seconds are slowly revealing someone I would not have recognized forty years ago.

The change is evident: My hair is gray, my gait is slower, and my words are fewer. The change I notice most, however, is how I think. No, I'm not talking about forgetfulness or the inability to remember names. I'm talking about something deeper, more personal, perhaps more significant—something weighty that leaves the testimony of one's life more clearly written in the chronicle of time. My thoughts have largely moved from my head to my heart.

I still mentally process the events of life, but I ponder their meaning more deeply than before. In my quietest hours, I think about God, people around me, the church, Christianity, and heaven differently than I once did.

Age has taught me the difference between the thoughts of your head and the thoughts of your heart. Thoughts are ordinarily associated with the mind, not necessarily the heart. But, in a broad sense, the mind deals with analytical ideas and determines our actions. Figuratively speaking, the heart, however, is the seat of our emotions and determines our feelings and attitudes toward both life and others. Thoughts of the heart are deep-seated, long-term, and form the basis of character and personality. They are the source of our most personal thoughts about others.

Thoughts of the mind can change rather quickly based on new facts, whereas thoughts of the heart can take years to change, or even a lifetime. Indeed, as one thinks about life, God, and his fellowman within the secret confines of his heart, so he is for a considerable portion of his life.

A person can change their mind fairly easily and quickly. But, changing the thoughts of their heart is something, quite often, that only God can do. That's why the wisdom of Proverbs states, regarding the impact of an individual's deepest thoughts, "For as he thinks in his heart, so is he."

It is easy to say to someone whose opinion has changed, "I see that you have changed your mind." But, saying to someone "I see you have had a change of heart" is much deeper in meaning and is made in response to a noticeable change of moral and emotional attitudes about something or someone.

Changing one's mind often does not alter the course of their life too greatly; changes of the heart often make them a different person. Changes of the mind may not have that great of an impact on others, whereas changes in thoughts of the heart can permanently alter the course of an individual, a family, a church, or even an entire nation.

What this nation needs more than anything else is for Christians to stop worrying about the thoughts of their mind caused by the chaos and confusion all around, and instead regularly and quietly get alone with God and let Him change the thoughts of their heart.

VI

When I was in seminary, I heard about someone going into an elderly professor's office and finding him sitting at his desk in tears and holding his Bible. The visitor asked if he was OK. The old professor pointed to a scripture verse, and with a quivering voice replied, "I've been reciting and teaching this passage for forty years, and I just now see its deeper truth. Oh, if I had only known. "

I can relate to his emotional and spiritual struggle. I have a confession that may surprise some of you: I don't think God is who I have always thought He was. Yes, I surely know He is holy and all powerful, and He is my loving heavenly Father. I don't doubt any of that. But age has taught me something about God that is deeper than I've known before. Allow me to explain.

Jesus said two things that defy my comprehension: "I and the Father are one" and "If you have seen Me, you have seen the Father." Those statements, and John's statement that "the Word became flesh and dwelt among us and we beheld His glory," weigh heavily on my aging mind in my quiet hours of spiritual reflection. In truth, when Jesus lived on Earth, multiplied thousands looked into the face of God, heard His words, saw His miraculous works, and simply could not believe that God was like that.

Is it possible that in all those years when I pounded the pulpit and described God in His transcendent holiness, His unlimited creative power, His majesty, and the eternal nature of His heavenly kingdom that I missed and failed to grasp some of the most fundamental qualities about His divine nature?

If Jesus was the human incarnation of God, then Jesus was like God, but that also means that God must be like Jesus. And if God is like Jesus, then God is a lot different from what most people believe Him to be—and probably a lot different than they want Him to be.

With all the condemnation of people who are different that we hear today, can you visualize holy God sitting down at a table with a bunch of sinners and being friends and having dinner with them? Jesus dined with sinners numerous times, so wouldn't God do that, too? And if God would do that, why aren't we willing to do the same and reach out to them in love and friendship? We are far more comfortable with a God who will judge and condemn sinners, like we do, rather than a

God who loves them and goes to their house and—to use today's expression—hangs out with them.

If God is like Jesus, then is He really willing to bless America more so than He is willing to bless other nations and other people? We have convinced ourselves that God loves America more than He loves Canada or Mexico or any other country, but does He? The Bible says God loves the world, but we never ask Him to bless any other nation but us. Jesus told us to go into all the other nations and make disciples of them, but very few people today even consider that.

Jesus had no interest in politics, and thus it doesn't interest God much either. Jesus could have been the world's greatest leader, but He chose to be the world's greatest servant. Where in the gospel does Jesus endorse a conservative, religious oriented government on Earth? He didn't. If God is like Jesus, then what must God think about politicians using Him to advance their own politics, power, and petty egos?

Have you ever considered that the sham of Christian-oriented politics that tries to make Christianity a part of a modern-day political party might actually disgust God? Is that maybe why a spirit of confusion has fallen on our national leaders? Maybe we should prayerfully reconsider what it really means to "render unto Caesar the things that are Caesar's and unto God the things that are God's."

If God is like Jesus, then God is willing to set aside His purity and get dirty and mercifully touch and heal those who are terribly sick and are difficult to be around. Lepers were pitifully diseased, like so many today, yet Jesus violated all norms and compassionately ministered to them. Lepers were covered in open sores and they stunk; but Jesus went right into their midst and helped them.

If God is like Jesus, then God is not reluctant to get His hands dirty caring for dying people just as Jesus did. Why, then, are so many Christian people today not trying to comfort those who are sick and hurting all around them and instead are making some foolish political ploy over being protected from this deadly virus?

If God is like Jesus, then how does He really feel about our ceaseless prayers for greater worldly goods, a better job, a bigger house, and more earthly treasures? When Jesus said, "seek first the kingdom of heaven and all these things will be added to you," is that God's answer to my prayers about stuff that garners my interest? Have I spent a lifetime seeking the wrong things? Jesus' words surely make me wonder.

Perhaps most important, if God is like Jesus, then He wants me to take the covenant that He made with me through Jesus' blood more seriously than I have. Through the new covenant, I am in Jesus and Jesus is in me, and if God is Jesus, then I am eternally one in covenant unity with God. I am His servant, His witness, His ambassador and messenger to the world around me. I have His power and His purpose in my life, and there is no limit to the things that He can do in me, with me, and through me that bring honor and glory to His name. My life is just a small portion of God's proof to the world that He is real.

I am a new and different person in Him. The days of childhood poverty and loneliness are gone, my future is secured through faith in Jesus, and my present experience is peace through the indwelling of the Holy Spirit, who daily declares the eternal truth of Jesus to me. I have spiritual riches and treasures laid up in heaven that I can never lose, so none of this earthly stuff interests me much anymore.

If God is like Jesus, I only wish now that I had spent less time pounding on a pulpit on Sunday and spent more time getting dirty for Jesus by going into the highways and byways of life and inviting those who have never imagined that God loves them to dine at the table of fellowship with Him. Jesus did that tirelessly. Oh, if only I had better understood the depth of His love over all these years.

VII

When I was a young boy, my mother took me to Good Hope Baptist Church and then First Baptist in Purvis, Mississippi, where I was baptized. Later in life, I served as pastor at three different churches over a twenty-year period. For all those years, the idea of "going to church" was drilled into my head as a fundamental Christian responsibility, and also for all those years I misunderstood in many ways what the church was truly about.

Age has refocused my clouded vision of this holy body of Christ. Maybe my ministry would have been more meaningful if I had more clearly seen these truths forty years ago.

Virtually everything I learned and thought about church in those days was physical in nature, such as the building, the congregational size, various activities, the quality of preaching and singing, and the growth and outreach to new members.

However, the true church is not physical at all; rather, it is spiritual and in many ways is the fulfillment of the ancient concept of the tabernacle. Yes, I fully know there are physical aspects about the church, such as the facilities in which people gather to worship, that are meaningful, but the church's true purpose is spiritual in a way that would shock most Christians if they really thought about it. Allow me to challenge you with some deeper thoughts about church that will directly end with you.

From the earliest days of God's covenant with man, the tabernacle and the temple were envisioned as God's physical dwelling place on Earth, much like our present-day description of the church as "the house of God." However, the tabernacle and temple's most meaningful feature was a small room called the "holy of holies," which held the ark of the covenant. Above the ark was the "mercy seat," and God's Spirit was thought to hover over the mercy seat, thus making God present with His people. The heart of this ancient concept is that God's Spirit hovers over and nurtures the source of the greatest mercy God can physically reveal on Earth. Think about that for a moment as it relates to your Christian life.

Let me cut through the religious description and say all this another way: First of all, the ancient Hebrew language didn't have a superlative, such as "holiest," so the phrase "holy of holies" describes the most sacred, holy, and divinely personal place God could create on Earth. In other words, of all the holy places God could establish, this is the most holy of all.

At the very center of that holiness is the seat—or center—of God's mercy on Earth, and God's Spirit continuously hovers over and guards the most basic spiritual feature of His nature and His covenant presence with mankind—the Mercy Seat, or the seat and source of His greatest mercy. Think about that for a second: The holiest thing that God could create on Earth was the center and source of His divine mercy.

Centuries ago, the High Priest annually entered the Holy of Holies and sprinkled the blood of the perfect sacrificial lamb on the Mercy Seat in atonement for the people's sins. But, the new covenant in Jesus' blood changed all of that, for as God's true High Priest, Jesus entered into the Holy of Holies and sprinkled His own blood on the Mercy Seat as the final and full atonement of sin for all believers.

Grasp the full meaning of this: Jesus became the eternal seat of God's mercy through His death on the cross. No further sacrifice will ever be needed. His life is the most holy of all the holy things God could place on earth, and His mercy is the center of that holiness.

The new covenant in Christ also accomplished something further that is mindboggling for you and me. In our personal covenant of faith with Jesus as Christians, we enter into and receive by grace the life of Jesus, and that means we also enter into and receive His mercy. Thus, individually and collectively, we enter into and become a part of God's manifestation of mercy on earth, and we personally share with Jesus the most holy life and the greatest source of mercy God can reveal on Earth.

There is a fundamental truth about the new covenant that is overlooked by many Christians: The Mercy Seat moved into a new tabernacle. The Spirit of God does not dwell in a building. Instead, through the indwelling of the Holy Spirit and the new covenant with Jesus, God's Spirit dwells in the hearts of all who believe in Christ. That is why the Bible specifically states, "Behold, the tabernacle of God is with men, and He will dwell with them...." The dwelling place of God on Earth is not a building, but the redeemed body of believers known as the church—the "called-out ones." The church is not a building, but rather the collective, redeemed, purified, and sanctified body of believers who are in a life-transforming new covenant with Jesus and who are His true witnesses to the world around them.

We do not go to church as if it were a weekly routine; we are the church. We do not go to God's house once a week, as if God lived in a brick building at 100 Main Street, Everytown, USA. Our transformed life in Christ is His dwelling place. We do not enter God's presence by going through the front doors of a building; rather, we are the manifestation of His presence on Earth through the new covenant with Jesus.

And if we are the tabernacle of His Spirit, and if we are in covenant with Jesus, then our individual Christian life should be the source of the greatest display of God's mercy that a hurting sinner can find. If your life is the seat of God's greatest display of mercy and compassion to hurting people around you, then the Spirit of God continuously hovers over you and empowers you to reveal His mercy to others just as He revealed it to you in Christ.

Thus, Jesus profoundly changed the purpose of our life as Christians. We are the light of the world in the darkness of sin around us. We are the salt of the earth—the living, present-day fulfillment of God's ancient, merciful salt covenant with His chosen ones. The

Christian church is called and divinely empowered to be the greatest source of mercy that God can physically create on Earth! May God forgive us for any hurting, struggling soul who has been turned away from the love and mercy of Jesus by any judgmental attitude or action, any snide comment or haughty look, or any evil gossip that has come from any Christian who was empowered to reveal God's mercy to them.

You may have never seen yourself this way before, but in your Christian life in the midst of your family, friends, and the world in which you live, you are now the tabernacle of God's Spirit, the living proof of His mercy, and the physical source of God's greatest mercy for others.

When I reflect on these truths in the autumn years of my life, I feel as though I failed, even if I tried the best I knew how. If only I had spent more time telling people what Jesus said: "But go and learn what this means: I desire mercy and not sacrifice" Indeed, as Jesus said, "Blessed are the merciful, for they shall receive mercy."

VIII

The older I become, the more I realize the profoundly deep and challenging nature of Jesus' teachings, especially what He taught about death and heaven. Both as a minister standing by a bedside and as a hospital administrative employee who was occasionally involved in some stressful end-of-life decisions, I am not a stranger to life's final moment. I have watched several people take their last breath.

Jesus made some startling claims and promises in His earthly ministry. Many were so shocking and radically transforming that most Jewish religious authorities of His day considered Him to be mentally unstable, if not demon possessed. None, however, exceed His statements about death. With all the suffering occurring around us today, we can find immense comfort in His promises about this inevitable human experience.

The ancient Jewish religion was somewhat unclear about what happened to someone at death. The conservative Pharisees believed there would be a resurrection of the dead, but the Sadducees, the slightly more moderate religious party, did not.

Two concepts reveal the believed destiny of souls after death. Sheol is mentioned in the Old Testament, and it was generally believed to be a dark, uncertain place buried within the earth known as the "abode of the dead."

However, the New Testament parable of the rich man and Lazarus reveals the belief that departed souls would go to "Abraham's bosom," wherever that may have been. In either case, death was an accepted reality until Jesus shattered existing religious beliefs by saying that, for Christians, death doesn't exist.

I cannot think of a statement more difficult to believe than being told that I will never die, but that is exactly what Jesus said. And He made that statement several times, and not just once. The most basic statement of Christian doctrine, John 3:16, promises that whoever believes in Jesus "will not perish but have everlasting life." In fact, Jesus specifically stated, "And whoever lives and believes in Me shall never die. Do you believe this?"

So how do I reconcile my bedside view of death with Jesus' promises? When I read His words and imagine Him intently gazing at me, as if He were asking me personally, "Do you believe this?" what is my response? Age has taught me a different understanding about the death of a Christian, and I hope my thoughts will be meaningful and comforting to you.

When you become a true Christian through faith, you enter into a different realm of physical reality. You become a citizen of the kingdom of heaven. You enter into a covenant with Jesus and you share His life. What you must grasp is that His life is not dictated and determined by physical rules and laws. You enter into a living realm where the impossible not only becomes possible, but in fact is a common, everyday occurrence.

You have eternally bound your life to The Life that has no limits. What we consider as miracles is just simply Jesus doing what Jesus does—giving sight to the blind, causing the lame to walk, forgiving sin, and defeating and reducing to nothing the concept of death. This Life to which you have bound yourself has always existed with God and always will for all eternity. When you enter into this Life, you are in an eternal covenant bond with a divine Life that knows no human limitations. This Life is not touched by nor in any manner limited by what we call human death. When Jesus died on the cross, you must understand that He willingly and triumphantly entered into the experience of human death in order to atone for sin and destroy death's claim on you through the power of His resurrection. He was not bound by death; rather, He was the master over it. Jesus was not the victim of death: He was the victor.

Therefore, though a Christian may cease all respiratory function, have no cardiac activity, and also have no brain-wave response, and therefore totally meet the clinical definition of human death, in truth he or she isn't dead. What you see while standing at the side of a death bed is not reality. The true reality is that this Christian's life has already transcended the physical bonds of human life and forever entered into the joyous experience of everlasting life in Christ in His presence.

If you can hear Jesus asking you personally, "Do you believe this?" then indeed, as the Bible says, the sting of death is gone and the grave will never claim victory over you.

In your covenant with Christ, you step over the line of limitations into the miraculous, heavenly realm of the boundless, limitless, and ageless eternal life of Jesus. Death is not the end, nor is it the beginning. It is only a continuation—and a momentary transition—of your glorious experience of the Life given to you by God's grace that has been prepared and reserved for you since the beginning of time, and it will be yours until the end of time. That is not a reason to grieve, but rather a reason to joyfully celebrate the gift of eternal Life.

Grandpa's America

His old cotton field is now my backyard, where he labored long and hard to raise a crop and feed the family he loved. With a one-eyed mule named Sadie Kate, he plowed his furrows long and straight, and he sought no man's help, just the blessings of the Lord above.

In the July heat, with blistered feet, he'd follow ole Kate until he couldn't take another step. He chopped his cotton with a worn-out hoe and plowed the grass from every row, and I don't know how he did it, but he did.

He read his Bible every day and taught his children how to pray, and he always thanked the Lord for the blessings he had. He sent his sons across the sea to fight a war that kept us free, and I don't know how he did it, but he did.

They all came home, except for one who lost his life to an enemy's gun, as his blood soaked the soil of a foreign land. He would hold the picture of that handsome lad, who patted him on his back and called him Dad, and yearned to hug his boy just one more time.

His fallen son's picture hung on the wall, beside his bedroom door just down the hall, and the old man talked to him every time he walked by. Beside the picture was his Purple Heart, which was all he got for doing his part to win a war and keep America free. Not a day went by that he did not try to share his love with that face on the wall. He would tell him about his mother, his sister and brothers, and how his dog howled all night the day he died.

He always sat an extra plate at the dinner table and prayed for his family as long as he was able to bow his head and name them one by one. He never spoke unkindly about any man and always extended a helping hand without wanting anyone to know what he had done. And it's unknown to this day just how much he gave away, and I don't know how he did it, but he did.

He listened to FDR and his fireside chats and always stood and removed his hat any time the American flag passed by. He knew the cost of freedom in a personal way and how he quietly grieved it's hard to say, but he always choked up when he spoke about his boy and the flag.

I stood by his bed the day he died, and I told him I loved him and then I cried, but with his last breath he whispered these words of joy, "Lord, I'm coming home, and it won't be long, and in just a little while I'm going to hug my boy."

He was a man of God and the path he trod helped make America what she is today. I earnestly pray that we don't drift away from the faith he lived by until his final breath. Just one old man, and his one-eyed mule, who lived his life by the Golden Rule, and I don't know how he did it, but he did.

When Pentecost Becomes Personal

Pentecost was one of many ancient Jewish religious holidays, and it was celebrated fifty days after Passover. Historically, Pentecost focused on a celebration of thanksgiving for the first fruits of the wheat harvest, but it later included a celebration of the giving of the law to Moses.

In the Christian faith, however, Pentecost is known as the time when the Holy Spirit first moved powerfully and miraculously in the lives of the disciples, and the Christian church became a dynamic, earthly reality. These events are recorded in the early chapters of the Book of Acts. For most Christians, Pentecost is known for the disciples' powerful preaching, the numerous miracles that occurred, and the ability of the disciples to speak in tongues, or the languages of those people from various countries who were present.

But Pentecost is much more personal than many comprehend, and it is one of the most defining moments in Christianity, not only historically, but also personally for each believer. If one focuses only on the historical nature of Pentecost and the mystery of various miracles, then the transforming spiritual power promised to every believer is largely missed.

Many today associate Pentecost with the Pentecostal Church and the practice of charismatic worship, faith healing, and even speaking in tongues. But the divine promise of Pentecost is intended for every Christian, and it is not limited to worship practices. In fact, Pentecostal power is one of the most transforming personal experiences in a Christian's life.

To better understand the concept, a Christian must seriously study the role and purpose of the Holy Spirit in our life. In truth, the Book of Acts marks the beginning of the dynamic work of the Holy Spirit in not only creating the Christian church, but also empowering the church to be the living witness of the power of Jesus' resurrection throughout the world.

The purpose and power of Pentecost can become a dynamic, life-transforming experience for every Christian. Don't think of it only in the traditional manner of charismatic worship or faith healing, which for some is a very personal method of worship, but rather think more broadly about the power of God's Spirit moving in the lives of ordinary people through signs and wonders that gave clear proof of God's work in everyday life.

As a personal experience, begin to prayerfully consider the nature of the Holy Spirit as the spiritual force and power of God working mightily in you to empower your personal Christian life and your witness regarding the truth of the gospel and of the resurrection of Jesus. How is the nature of Jesus' resurrected life, which is given to you by grace through your faith, energized and vibrantly empowered in you? What spiritual change occurs in your life when the power of the Holy Spirit "comes upon you," as He did with the disciples at Pentecost, and begins working signs and wonders in your life that are beyond human explanation? How are you given the power to speak in the "tongue" of others around you, so that your communication of the gospel truth to them is clear and convincing? These are just some of the many things to consider when Pentecost becomes a truly personal spiritual experience for every Christian believer.

II

Christianity has a unique concept of a loving God who reveals Himself to us as three different "Persons": Father, Son, and Holy Spirit. But He is not three different Gods. He is one God who loves us in three different, life-changing ways. Think of it in this way: If one is blessed with a loving father, he knows his father's love is unconditional, his providential care is unlimited, his mercy is great, and his devotion to his child is eternal. He is at all times "Father" to his child.

But, this father can also at the same time be his child's best friend. He is a constant companion, a fellow-laborer, one who shares the burdens of life, and one who would give up his own life to help and defend his friend, and it is indeed true that there is no greater love than to lay down one's life for his friend. He commits himself to being his friend's savior and devotes his life to his well-being.

If this friend of yours is Jesus, then you know that the Father has revealed Himself to you in the person of the "Son," who is identical in nature with His Father, but who reveals God's love to you as your savior and friend. It is one God who lovingly reveals Himself to you at all times as "Father" and as "Son."

41

Your Father's love doesn't stop there, though. His influence and loving nurture in your life is constant, and you always feel the presence of His Spirit and His influence in your life. It makes you think of him, talk to him, and go to him with all the burdens and challenges of life. His Spirit is constantly with you and sustains you.

Thus, God is at all times and in all ways in your life Father, Son, and Holy Spirit. He is one God who works in your life in three different yet profoundly powerful ways to make you a child of His own.

When God adopts you as His child through your faith in Jesus, He pours His divine blessings out in your life as your Father, He lays down His life for you as the Son of God, and He constantly ministers to you through the power and purpose of His eternal Spirit. All three are working constantly and without condition or compromise to redeem you to God. One God. Three "Persons" of the divine, blessed Trinity. One divine Life. One salvation. One promise of an eternal home in glory.

When the Holy Spirit begins to miraculously work through signs and wonders in your life to make you more like the Son, for the glory of the Father, then the power of Pentecost becomes an amazing, personal experience in your life.

III

Peter's sermon at Pentecost, where three thousand people responded in faith, was wondrous in nature. The sermon was a powerful presentation of the life and work of Jesus and Peter's personal testimony regarding Jesus' resurrection. In truth, the sermon was out of character for Peter.

Peter was a fisherman, not a scholar of the Jewish law, yet the sermon was substantively deep and persuasive. Peter wavered in his commitment to Christ, and his well-known denials of knowing Jesus when He was arrested are a part of Christian history. Yet, at Pentecost this fisherman became a dynamic preacher without a hint of hesitation. Why is there such a difference? How can we be personally influenced by the change from Peter the cowardly denier to Peter the powerful proclaimer?

Jesus once specifically explained the purpose and power of the Holy Spirit to His disciples, and one word that He used opens a window of understanding that can profoundly impact your Christian discipleship. Jesus said:

> "However, when He, the Spirit of truth, has come, He will guide you into all truth; for He will not speak on His own authority, but whatever He hears He will speak and He will tell you things to come. He will glorify Me, for He will take of what is Mine and declare it to you. All things that the Father has are Mine. Therefore I said that He will take of Mine and declare it to you" (John 16:13-15).

You should carefully read Jesus' statement. The Holy Spirit is co-equal with the Father and the Son in the triune Christian concept, or as the hymn states, "God in three persons, blessed trinity." Therefore, with the same power of God and in the power of Jesus' resurrection, the Holy Spirit works in a way that will radically transform your Christian life, if you will let Him.

Jesus said, "All things that the Father has are Mine." He stated that the Holy Spirit "will take of what is mine and declare it to you." Adding these two statements together, you realize that the fullness of God's power and holiness was in Jesus, and that the Holy Spirit will take all that Jesus possesses and "declare" it to you.

The ancient definition of "declare" means to make a report, utter a declaration, or make an important announcement. However, the importance of the declaration does not mean a preliminary report, but rather something that has gone through all essential stages of completion and clarification so that the declared truth is fully mature, complete, and final. For example, the Declaration of Independence fully sets forth the reasons for America's independence from England.

Herein is the work of the Holy Spirit in growing a new Christian into a mature disciple of Christ. The Spirit completes the words and works of Jesus in His covenant disciples, spiritually maturing them and enabling them to function as effective witnesses and ambassadors for Jesus in the world. The ability to love one's enemies, turn the other cheek, and go the extra mile are manifestations of the harvest of spiritual maturity and are visible fruits of the unseen Spirit at work. The Holy Spirit does not reveal partial truth to you; rather, He will declare to you the full life-changing truth about Jesus, filling you with divine wisdom, understanding, and empowering a previously unknown commitment in you. The potential impact this divine declaration in your life is incalculable.

Here's what I think Peter experienced at Pentecost: The Holy Spirit suddenly came upon him with spiritual power that he had never known before and declared to Peter the truth about Jesus! It was not partial truth that he realized, but rather the eternal purpose and truth of God in the life and work of Christ. It was like a divine lightning bolt of wisdom and insight that transformed this once crusty, wishy-washy fisherman into a dynamic "fisher of men," as Jesus once described the disciples' work.

There is a two-fold concept of Holy Spirit work here that must be understood. Not only did the Holy Spirit declare the final truth about Jesus to Peter, but the Spirit then declared the truth about Jesus through Peter to the assembled multitudes, thus giving birth to the Christian church. Would you allow me to give you a personal testimony about how that spiritually feels?

In my former years as a preacher, there were countless times when, in the midst of a sermon, I would suddenly see a divine truth that I had never known, and just as suddenly as I saw it, I would proclaim it without hesitation. The experience would leave me startled, even as I spoke, because I was just as enthralled with this new revelation of truth as I hoped the congregation would be. I was not some religious scholar steeped in wisdom. I was simply a conduit of divine truth, a living witness to the power of Jesus' resurrection, and a channel used by the Holy Spirit in which He simultaneously declared truth about Jesus to me and through me. That is just an example of the amazing experience of Holy Spirit empowered preaching.

When the power of Pentecost becomes personal for you, and it is no longer just a quaint and interesting Bible story, you will experience unlimited occasions when the Holy Spirit will declare truth about Jesus to you, and then through signs and wonders, declare that same truth about Jesus through you to others. That is how you become a true and faithful witness of the power of Jesus' resurrection, and your Christian life will be forever changed.

Miss Cora's Gladiolus

Flowers fascinate me. The rich variety of colors, combined with the subtle fragrances wafting across a flower garden on a dewy summer morning, is captivating. There are many varieties of flowers in my yard, but none intrigue me more than Miss Cora's gladiolus.

I bought an old farm in 1983 that had been the home of an elderly couple for decades prior to their deaths. I often visited them when I was a teenager, and I loved them like they were family. Miss Cora had a few flowers in her yard, but something happened after I bought the property that amazed me.

I had lived there several years when a beautiful salmon-colored gladiolus unexpectedly and mysteriously emerged from the ground and began to bloom. I didn't plant it, and I have no idea where it came from, other than Miss Cora had planted it years earlier. The color was stunning, and the smaller blossoms indicated it was a much older variety that had sat dormant in the ground for a long while.

Once it came to life, it has bloomed every year since, and I have been very protective of it, especially when moving and transporting it here to its new home. It bloomed again recently, as beautiful and unique as always.

It amazes me that the bulb and its roots sat dormant in the ground for so long. Questions about it fill my mind: How old is the flower? What traumatic stress caused it to stop blooming and retreat into subterranean safety and security? How did it survive dormancy so long? What caused it to suddenly emerge from its long sleep and again reveal its natural beauty?

Thinking about Miss Cora's gladiolus can be insightful and instructive to each of us as Christians, especially if one considers the power and potential of spiritual gifts. Does talent spontaneously develop, or does it lie dormant in us for years before emerging? Is a spiritual gift suddenly bestowed by the Holy Spirit, even at middle age or later, or has it been within us unseen and undeveloped since birth? Do we possess only one dormant talent, or are there other gifts? If so, how many?

I reflect on my writing in asking these questions. I had never written anything other than term papers in college, law school, seminary, and some legal briefs while working as an attorney. I was past fifty years of age when I began to feel a deep urge to start writing—almost like a divine calling. Now, it is the ministry to which I am committed. Was the gift of writing there all along, lying dormant somewhere within my mental and emotional capabilities for over fifty years, waiting for the creative juices to begin flowing?

I never envisioned myself as a published author, but I am, and there are more books on the way. Are there other spiritual gifts lying silent within me yet waiting to come to life? Only God knows.

It also makes me wonder about each of you. What may be the amazing variety of spiritual gifts silently lying dormant in Christians around us awaiting the moving of the Holy Spirit, stirring them into creative life? What could be the impact on our country and the world if our true potential as God's redeemed people began to emerge, and we boldly and joyously came forth in the beauty and power of Christ's resurrection to live our new life in Him?

On a personal level, what would be the impact and influence of your life if you came alive in Him spiritually, after a long period of spiritual dormancy, and began to bear fruit consistent with the power of Jesus' resurrection and the new life He has given to you?

I truly believe each of you is gifted for greater works than you now envision. You may not write or sing, but I feel God has blessed you with a unique ability to richly bless the lives of others more than you imagine in a way that glorifies Christ and brings you greater spiritual maturity and satisfaction.

If you feel the desire within you to use and develop your gift, don't suppress it. Let it emerge and bloom forth. You have no idea how many lives you may touch for Jesus and how rewarding the change in your life may be.

Just think about Miss Cora's gladiolus. It quietly sat dormant for years until it bloomed out in rich, radiant beauty that blesses all who see it. Your life can be the same.

Two Sparrows for a Farthing
(Matt. 10:29)

A large flowering quince dominates a circular portion of my driveway, and a four-foot octagonal picnic table is tucked under its orange-flowered branches. I don't eat at the table; it belongs to the birds. For years, I have enjoyed the serene beauty of feeding birds and observing the many kinds and colors of feathered creatures eating at this table. They each have their own peculiar habits, eating methods, songs, and preferential feeding times. For example, a blue jay will crack open a sunflower seed by banging it against the table, while a red bird will twist the seed open by grinding it between its upper and lower beaks. They are all unique creatures of God, just as we humans are.

The most prolific, and in some ways the most interesting, is the common sparrow. There are over thirty subspecies of sparrows, and how they each developed their unique color pattern and songs, yet remain true to their identity as a sparrow, is a fascinating work of nature. Often, there are so many of them eating that an individual bird can lose its sense of identity and worth in the feeding frenzy under the overlapping quince limbs.

It's the feeling you and I get sometimes when we feel overwhelmed by the impolite persistence of people and the pressures of life. A healthy sense of self-worth can get crowded out in the madness and mania of living life in the fast lane. Just watching the sparrows eat, you can get the feeling that one little sparrow is not that significant, which is kind of how each of us feels in those moments when, as Herman Melville poetically stated, "I feel myself growing grim about the mouth; whenever it is a damp, drizzly November in my soul...."

But Jesus did not see the common little sparrow in that way, and we can learn a great lesson about our own self-worth in the eyes of God from His statement about them. Sparrows were so plentiful they were considered a nuisance by many people, and if they could be caught, they were practically worthless—but not to Jesus.

Our Lord knew His disciples faced enormous struggles in living for Him, and there would be days when the pressure of life, the rejection and persecution they would face, and the physical and emotional pain they would endure would make them feel defeated, demoralized, and worthless.

Thus, with understanding and compassion, Jesus chose the least important creature to encourage His disciples and instill in them a renewed feeling of self-worth. In addition to using an insignificant bird as a teaching example, Jesus reminded them that an individual sparrow was of lesser value than the least valuable coin.

Interestingly, in order to assure His disciples they were not worthless, Jesus used the best example of worthlessness He could create. Think of a farthing as a penny: A sparrow was thus worth about one-half cent. Remember when pennies were made of copper and a new penny had a bright reddish-copper color? That is where the expression "not worth a red cent" originated. You've had those days when you felt that way about yourself. I know that I have.

But Jesus said even though two sparrows were worth only one farthing, yet God knew them individually, each was special and of great value to Him, and each one lived within the purpose of His will for them. There is, therefore, no reason for us to fear and be filled with worry and anxiety. As Jesus said, "…you are of more value than many sparrows."

Each of us, even on days when we don't feel like we're worth a red cent, is unique, special, and of great value and meaning to God. Don't get beaten down by the bird-feeder battles of life. There will be days when you will feel too fatigued to fly very high because of the weight on your shoulders, but regardless of how ruffled your feathers might be by the unpredictable winds of life, you can still fly to Christ. You may feel like an insignificant sparrow, but if His eye is on each little sparrow—and you are worth more than many sparrows to Him— surely he is watching you and encouraging you to soar above this life to Him.

Holy Week: Sunday

Thoughts About Cutting Palm Branches

Palm Sunday is a uniquely interesting day on our Christian calendar. It is often referred to as the day Jesus made His triumphal entry into Jerusalem, yet by the end of the week the adoring Palm Sunday crowds were screaming for His crucifixion.

When Jesus rode a donkey into Jerusalem, He was fulfilling Old Testament prophesies stating that the Messiah would ride on a donkey colt. The atmosphere was charged with anticipation that Jesus was about to usher in the Golden Age of messianic rule, and thus the throngs cut palm branches—which symbolized victory, triumph, and peace—and laid in His path. They shouted "Hosanna" (save us!) and cried out "Blessed is He who comes in the name of the Lord." "The Coming One" was a messianic title, as demonstrated when John the Baptist had messengers ask Jesus, "Are You the Coming One, or do we look for another?"

One could say this was indeed a triumphal entry. The tragedy of Palm Sunday, though, is the multitudes had it all wrong. Jesus was not entering Jerusalem as a military savior, but rather as the Suffering Servant, promised centuries earlier by Isaiah, who would save His people through His death so they might have eternal life. He did not speak of killing the enemies of Israel, but rather having an attitude of prayer for them.

The sad truth is Jesus was not the kind of messiah the people wanted, and the means by which He would save people from sin was not what appealed to them. They had no interest in a heavenly kingdom that was within them. They wanted a kingdom like King David had that would be unrivaled in military, political, and economic strength. The people cried out "Hosanna" because they thought that kind of a political, messianic kingdom would save them. Thus, when Jesus was arrested, and He did not divinely and powerfully deliver what they wanted, the once jubilant throngs vengefully turned against Him and screamed for Him to be crucified as an impostor.

Palm Sunday has this unique capacity that compels us to ask what kind of savior do we want, also. What do we really want Jesus to do for us individually and for America collectively? Do we most fervently want economic prosperity, military superiority over our enemies, and laws and legislation that would right the perceived social and civil wrongs in our land?

Or do we want Jesus to powerfully change us inwardly? Do we yearn to experience the kingdom of heaven within us by being spiritually reborn; do we really want spiritual power to love and pray for all others; do we truly desire the strength to go the extra mile, turn the other cheek, and be a servant to our fellowman? Do we pray for the personal ability to be kind, compassionate, longsuffering, patient, and forbearing? Do we actually pray for the spiritual strength to forgive seventy-times-seven, or do we just talk about it with high sounding religious platitudes? Do we want to experience forgiveness of sins and the guarantee of everlasting life that fills our heart and soul with peace and joy that is beyond understanding? On a personal level, do I truly want Jesus to transform America by first transforming me, so that I love my neighbor as much as I do my own self?

Here is a suggestion for how to celebrate Palm Sunday: Get in a quiet place and imagine yourself cutting palm branches symbolizing peace and victory and laying them in His path. Cry out to Him in your mind and heart, "Hosanna. Blessed is He who comes in the name of the Lord!" and experience His triumphal entry into your life today. Then, with a heart filled with praise and thanksgiving, tell Jesus how you want Him to save and transform you.

Be honest with yourself and with the Lord. What is it that you truly and deeply want Jesus to do? Palm Sunday has a strangely divine capacity to change the thoughts of your heart, if you are sincere about being a faithful, living witness for Him.

Holy Week: Monday

Confronting the Merciless Moneychangers

After spending the night in the village of Bethany, about two miles from Jerusalem, Jesus returned to Jerusalem on Monday morning with His disciples. Upon arriving at the Temple, He confronted leaders of one of the most corrupt and merciless practices of His day. Temple religious ritual and sacrifices were required by Israel's religious laws. But the Temple operated financially independently with its own Temple tax and currency. In order to pay the tax, a worshipper had to exchange his own currency for Temple currency. Tables were set up in the Temple courtyard where this exchange was handled by "moneychangers." The system was rife with fraud, and the currencies were exchanged at a huge profit to the Temple authorities.

The system had other financial traps. All adult males within a specified distance from Jerusalem were required to bring a perfect sacrificial lamb, without spot or blemish, to be offered as a sacrifice at Passover. Each lamb was inspected by a priest, and if found unacceptable, a perfect lamb could be purchased at an inflated price. The worshipper had little choice because the law required the perfect sacrifice. It is likely that the unaccepted lamb was taken and later sold to someone else as a perfect lamb. It was an endless, evil circle of fraud in the name of God.

Viewing Himself as God's perfect sacrifice and seeing the heartless manipulation of innocent worshippers, Jesus angrily confronted the moneychangers, turned over the money tables, and cleared them from the Temple, while pointedly saying, "The scriptures declare, 'My house is a house of prayer,' but you have made it a 'den of thieves.'"

Is there a modern-day message in Jesus' actions? I think so. Throughout the Old Testament, the Temple (and the temporary tabernacles) was viewed as the dwelling place of God in the midst of His people. The new covenant in Jesus changed that. Through the indwelling of the Holy Spirit in believers, the dwelling place of God's Spirit now is in the lives of all redeemed believers.

Looking at many religious practices today, especially media ministries, the moneychangers are still in our midst. I simply cannot understand the cold, calculating mindset of anyone who would defraud another person and harm them financially in the name of God, but it happens every day.

Maybe Jesus' devotion to cleansing the Temple will inspire each of us to examine our own spiritual dwelling place and remove sinful actions and attitudes that grieve the Holy Spirit. Most all of us would benefit from a good, old-fashioned spring "heart cleaning." Because our Christian life is the tabernacle of God's Spirit among men, let each of us enter into this holy week with the words of this old hymn in our heart,

"Search me, O God, and know my heart today. Try me, O Savior, and know my thoughts, I pray. See if there be some wicked way in me, cleanse me from every sin, and set me free. Lord, take my life, and make it wholly Thine. Fill my poor heart with Thy great love divine; take all my will, my passion, self and pride. I now surrender, Lord, in me abide."

Holy Week: Monday Afternoon and Evening

"What Do We Do About Lazarus?"

Following His confrontation with the Temple moneychangers earlier in the day, Jesus and His disciples returned to Bethany to the home of Mary, Martha, and their brother Lazarus, who were Jesus' close friends. There is an often overlooked yet highly significant role in the dramatic events of the week that focuses on Lazarus, and one can only imagine that was a topic of discussion as they ate their evening meal together.

Jesus had earlier miraculously raised Lazarus from death in a manner that defied both Jewish tradition and human understanding, having intentionally waited until the fourth day after Lazarus died to resurrect him. Jewish tradition held that a person had no chance of resuscitation after three days, and in fact by the fourth day the smell of death was coming from Lazarus' tomb. But Jesus raised him back to life to the utter amazement and astonishment of everyone.

For Jewish authorities, Lazarus' resurrection was more than a miracle. It was a serious problem for them and their whole religious system for which they had no response, and the problem would only worsen unless an answer could be devised.

Jewish tradition held that the messiah would appear on "the great day of the Lord" that would involve cataclysmic events of nature, miraculous displays of power, and divine signs and wonders beyond human explanation. Messiah's unlimited power would even enable him to raise the dead back to life.

With Lazarus, Jesus had done just that, plus countless other displays of miraculous power, but Jesus was the exact opposite of the Messiah the leadership wanted. In fact, Jesus was so totally opposite to their messianic vision that most Jewish religious leaders wrote Him off as demon-possessed and mentally deranged.

However, in their efforts to deny Jesus' messianic claim, they faced one major obstacle: What do we do about Lazarus? There was no immediate answer, and the two choices they faced were extreme. They could either accept Jesus as the Messiah, which was unthinkable to most, or remove the problem and kill both Jesus and Lazarus. Soon after Lazarus was raised, serious discussion and plotting began among Jewish authorities about the best way to kill both of them.

Now the issue had become urgent. Knowing that Jesus had arrived in Jerusalem and was staying with Mary, Martha, and Lazarus, a higher level of fear and uncertainty would have surely arisen among Jewish authorities. What if Jesus were to bring Lazarus to the Temple at Passover as a living witness to Jesus' messianic power? What counter-strategy could they employ to prevent the mass acceptance of Jesus as the Messiah? The only answer was to kill Jesus as quickly as possible, but how? The scheming and plotting would continue all week.

As He dined with Lazarus, Mary, and Martha, Jesus knew what was happening behind the scenes among His enemies? By late Thursday, He would see their plot unfold. As He ate His evening meal on Monday, the realization of what lay ahead surely became more vivid, and His sense of anticipation and anxiety steadily grew.

Holy Week: Tuesday

A Fundamental Truth

Ever since the spiritual downfall of Adam and Eve in the Garden of Eden, two great forces have separated man from God and prevented a perfect covenant union between them—sin and death. God is sinless and man is not, and God has everlasting life and man is mortal and will die. As long as that difference remains, it is impossible for a man to experience and share God's life within the kingdom of heaven, for they are eternally separated.

In order to experience the personal victory Jesus won for you during the events of Holy Week, you must grasp the magnitude of His personal struggle. In order to establish a new covenant union between man and God and provide redeemed believers with the riches of the kingdom of heaven, these two great separating forces of sin and death would have to be defeated and destroyed and their death-grip on man permanently broken. The old covenant of law had not done that, and thus Jesus was committed to creating a new covenant of grace in which victory over the personal consequences of sin and death would be freely given to every believer through their faith in Him, or as He stated, "Whoever believes in Him would not perish but have everlasting life."

Since Jesus was the physical embodiment of eternal, sinless God, in order to destroy and defeat sin and death, Jesus would have to enter into and become the exact opposite of His divine nature and become the nature of sinful man in order to bear the punishment of sin, and He would have to enter into human death in order to provide eternal life.

Thus, He would have to be condemned to death to atone for sin and He would have to be dead and buried to destroy the consequence of death. The cross and the tomb are the two central focal points in Jesus' battle over sin and death, and they must be considered together.

In order to better experience the passion of Holy Week, you must grasp Jesus' struggle with the reality of betrayal and rejection, but you must also grasp His growing anguish over the pain of willfully entering into human sin and death in order to save you and me. His anguish would later become so intense that drops of blood literally fell from His face.

It was now Tuesday morning, and He knew the plotting and scheming that was taking place in order to kill Him. The cruelty of the Cross was looming closer each day.

Holy Week: Tuesday Afternoon

The Issue of Moral and Spiritual Authority

Jesus returned to the Temple on Tuesday afternoon. As He was teaching a group of worshippers, He was angrily confronted by the chief priests and elders regarding the basis of authority for His teaching, and they pointedly asked Him, "By what authority are You doing these things? And who gave You this authority?" The issue of moral and spiritual authority for the interpretation of scripture and the law was fundamental to Judaism, and it was one of the crucial issues of Holy Week.

The concept of *stare decisis* in American law is a good parallel. Stare decisis is the concept of precedent that obligates courts and judges to rule in a similar manner as prior decisions on a given point of law. Only the Supreme Court (or a state supreme court) can change established precedent.

The same was true in Israel. Once a question of scripture, or an interpretation of religious law was made, all subsequent similar questions must adhere to that precedent. This concept of interpretation was as entrenched in the religious traditions of Israel as stare decisis is entrenched in ours. Every rabbi, teacher, or scribe always cited prior authority for their opinion, and no one would have dared do otherwise, except Jesus.

Matthew 7:29 records that, following one of Jesus' sermons, the multitudes were astonished, "because He taught them as one having authority, and not as the scribes." You probably have read scriptures where Jesus stated, "You have heard that it was said, but I say unto you. " The ancient word for authority describes an inherent power naturally flowing from within that creates an unquestioned response. In other words, because of the perceived moral and spiritual power being projected by an individual, they are believed above all else and become the final authority on a point.

To better understand the bitterness that the religious leaders had toward Jesus and their blind determination to kill Him, consider the implications of Jesus' phrase, "you have heard that it was said, but I say unto you. " Because of the overwhelming power and impact of the moral and spiritual authority that naturally flowed from Him, Jesus had the divine authority to supersede every aspect of the revered law and the ancient traditions of the elders with His own words, and He needed no other authority other than Himself.

The religious leaders perceived this as an unparalleled threat to Judaism. If He can teach by His own authority, then He can transform the ancient law and the traditions of the elders in whatever way He decides, they reasoned.

Realizing the magnitude of the threat posed by Jesus' authority, the elders concluded there was but one option to prevent this from happening, and the plotting about how to kill Him became more intense.

Holy Week: Wednesday

The Price of Betrayal

Word had started circulating that Jewish religious authorities were willing to pay anyone who could deliver Jesus to them. The chief priests, scribes, and elders had met in the palace of Caiaphas, the high priest, to form a plan to seize Jesus, but backed out fearing hostile reaction of the crowds around Him. The preferred arrangement would be somewhere quiet and secluded, perhaps at night, where nothing would interfere with Jesus' arrest.

Two days before the Passover celebration, Judas Iscariot, one of the disciples, secretly went to the chief priests and asked, "What are you willing to give me if I deliver Him to you?" They counted out thirty pieces of silver, and Judas accepted it. He then began looking for the best opportunity to carry out the agreement and betray Jesus to them. Judas would later suffer for his deed. After Jesus was condemned, Judas was filled with remorse for having betrayed an innocent man, and he sought to return the thirty pieces of silver to the chief priests and elders. They scoffed at him and said, "What is that to us?" Judas then threw the silver down in the Temple and went out and hanged himself.

Jewish authorities were unsure what they could do with blood money, so they bought a piece of property with it to be used as a burial ground for the poor and for strangers. For a long while afterward, this burial field was called the "Field of Blood."

Holy Week: Wednesday Evening

The Costly Anointing

Jesus and the disciples were again at Bethany, two miles from Jerusalem, where they gathered in the home of Simon the Leper for an evening meal. As they ate, Jesus remarked that the Passover was two days away and "the Son of Man will be delivered up to be crucified."

Shortly afterward, a woman guest slowly approached Jesus with an alabaster flask of very expensive oil and poured it on Jesus' head. If this was the flask of oil of spikenard mentioned in other passages, it was valued at 300 denarii. A denarius was the equivalent of a day's wage, and thus this oil was equal to nearly a year's wages.

Some of the disciples were shocked and considered it a huge waste, saying the oil could have been sold and the money given to the poor. Jesus saw her merciful act differently, "For in pouring this fragrant oil on my body, she did it for My burial."

Jesus consistently told His disciples that He would be crucified and buried, saying "The Son of Man must be delivered into the hands of sinful men, and be crucified, and the third day rise again." This had always been His ultimate fate and His ultimate mission. As He dined, He well knew the devious plotting that was occurring, and He quietly prepared Himself for death.

Holy Week: Thursday Afternoon

The Passover Supper

Following Jesus' instructions, Peter and John went into the city and found a certain man carrying a pitcher of water, just as Jesus had said, who led them to a second-story room in a compound area known as David's Tomb, which became known as the Upper Room. There the two disciples prepared the Passover meal.

Since the exodus from Egyptian slavery, Passover is the most important observance in Judaism. The meal celebrates the Israelites' deliverance when the death angel, who was unleashed on Egypt, passed over the homes of Jewish slaves because of the blood of the sacrificial lamb on the doorpost of each house.

Immediately thereafter, the Israelites hurriedly left Egypt without putting leavening in their bread (their kneading bowls were wrapped up in their clothing), which made them eat flat, tasteless unleavened bread. Thereafter, unleavened bread became the central portion of the Passover meal, and the Feast of Unleavened Bread was a major part of the Passover celebration. Once the Passover lamb was slain, which had to be perfect and without spot or blemish, the entirety of the Passover meal took priority.

The Passover meal eventually became the basis for the Lord's Supper celebrated by Christians, and traditionally the bread component of the Lord's Supper is unleavened bread.

Jesus and His disciples would share this last meal together later in the evening.

Holy Week: Thursday

The Issue of Betrayal

One of the undertones of Thursday must have been the profound loneliness that Jesus felt. Throughout the three years that His disciples had been with Him, none of them really understood His divine nature or the nature of His heavenly kingdom. Only Peter seems to have had some basic belief that Jesus was indeed the Messiah, the Son of God, but that did not prevent him from denying his association with Jesus in the final moments.

Instead, the gospel record reveals that the disciples were consistently obsessed with Jesus creating an earthly kingdom in which they would have major roles. The disciples would often argue about which of them would have the most important position, or who would be greatest in the kingdom, and even the mother of James and John became involved when she asked that her sons be allowed to sit at His left hand and His right hand in the kingdom. The disciples' blind obsession with earthly political power continued until shortly before Jesus' ascension into heaven when they pleadingly asked one last time, "Lord, will you at this time restore the kingdom to Israel?"

As they increasingly realized that Jesus was going to be crucified, fear that the same could happen to them became very real. It would only be logical that self-preservation became a personal motive for each one. It is entirely possible that there were hushed conversations among the disciples about the best possible way to escape, and, if necessary, how each of them might gain the favor of religious authorities and escape with their life. Not one of them was brave enough to stand with Jesus through His arrest and trial. Instead, they denied Him and fled in fear.

So, in reality, it wasn't just Judas who thought of betraying Jesus in an effort to save himself. They all had considered it. When Jesus said, "One of you will betray Me," it is astonishing that all of the disciples asked, "Is it I?" Realistically, I doubt their question revealed some deep, introspective soul searching. Most likely, they each were gripped with the embarrassing fear that He had heard all of them discussing the possibility.

So, who betrayed Jesus? Judas Iscariot. Who could have betrayed Jesus? Each and every one of the disciples. Knowing this, Jesus died friendless and alone.

Holy Week: Thursday Night

A New Covenant

While Jesus and the disciples were eating the ancient Passover meal in remembrance of God's covenant with Israel, Jesus used the meal and its elements to establish a new covenant relationship between God and man that would forever change the course of human history. Jesus took the Passover unleavened bread, said a prayer of thanksgiving, broke the bread into pieces, and gave the bread to His disciples. As He did, He said, "This is My body which is given for you; do this in remembrance of Me." Then He took a cup of wine and said to them, "This cup is the new covenant in My blood, which is shed for you."

A covenant is the highest, holiest, and most personal and life-transforming relationship that can exist between two individuals. We often hear it used to describe an ideal covenant marriage between a husband and wife. Think of that same perfect relationship existing between Christ and His bride, the redeemed Christian church. More importantly, think of this ideal relationship existing between Jesus and you.

No longer would God relate to His people through cold, religious law and methodical ritual, but this new covenant would occur through Jesus graciously sharing the fullness of His life with whoever would believe in Him.

His body would be broken and crucified in order to defeat the stranglehold of sin on believers and free them from its consequences. A new life would be given to them through the power of His blood covering their past and giving them new life, as if they had been reborn. Because of Jesus defeating sin and death, life through this new covenant would be His life freely bestowed on believers which would redeem them, justify them before God, grant them His everlasting life, and make them a joint-heir with Him to all the riches and wonders of heaven.

This new covenant became the basis of the New Testament, the foundation of the Christian church, and the basis of our salvation and our eternal life in Christ. Jesus did this out of redeeming love for you and me!

But other developments were also occurring on this night. When the Passover meal was finished, Jesus and His disciples retreated to the seclusion of the Mount of Olives and a special area called the Garden of Gethsemane. As they did so, Jewish authorities were meeting and planning how and when they could best seize Jesus and arrest Him. It would need to be done tonight and done quickly, so He could be crucified before the Sabbath.

Holy Week: Thursday Night

The Garden of Gethsemane

The reality of what lay ahead began to deeply affect Jesus as He prayed in the Garden of Gethsemane, and He became deeply sorrowful and distressed. He cried out to His heavenly Father, "O My Father, if it is possible, let this cup pass from Me; nevertheless, not as I will, but as You will." His agony was so intense that the small blood capillaries in His face ruptured and drops of blood fell from His face. Jesus' anguish was so intense that He was near the point of shock and death.

He had taken Peter, James, and John with Him, and He asked His disciples to pray with Him. But as He prayed alone, the disciples ignored His request and fell asleep.

When He told them they would all be made to stumble this night, Peter vigorously declared that he would never leave Jesus. Pausing for a moment, Jesus looked at Peter and said, "This night, before the rooster crows, you will deny Me three times."

Then, as they were about to depart the Garden of Gethsemane, suddenly there was a noise and the sound of men rushing in. Judas had told the chief priests and elders where Jesus could be found, and a crowd of men armed with swords and clubs approached.

As Judas had prearranged a means to identify Jesus for this mob, He approached Jesus and kissed Him on the cheek. They roughly grabbed Jesus and led Him away. Ahead of Him lay a night and day of agony that we can't begin to imagine.

Holy Week: Friday Morning

Jesus is Crucified

Following His betrayal and arrest, Jesus endured a night of agonizing beatings, false accusations, humiliation, mockery, and abandonment by His disciples. Indeed, just as He had stated the night before, before a rooster first crowed and welcomed the dawn light, even Peter had denied knowing Him three different times.

Following a sham trial, Jesus was condemned to death by crucifixion, the most painful and horrible method of execution known at that time. The Romans used crucifixion both as a means of public execution of criminals and as a crime deterrent. The condemned was laid on a wooden cross with their arms outstretched and feet atop each other. Large nails were driven through their hands (or wrists) and feet. The cross was lifted up and the condemned hung there in agony for hours, or even days, until they died.

Crucifixions were done in areas most visible to others, often alongside heavily traveled roads, in order to deter potential criminals. Outside of Jerusalem, there was a noticeable outcropping of elevated rock strangely shaped like a human skull where most Roman executions in Jerusalem took place. The Jews referred to it as Golgotha (place of the skull) and the Latin name was Calvariae, which later became translated into English as Calvary, or Mount Calvary.

Before Jesus was taken away to be executed, soldiers again spit on Him and painfully forced a crown of thorns down on His head, mocking Him as King of the Jews. Even though weakened by beatings, Jesus was forced to carry His heavy cross to Calvary until He collapsed. A man from the crowd of onlookers named Simon of Cyrene was then forced to carry the cross for Him. When He reached the site of His crucifixion, Jesus was again mocked by Roman soldiers as they nailed His ravaged body to the cross.

Jewish daylight hours were calculated beginning at sunrise, the first hour. At the third hour, or 9:00 a.m., Jesus was crucified on Calvary.

Holy Week: Friday Afternoon

Nature Bears Witness

From the sixth hour (noon) until the ninth hour (3:00 p.m.), unexplainable natural events took place that left many onlookers in fear and caused others to wonder if, in fact, the true Messiah was being crucified.

From the sixth hour until the ninth hour, darkness covered the land, and there was no explainable answer. Old Testament prophets had said the Messiah would appear on the "great day of the Lord," which would be marked by cataclysmic natural occurrences, such as stars falling from the sky or the moon and sun standing still.

Other traditions held that the prophet Elijah would also appear to proclaim the messiah. When Jesus cried out, "My God, My God, why have you forsaken Me?" some thought He was calling for Elijah, and they huddled in anticipation of him suddenly appearing.

The combination of Elijah's possible appearance and natural phenomena consistent with the great day of the Lord had many people gripped in total fear, unsure of what might happen next. What would God do to them if they had killed the Messiah?

Holy Week: Friday Afternoon

It is Finished

At the ninth hour (3:00 p.m.), Jesus cried out in anguish, "It is finished." His head dropped down on His chest, and He died.

Nature exploded, as if enraged. An earthquake shook the area, rocks suddenly split into, tombs opened, and dead saints appeared. The darkness was intense, and the veil in the Temple that had historically hidden the Spirit of God from public view suddenly was torn into two pieces from top to bottom.

Seeing all of this, the centurion and those with him who were guarding Jesus were gripped in fear. The centurion looked up at Jesus and said, "Truly this was the Son of God."

Holy Week: Late Friday Afternoon

A Borrowed Tomb

Following Jesus' death, the question of a suitable burial tomb became critical, because according to religious law, He would need to be buried before the Sabbath began at sundown. Since Jesus had no prearranged tomb, and there was insufficient time to find one, it became necessary to quickly bury Him in a borrowed tomb and make permanent burial arrangements after the Sabbath, including anointing His body.

A wealthy man named Joseph, who lived in Arimathea and had become a follower of Jesus, went to Pilate and requested Jesus' body. Joseph wrapped Jesus in a linen sheet and placed Him in his new tomb, which had been hewn out of rock. He then rolled a large stone across the tomb's entrance and departed.

By late Friday afternoon, Jesus had been crucified, and He was dead and buried. To the Jewish religious leaders who had cruelly plotted to kill Him, it seemed like all of the drama over this man, Jesus, was finally over. But it wasn't; it had only begun.

Holy Week: Sunday Morning

April 15, 1979

I preached my first sermon on Easter Sunday, April 15, 1979, at Good Hope Baptist Church, Purvis, Mississippi. It was a morning of uncertainty and anxiety for me. A devastating flood had inundated large portions of my hometown, Jackson, and I was deeply worried about areas around my own home, in addition to the homes and businesses of friends.

I had taught several Sunday School classes at First Baptist Church, Jackson, but this experience of actually preaching a sermon, especially in front of friends and family on Easter Sunday, was new and quite unnerving. I was worried sick that the sermon would be so short that people would still be looking up the Bible verse when I called for the Hymn of Invitation. I had enough sermon notes to fill a binder, just in case.

The title of the sermon was "Woman, Why are You Weeping?" and it was about Jesus appearing to Mary outside of His tomb following His resurrection. "Whom are you seeking?" He asked her, or as the two angelic figures had asked, "Why are you seeking the living among the dead?"

On April 15, 1979, at about 11:30 a.m., I began to understand the power and meaning of Jesus' resurrection in a personal way. Forty-three years later, and after a few thousand more sermons, two books, and hundreds of devotional media messages, I'm even more amazed at the power of His resurrection in my life.

On that Easter Sunday morning, as I began talking about Jesus' resurrection, something happened to me that I'd never experienced before. Standing behind that pulpit, I felt myself transformed into a different person. Suddenly, I was no longer afraid, and a sense of power and purpose enveloped me. I spoke clearly, powerfully, and with conviction that soon touched many people in attendance.

I knew that God had called me to preach, but that morning the Holy Spirit began showing me how to preach. In all the years that I proclaimed the gospel, I had the same experience each time. I am normally a quiet, somewhat shy person who can be an introvert, and I struggle to find the right words to say—until I step behind a pulpit.

Then the power of the resurrection explodes within me and I lose track of time, my mouth can't keep up with my mind, and I can't get it all said in the appointed sermon time. The words and wisdom pour out of me because they are first poured into me. After every sermon, I was always emotionally drained and weak feeling, as if every ounce of preaching power had been wrung out of me.

When I began writing, there was an initial moment where I clearly heard an inner spiritual voice saying, "Write down the words that I give you; I will teach you how to write." I'm not a scholar: I'm just a stenographer for the Holy Spirit. Sometimes I may wake up in the middle of the night and write down the words that I'm given. It's been that way since 11:30 a.m. on April 15, 1979.

The New Testament speaks of power in many places, and if you are to understand Jesus' resurrection, you must grasp the meaning of resurrection power in your own life. The Greek word for power is the basis of our English word "dynamite." That's what happened in the tomb on the first Easter morning. The power of the resurrection is best understood by visualizing the moment when the unrestrainable power of Almighty God ignited, filling Jesus with eternal life again and causing the powerful angel from heaven to roll away the stone that sealed His tomb.

Death was forever defeated by the dynamic, explosive power of the resurrection. Resurrection power can empower and transform any person it touches, and it can transform the lowest sinner into the most dynamic servant for Christ. Resurrection power can make the spiritually blind see God's truth for the first time; resurrection power can right any wrong in your life; resurrection power can give you a new purpose and passion in life that you've never known; resurrection power can make you bold and courageous enough to spit on the devil and dare him to ruin your life; resurrection power can make you bear spiritual fruit and touch and influence the lives of countless people for Christ; resurrection power can explode within you and make you a true, living witness to the power of the gospel; and resurrection power can destroy your fear of death and fill your life with a determination to proclaim the lordship of Jesus until you draw your final breath.

After Jesus' resurrection, why do Christians even consider the issue of death? "Woman, why are you weeping?" Jesus would say the same to you that He said to Mary, "Don't look for Me among the dead!" The resurrection has changed all of that forever! We are eternally alive in Christ, and death is merely the transition from an earthly walk with Christ to being with Him forever in our heavenly home. The new covenant means He is eternally with us, and we will never to be separated from Him and the power of His life again.

The resurrection of Jesus has changed your life forever. By your faith in Him as your Lord, you are in a living covenant with Him through the power of His blood and through the power of His resurrection, and His bond with you cannot be greater, nor can it be broken. His resurrection power is now your resurrection power, and you are transformed in Him. The horror of your cross and your sins has been forever replaced by the power of His resurrected life in you.

So, shout for joy! Shout Hallelujah to High Heaven! Your sin is atoned for and you are alive evermore in Christ, and no power on earth and no scheme of the devil can hold you back and restrain you from living a powerful, dynamic, life-changing Christian life that glorifies Jesus.

Sin is forgiven, death is defeated, and you are redeemed, saved, justified, sanctified, and set apart for good works through faith in Jesus and the power of His resurrection.

Jesus has taken care of your future just as surely as He has taken care of your past. If you're willing to strike the match, the Holy Spirit will set the fuse, and the power of Jesus' resurrection will explode within you. When the dust settles, your past will be blotted out and you will be a new person in Christ with your eyes forever set on the things that are above, and not on the things of this earth! And it will all be because of your loving Savior, His empty tomb, and the power of His resurrection!

Walking the Road to Emmaus

A few hours after Jesus' resurrection, two individuals, one of whom was named Cleopas, were walking to the village of Emmaus, about seven miles from Jerusalem, while sadly discussing the day's events. Mysteriously unrecognizable, Jesus joined them, and He asked what they were discussing.

When they told Him how the chief priests and rulers had delivered Jesus to be condemned and crucified, Jesus responded, "Ought not the Christ to have suffered these things and enter into His glory?" He then taught them the meaning of various scriptures, beginning with Moses' writings and then the prophets, concerning the true messiah. Later as they dined together, Jesus broke bread and gave it to them. They immediately recognized Him, and He then vanished from sight.

Realizing Jesus was alive, they commented, "Did not our heart burn within us while He talked with us on the road, and while He opened the Scriptures to us?"

The greatest need of Christians in America today is to walk the road to Emmaus in their own life and hear the truth about the scriptures anew and afresh. Contrary to current trends, the Bible is not a political playbook for how the right can gain victory over the left, or vice versa! It is, in truth, a message of divine love and a passionate plea from God for each of us to enter into an eternal covenant of life and love with Him.

The Emmaus Road experience of these two is an early picture of the work of the Holy Spirit. With church attendance declining and Christian influence reaching low levels, the power of the Holy Spirit needs to fill our minds with divine truth as never before and ignite our hearts with a renewed passion for Christ.

We have lost our way, our passion, and our purpose. The redeemed church of Jesus Christ is not a political party, nor a branch of one, and it is a blasphemous insult to the resurrected Jesus to tarnish His holiness with foolish politics. We are the unique, holy covenant, blood-bought body of believers united with Jesus in an unbreakable bond for the sole purpose of being His living witnesses in this world and proving by our own life, work, and testimony that the resurrection of Jesus Christ is true, real, and life-changing. Walk to Emmaus with Him and see if He won't burn that truth into your heart and mind!

We have converted the Holy word of God into a spiritual menu in which we pick what we like and ignore the rest. For example, we can use the laws of the Old Testament that condemn those we don't like and preach hell-fire and damnation against them like self-righteous Pharisees, while totally ignoring Jesus' command to lovingly redeem them. Walking to Emmaus with Jesus can ignite a renewed passion in your heart for the life of all people.

Most Christians need a renewed vision of their own redeemed life. We have ignored Christ's purpose in our life too long. We have grown complacent about our holy calling. We have been bought at a great price for a great purpose, and it is time for renewed commitment to Christ's claim on our life.

Jesus specifically told us that we are the light of the world. We are a gleaming city on a hill, to use Jesus' words. If the resurrection of Jesus doesn't change your concept of yourself and your passion to serve Him, something is wrong! No one should ever take the amazing gift of a new life in Christ, empowered by His resurrection, and hide it under a proverbial bushel basket, but millions of Christians do every day.

Just like Samson with his hair cut off, they are blind, bound, powerless, going in circles without spiritual direction and have become spiritually weak and ineffective "just like any other man." No other people on Earth have the divine power within us that Christians have, but it's meaningless unless it burns within you and makes you different from the world, sanctifies you, and sets you apart for good works for the sake of Christ. Maybe a walk down the road to Emmaus with Him will make the truth about your redeemed Christian life burn with new brightness within you so that people will "see your good works and glorify God" because of the power and testimony of your transformed life.

Most Christians never see our relationship with Jesus in terms of a covenant marriage, but that's what it is. As the church, we are the Bride of Christ! He has redeemed us with His life; washed us clean with the power of His blood; given us eternal life with Him through the power of His resurrection; and placed the light of divine truth within us so that, through the power of His resurrection, we may gloriously radiate His love and truth to the world. His love for us is unconditional; His presence in our life is eternal; His passion for us is personal; and His power within us is without restraint. Can we not love

Him in return with the devotion of a glorious bride thankful for the new life He has given us?

If ever there was a time when we as Christians need to recapture a vision of our holy relationship with Jesus and our holy purpose in the world for Him, it is now. Walk with Him down the road to Emmaus, and let His divine truth burn within you again!

Dark Days and an Old Hymn

The early days of 1991 were the darkest days of my life. I had left a lucrative legal position in order to concentrate exclusively on the ministry, and it had proven to be a decision that taught me more about faith than I ever imagined.

I truly felt this was God's will and purpose in my life, but my decision of faith substantially reduced my income, and I was soon behind in the mortgage payments on my home and farm. The emotional and spiritual pressure was mounting daily. I knew the eventual outcome if something didn't change. I would be homeless.

But, every time I begged God to help, it was as if an angelic choir sang the words of an old hymn to me, "Have faith in God when your pathway is lonely, He sees and knows all the ways you have trod, never alone are the least of His children, have faith in God, have faith in God!"

Then the miracles began. First, the mortgage company lost my file, and I heard nothing from them for months. In the course of business, that just doesn't happen. It took the pressure of persistent demands off, but I knew the debt was mounting monthly.

I would take long, lonely walks and cry and pray. I would scream out in the darkness of the night, "Dear God...help me, please!" And the angels would sing, "Have faith in God when your prayers are unanswered, your earnest plea He will never forget, wait on the Lord, trust His word and be patient, He'll answer yet, have faith in God."

Months went by, and the debt mounted. Then the mortgage company found my file and the demands for payment entered a final stage. More pleas to God for help, and more singing of the old hymn, "Have faith in God in your pain and your sorrow, His heart is touched with your grief and despair, cast all your cares and your burdens upon Him, and leave them there, oh, leave them there."

Finally, the mortgage company began foreclosure proceedings. In about a month, I would be homeless. I was desperate, despondent, and spiritually drained dry, helpless and hopeless. And the angels sang, "Have faith in God though all else fail about you, have faith in God, He provides for His own; He cannot fail though all kingdoms shall perish, He rules, He reigns upon His throne."

By then I had started doing some part-time work with the Mississippi Baptist Convention, and on one of my trips to Jackson, I had this overwhelming desire to go talk to my former pastor at First Baptist Church, Frank Pollard, and ask him to pray for me. I shared my situation with him and how it had developed. We had a precious time of prayer, and I left.

A couple of days later, I was back in Jackson and Dr. Pollard invited me to lunch. Before leaving his office, he handed me an envelope and said he hoped that would help me some. As we began eating, I opened the envelope and began crying upon seeing the contents. It was his personal check for $10,000. When I finally was able to speak, I asked, "How can I ever repay you?" This great man of God lovingly responded, "Don't even say that. You won't pay me back. If you do, you will steal my blessing."

I joyously came home and went to the mortgage company and paid my account current. And the angelic choir sang again, "Have faith in God when your prayers are unanswered..."

Some of you may be walking a dark, lonely pathway today, struggling to understand why your prayers seemingly are unanswered. I can only urge you to trust God's word and be patient. He will answer yet; have faith in Him. His answer may be different, and it may come in a way you never imagined. Just always remember, "He cannot fail, He must prevail, have faith in God, have faith in God."

When Faith Looks Foolish

I

Step into the Water
(Joshua 3:13-17)

The Jordan River is normally a serene, slowly flowing river that traverses a descending course from the Sea of Galilee in northern Israel to the Dead Sea in southern Israel where it ends. Because the Dead Sea has no outlet, centuries of steady evaporation of water have left a salty mineral deposit that cannot sustain marine life.

Occasionally, however, the Jordan can reach flood stage and flows quite rapidly and dangerously. It was during such a high-water time that Joshua stood on the bank of the Jordan, virtually drained physically, emotionally, and spiritually. He had been divinely vested with the responsibility of finally leading the Israelites into the Promised Land, and that journey had brought them to this impossible and impassible barrier to their goal. It was like crossing the Red Sea again. How could he possibly get all these people across the flooded, raging river?

Joshua stood on the river bank feeling spiritually overwhelmed by the challenge before him. God had spoken, but what God said must have seemed like the most incredulous, divine instruction he could have possibly heard. The priests who bore the ark of the covenant, which represented God's power and presence, were to step into the Jordan's waters, while carrying the precious ark, and God would empower them to cross over.

"Step into the water," God said. It was as if God were saying, "I know this looks impossible, but trust me. You can do this; you can cross this flooded river and get to the place I've promised you. You will make it. It will be My power that will get you there, not yours."

Joshua must have thought how foolish his faith and his instructions looked to all those around him. "Wade out farther. Get a little deeper. Keep going," God softly said. It would only be human nature if Joshua thought to himself, "This is about the craziest thing I have ever done...telling these priests to wade into this river carrying the ark, when common sense says there's no way we can get across."

And then it happened: God took over. Suddenly, the raging Jordan River began to flow more calmly, and more slowly, until it stopped altogether, and the water backed up and piled up in a heap far upstream. Joshua's faith had been honored by God, and the wandering Israelites crossed to the other side.

Maybe you're standing on the bank of your own flooded river this morning...some physical, emotional, or financial obstacle that seems impossible to overcome and you are filled with a sense of hopelessness, helplessness, and despair. I know the feeling; I've been there before. Get alone with God for a few minutes. Let Him calm your fear. Sometimes He uses obstacles to turn us around. But many times, He uses impossible obstacles in our life to show us His power and love.

Listen closely to Him. If you hear this quiet voice of resolve and faith in your heart saying to you, "Step into the water. Wade out a little deeper," then regardless of how foolish your faith may look to others, don't give up and don't turn back. Whatever it is you face, with God's help you can make it to the other side.

Let's pray together: "Heavenly Father, I know that there are many hurting and scared people who may read this, and I know that You love each of them. Many face obstacles that have stopped them in their tracks in their journey of faith, and they don't know what to do. Fill them this day with a sense of faith, courage, resolve, and spiritual fortitude that flows from Your heart into theirs. I ask You to honor their faith in you and open for them a divine passageway to the other side, so that each of us may draw closer to you in faith and service. In the blessed name of Jesus, I pray. Amen."

The Awfully Sad Year When Grandpa Drowned

No, no, don't be shocked. It wasn't my grandpa who drowned; it was Noah's who may have drowned. In all honesty, the Bible doesn't specifically tell us that, but there is some fascinating scriptural evidence that he did.

You're probably wondering what is the significance of the manner in which Noah's grandfather died. I once stumbled across this interesting historical gem while reading Genesis 5:21-32, and it gave me an entirely new appreciation of Noah's struggle to be faithful to God, when virtually everyone around him considered his actions in building an ark somewhat foolish. I've personally come to believe that even Noah's grandfather may have had that same opinion.

You probably have heard of Methuselah, the oldest man who ever lived. The Bible states that he lived to be 969 years old. Well, Methuselah was Noah's grandfather. In between them was Lamech, Noah's father. Because of the sequence of their deaths, Methuselah, no doubt the oldest and most revered man of his day, would have exerted enormous influence and control over Noah in the patriarchal society of that time. It would only be logical that Methuselah observed Noah building the ark and shared his opinions about the project.

So, here's the historical nugget that will make you think deeper about Noah's faith. The narrative indicates that Lamech, Noah's father, died five years prior to the great flood when he was 777 years old. It further states that Methuselah lived 782 years after Lamech was born, or five more years after Lamech died. If Lamech died five years before the flood and Methuselah lived five more years, that means that Methuselah died the year of the flood. Did he drown in the flood with all the other unrighteous people? The Bible doesn't specifically tell us. If he drowned in the flood, one can only imagine Noah's anguish in knowing the fate of his grandfather.

Noah's family wasn't righteous, but through God's mercy, they survived the flood in the ark because of Noah's righteousness, because "Noah found grace in the eyes of the Lord." It's kind of an early picture of us surviving judgment based on our faith in the righteousness of Christ.

It's fascinating that Methuselah was not invited onboard the ark with Noah's family members. If he were alive when the flood began, it would imply that, despite his age, he was an unrighteous man like everyone else but Noah. Maybe he was just a crusty, ornery old man who had told Noah so many times how foolish he looked building this ark that he just couldn't swallow his pride and join the family. And then it started raining.

There's an old expression stating that it's not the mountain you face that causes the most grief, but rather the small pebble that's in your shoe. In like manner, often the biggest challenge to our faith isn't some great obstacle in front of us, but rather our family and friends around us. A wife's faith can be battered by a hard-hearted husband who refuses to attend church with her and who curses every time it's mentioned. Family and friends who turn a deaf ear to your testimony can quickly take its toll on your faith, and the negative comments of co-workers who chuckle about you leaving work on Wednesday afternoon to attend mid-week Prayer Meeting can be quite hurtful.

Maybe you face a similar situation today. Please know this: Your faithfulness to God may not be appreciated by everyone around you, but it does not go unnoticed by either man or God. Just think about Noah: You and I are here today because Noah kept faithfully building while others laughed and joked about his work. You have no idea what the long-term impact of your faith might be. So, just keep on faithfully serving the Lord, live and share your faith in Him, plant the seed, and leave the harvest to God.

The Parable of the Sheep and Goats
(Matthew 25: 31-46)

I

Although I have read this parable several times, it continues to grow in meaning for me. I am fascinated by Jesus' use of a shepherd separating his sheep and goats to demonstrate God's final judgment on mankind; I'm intrigued by the meaning of those on his right hand and those on His left hand; I'm amazed at the promised inheritance of the righteous; I'm spiritually captivated by the merciful basis on which the separation will be made; and I'm deeply touched that the separation of the righteous and unrighteous will be done by "the Son of Man" in the fullness of His glory and in the presence of the holy angels.

What is the significance of the title "Son of Man"? Throughout the gospels, the titles "Son of God" and "Son of Man" are used numerous times to describe Jesus, along with "Son of David." The ancient Jewish concept of a messiah focused on him being a divine figure vested with extraordinary power and righteousness. He would rid the nation of her enemies, restore her economic power, and re-create a political and military kingdom akin to that administered centuries earlier by King David. Thus, a popular messianic title was "Son of David," or one whose kingdom would be like King David's.

The phrase "son of" denoted not only a direct biological connection, such as a man's son, but it was also used to describe one whose characteristics and personality epitomized a certain trait, such as Judas being referred to as "the son of perdition."

Jewish messianic hopes did not envision the Messiah as the actual son of God, and they certainly did not focus on the Messiah being God in human form. In fact, Jesus' references to Himself as the Son of God were considered by religious leaders as blasphemous and worthy of death. The Messiah was to be the ultimate human leader and figure, manifesting every quality of a divinely gifted person—strong, wise, courageous, righteous, and committed to fulfilling God's will for Israel. Thus, as the ultimate human embodiment of every characteristic of goodness and godliness, the Messiah was to truly be "the Son of Man."

But Jesus was uniquely both. He was fully God, and God's only begotten Son, and He was also the ultimate example of a godly man. Thus, only Jesus was both Son of God and Son of Man. More than any other traits, Jesus was the embodiment of divine love and mercy for others, both of which were noticeably absent under the cold, methodical practice of religious law.

Why didn't Jesus just say "I will come in My glory and judge the nations"? Why did He use the Son of Man messianic title to describe His role in judgment? A close reading of the parable yields some clues that are underscored by Jesus' words and deeds.

For example, the gospels record how the suffering plight of the poor was ignored, sinners were unmercifully condemned, and the sick and needy were shunned. The most frequently recorded plea from people in the gospels was "Lord, have mercy on me."

The Son of Man title describes the ultimate example of a truly compassionate, caring, merciful, and kind-hearted man who would love and show mercy to all he encountered, even the lowest in society and the least important person around him—traits that were noticeably absent in both religious and civic leaders under the judgmental law of Israel. Quite understandably, through His ministry among the hurting masses in Israel, Jesus gave final and true meaning to the title "Son of Man."

If one is to better understand the basis of judgment between the sheep and goats, then one must focus on the Son of Man's capacity to show love and mercy to those shunned and rejected under the law. Jesus infuriated religious leaders by befriending sinners, and even dining with them. He openly broke the religious law by touching and healing lepers. He defied expectations by refusing to condemn a woman caught in the act of adultery, and instead showed her mercy and understanding. And, He pointedly and powerfully used Samaritans—the most hated people in Israel—to make some of His most remarkable statements of divine truth.

When the Son of Man separates the sheep from the goats, He will look for those in His flock who both experienced and shared the love and mercy of their Good Shepherd with others, even the least among them. It's our sinful human nature to be a goat; but it's our divine nature given to us by the mercy, love, and grace of Christ to be a sheep in His flock. The Son of Man knows which of the two we are.

II

The meaning of words can change over time according to their usage, especially when they are translated from an ancient language into modern English. As used in this parable, "glory" is a good example. Our concept of glory isn't exactly the same as it was in the original Hebrew or the later Greek languages. Thus, when we look back at its earlier usage, we can find gems of spiritual truth not readily apparent today.

Interestingly, glory in the Old Testament was used in different ways and had multiple meanings. It was derived from a concept describing weight. When applied to money, for example, it could mean riches, such as the abundance or weight of wealth, or when applied to one's character, it could mean exemplary or radiant. But, when applied to personal wisdom, it usually meant that one was noticeably wise or thoughtful in his judgments and decisions as he pondered under the weight of the options being considered.

The Greek term for glory, *doxa*, has multiple meanings also, and one of them includes a similar idea of judgment, opinion, or personal honor derived from a good and godly reputation. In terms of rendering judgment, it is how one exemplifies and magnifies good and godly character under the weight of having to make a serious decision. We use a similar concept to describe the weight on someone's shoulders when they are vested with a serious responsibility and have to make major decisions that bring them personal honor and glory.

Thus, in the language of this parable, "when the Son of Man comes in His glory" denotes the weight of His godly character and the wise and thoughtful decisions He will be making. His wisdom, goodness, and merciful consideration of the issues He judges radiates from Him.

The matter that the Son of Man will decide is weighty and constitutes a heavy burden and responsibility. God has prepared a heavenly kingdom from the foundation of the world reserved for the redeemed, and the Son of Man must determine those who will inherit that kingdom.

Consider the weight on His shoulders. The Apostle Paul stated that, through faith in Jesus, we become "joint heirs" with Christ in all of the riches of the heavenly kingdom. Determining who will inherit those eternal blessings and who will not is a heavy decision not easily made.

Jesus stated that He did not come to judge the world, but rather that the world through Him might be saved. His divine purpose was ot to condemn, but rather to redeem. However, it is the responsibility of the Son of Man to make a final and fateful decision regarding those who believed in Him and those who did not, and thus Jesus said, "For judgment I came into the world." In other words, this fateful moment of judgment was inevitably destined by the demands of His teaching and preaching. Therefore, His greatest and most important decision will be to determine and judge between those redeemed through faith in Him and those who have rejected Him, or, in the words of the parable, to separate the sheep of His flock from the goats.

There is no other person in human history more qualified to make this judgment. As the Son of God, He will use all of His divine characteristics of love, mercy, and grace in making His decision. Equally, as the Son of Man, He will embody the wisdom and judicious insight granted to Him by God as the ultimate personification of human goodness. Our fate rests in the hands of the only One who was fully God and fully man.

In making this judgment, the Son of Man will execute righteousness on the Earth, and He will radiate the holiness and goodness of God's redemptive purpose for mankind. God will be glorified in the final judgment made by the Son of Man.

III

The parable begins with a perplexing statement: "When the Son of Man comes in His glory, and all the holy angels with Him. " Why would He bring multitudes of angels to assist in separating the redeemed from the unrepentant, or the sheep from the goats, as the parable phrases it? What will be their role in the judgment process?

The answer isn't specified in the parable, but an interesting hypothesis occurred to me, one that I've never considered, even after having read the parable numerous times.

Angels are special spiritual creatures with specific functions within the heavenly realm. In general, they maintain a continuous atmosphere of praise and adoration. Some have served as herald angels and delivered divine announcements or proclamations on earth, such as the birth of Jesus. Legions of warrior angels would have come to Jesus' side had He beckoned them. And there are angels who serve as ministering spirits to assist us, just as those who ministered to Jesus after the devil tempted Him.

Psalm 91:11 promises that God has given His angels charge concerning us so that they may guard and keep us in all our ways. Unseen angels care for us and provide protection in ways we do not always recognize, even though we refer to them as our Guardian Angel.

But the verse about angels that really intrigues me, and is at the basis of my hypothesis about the role of angels in separating the sheep from the goats, is Hebrews 13:2, which states, "Do not forget to entertain strangers, for by so doing some have unwittingly entertained angels." That verse merits serious consideration.

The Bible also states in Hebrews 12:1, after describing the heroes of faith, that we are "surrounded by so great a cloud of witnesses...." It does not specifically define who those witnesses are. They could include faithful servants who are deceased, but could this cloud of witnesses also include angels who are observing our actions and merciful attitudes toward others, including total strangers?

Here, then, is the hypothesis of the role of the "holy angels" that the Son of Man brings with Him. The judgment of who is a sheep and who is a goat focuses on acts of mercy either done or not done for those who are hungry, thirsty, and needy. What if some of those hungry, hurting souls were actually angels who will bear witness to the Son of Man about our words, deeds, and attitudes toward those in need of our love, compassion, and mercy?

What if we unknowingly meet and relate to angels in our everyday walk of Christian life whose purpose is to test our level of discipleship and who will eventually testify as a witness to the Son of Man, either for us or against us, regarding our actions and attitude toward them, as He judges whether we are a sheep or a goat? That thought should make each of us read afresh the Beatitude that states, "Blessed are the merciful, for they shall obtain mercy."

In closing, may I share a personal experience? Several years ago, I was traveling from Hattiesburg to Purvis at midday on a blistering hot July day. I noticed a car parked alongside Old Highway 11 in an unpopulated area with a young black woman and child inside. They were sitting in the glaring sun with the windows down.

I stopped and asked if she and her baby were okay. She said the car was broken down, and her friend had gone to find someone to get it running. Then she told me how miserably hot she and her child were, and she asked if I had some water.

I told her to trust me and to get into my air-conditioned car with this old white Mississippi man. I could see that her baby was nearly in heat distress, so I drove them several miles to a country store and bought both of them water and some cold drinks and food. I then took her back to her car and waited with her for several minutes until repair help arrived. She thanked me profusely for my kindness.

The whole event was so unusual, and I've thought about it many times over the years. After thinking about the opening words in this parable, now I wonder whether she will attend my sheep-and-goat judgment and testify as a witness to the Son of Man about my level of Christian mercy on that hot July day.

IV

I have owned many animals over the years, including cows, horses, dogs, cats, birds, and an assortment of fish. But I have owned only two goats—Bonnie and Charley—and I don't desire to own any more. Those two goats were unlike any other creatures I've had.

They were nosey and seemed to always be looking for something they could mess up or destroy, such as getting in the feed storage room in the barn and ripping holes in feed sacks. A fence was only an invitation to escape. Not content with remaining in the pasture, they much preferred to get into the yard and eat flowers and shrubs, or to strip my grapevine bare.

Smelly, independent minded, hard to control, prone to jump on top of any vehicle parked in front of them, they, more than any animal I've owned, could bring out in me the dirtiest and most hateful thoughts toward them, and make me ask myself, "What on earth were you thinking when you got those two?" Needless to say, Bonnie and Charley did not really have time to get their goat bags unpacked before they were gone. Oh, happy day!

If this parable is to grow in meaning for you, you must visualize how many people act in a similar way toward God—defiant, headstrong, refusing any moral or spiritual restraint, looking for ways to escape His sovereignty and control, refusing to partake of the spiritual nourishment of His word and choosing instead to feast on the moral garbage of a worldly life, and the list goes on and on.

From a shepherd's perspective, it is understandable that goats are used in this parable as the object of divine scorn. Even though the devil isn't described physically in scripture, early Christian art and writings often portrayed him as having goat-like characteristics. After owning Bonnie and Charley, I can understand why.

Conversely, sheep tend to be more docile and trust their shepherd's care and leadership. They desire the nourishment of the green pastures provided by their shepherd and remain together as a flock, while relying on him for protection. The sheep within a shepherd's flock seem to sense their shepherd's love for them and will follow the sound of his voice calling them.

Thus, the Psalmist used the example of trusting sheep when he poetically declared, "The Lord is my shepherd; I shall not want. He makes me to lie down in green pastures; He leads me beside the still waters. He restores my soul; He leads me in the paths of righteousness for His name's sake. "

It is important to note the spiritual basis in the parable on which the separation is made. Throughout Jesus' ministry, He demonstrated mercy and compassion toward those hurt and scorned by the rigid coldness of religious law. When He separated the sheep from the goats in the parable, it was because the goats on His left hand had shown no interest in following His merciful leadership.

Rather than following their shepherd to green pastures and still waters of faith, they rebelled and chose instead to eat the briars, brambles, and bitter weeds of sin. And if there was a vineyard nearby, the goats probably found a way into the vineyard and destroyed all the grapevines. And it wouldn't surprise me if right in the middle of this defiant herd of four-legged demons were two old goats whom the shepherd had named Bonnie and Charley.

V

I admire left-handed individuals. If I try to write with my left hand, it's illegible. If I try to throw a ball left-handed, it goes about ten feet in whatever direction it chooses. Interestingly, the left hand has historically been viewed differently than the right hand. Probably because most people are right-handed, the right hand is used as a metaphorical description for a variety of relationships and situations. For example, an indispensable assistant worker is often referred to as one's "right-hand man." Viewed as an extension of one's trustworthy character, it is the right hand that is raised when taking an oath. Friendship, loyalty, and commitment to an agreement are expressed by a right-handed handshake with another. The left hand is never used for these positive gestures.

The Son of Man reflects these attitudes in the parable when He places the sheep at His right hand and the goats at His left hand. This involves far more than just placement in a position. In fact, for Christians, it is one of the most amazing aspects of this parable and one of the greatest promises of spiritual blessings in the gospels.

An ancient concept about the right hand is premised on the belief that it's a total extension of an individual's personality and power. It was as if an individual completely gave himself to another through his right hand.

Therefore, when the Son of Man places the obedient sheep, who hear His voice and follow Him, at His right hand, He is strategically placing them in a position to receive the fullness of His love, mercy, and grace into their lives.

By extending the parable's truth to our Christian life, the redeemed of Christ sit at His right hand and receive unto themselves the fullness of the life of Jesus. Every Christian life becomes an extension of Jesus' life in the world.

But, there's more. The Bible states in Mark 16:19 that "...after the Lord had spoken to them, He was received up into heaven, and sat down at the right hand of God." Pause for a moment and consider the incredible depth and meaning of that verse as it relates to this parable and to your Christian life. If you are one of His sheep, then you are at the right hand of Jesus and Jesus is at the right hand of God, and all the power and might of God flows through Jesus into those redeemed by faith who sit at Jesus' right hand.

But, that's not all; there are even more blessings. Romans 8:34 states that Jesus sits at the right hand of God and makes intercession for us. What an amazing promise of love and grace! Not only is Jesus our merciful Lord and Savior, but He is our eternal advocate who assures our salvation, defends our faith in Him, and secures the fullness of the riches of heaven for us, because those at His right hand are a joint-heir with Him, and the riches of the heavenly kingdom that belong to Jesus flow through His right hand into us!

That is the power and promise of the resurrection of Jesus expressed through His new covenant with believers. A covenant is the basis of an unbreakable relationship between two individuals who so totally give their life to each other that they become one—one mind, one spirit, one body, and one love. Each lives through the other. That is what Christianity is all about. We live a dynamic Christian life because God fully placed His life in Jesus and Jesus fully places His life in us—those blessed sheep of His flock who are placed at His right hand.

There is no such relationship for the defiant, hard-headed goats who are placed at His left hand.

VI

The New Testament clearly teaches that salvation is by faith and belief in Jesus as Lord and Savior. The Apostle Paul expressed it very simply in Romans 10:9: "…if you confess with your mouth the Lord Jesus and believe in your heart that God raised Him from the dead, you will be saved."

But with faith comes the responsibility of discipleship and service to God and our fellowman. It's not salvation by works, but rather a demonstration of our faith through our work for Christ. But what kind of spiritual conduct best demonstrates one's commitment to Jesus? The gospels provide an answer in two different places.

When John the Baptist was in prison and facing execution, he sent messengers to Jesus asking, "Are You the Coming One, or do we look for another?" Jesus replied to the question, "Go and tell John the things you have seen and heard: that the blind see, the lame walk, the lepers are cleansed, the deaf hear, the dead are raised, the poor have the gospel preached to them." Rather than simply saying, "Yes," Jesus' answer to John affirmed a level of mercy so unheard of in Israel that only the Messiah would do it.

Thus, when the Son of Man separated the sheep and goats, He applied a similar test to their individual work and spiritual service. Why? Why wouldn't He just look at their level of faith? Jesus' words give us the answer.

As He journeyed through Israel teaching and preaching, Jesus was asked which of the commandments was the greatest, and He replied, "You shall love the Lord your God with all your heart, with all your soul, and with all your mind. That is the first and great commandment. And the second is like it: You shall love your neighbor as yourself. On these two commandments hang all the Law and the Prophets." The word "hang" denotes a peg driven into a wall on which weighty items are hung. If the peg fails, all that it supports crashes down.

One should carefully consider the depth of Jesus' answer. At that time, there wasn't a New Testament and the only concept of religion was contained in the religious law and the writings of the prophets, what we today call the Old Testament. Jesus declared a shocking and almost unbelievable new religious standard: If people did not love God supremely, and if they did not love and care for others—even the least among them—with a level of mercy and compassion they desired for their own selves, then the whole idea of a covenant with God would fail and come crashing down. That's why Jesus established a new covenant with God based on redeeming love and not religious law.

Jesus came to fulfill the spiritual and merciful meaning of the law and the prophets, and not to destroy them. Therefore, the peg standard still holds true today. Without an overriding love for God and a merciful love for others, our whole concept of Christianity, our concept of America as a Christian nation, and even our concept of ourselves comes crashing down, if the peg breaks. Through His life and ministry, Jesus provided an example of how to keep the peg from breaking, and His example is the model for our Christian life of faith.

VII

The power of words to describe intangible emotions, such as love or grace, is fascinating. In the New Testament, the ancient Greek word for mercy is derived from the name of the Greek god (or goddess) Eleos, who was believed to be the ultimate personification of compassion, pity, and mercy. In the mythology of the day, Eleos bestowed compassion on all who came to her, she provided care and succor to the needy, and her sense of mercy was shown to all without condition or qualification.

Understandably, when the ancient Hebrew concept of God's compassion, benevolence, longsuffering, and mercy was translated into the Greek language, the word *eleos* was used to describe divine mercy. It essentially means the highest level of compassion, pity, and charity shown by one person to another. *Eleos* conveys the idea of a god-like capacity of mercy so basic to one's personality that it comes naturally to them. It is neither pretentious nor a hypocritical religious display.

One may think of it in this manner: Mercy is the deepest characteristic of God, as He broods over the plight of man. When

God's nature is vested in a Christian through covenant faith in Jesus, mercy likewise becomes the deepest characteristic of a Christian's character as he broods over the plight of his fellowman. Mercy flows unabated from the heart and soul of a Christian. It is who he is and what he does. He can't help it. It is done because of his relationship with his merciful God, and not for self-glorification.

The Son of Man's separation of the sheep from the goats was based on the level of mercy that naturally flowed from them toward others. The Son of Man specifically described the opportunities both had to feed the hungry, provide drink to the thirsty, assist strangers, provide clothing to those in rags and virtually naked, assist those who were sick, and visit and help those hopelessly confined in prison.

The response from both the ones on His right hand and those on His left hand was diametrically opposite. Those at the right hand of the Son of Man—those into whom all the mercy of God naturally flowed—had no recollection of helping anyone in either of those categories in order to gain the Son of Man's blessing. Why? Because divine mercy for others just came naturally to them without even thinking about their actions.

"When did we do this?" they asked, and the Son of Man replied, "inasmuch as you did it unto one of the least of these My brethren, you did it to Me." That phrase literally means "the least and most insignificant thing you did to help one of My brethren." But, because it was such a part of their merciful personality, they had forgotten all about it.

In contrast, those on the left hand were stumped at the Son of Man's statement. "When did we not do this?" they asked. The Son of Man pointedly summarized their uncaring and unmerciful actions, in effect saying to them, "You saw hungry, hurting, sick people all around you every day. You saw people homeless, desperate, wearing nothing but rags, strangers who had nowhere to go and no one to help them. Yet, in all your religious pretense about being merciful, you never did even the smallest thing to help one of My brethren. Nothing. You saw the opportunities all around you, but you had no compassion on them whatsoever. You simply did not care."

Thus, the Son of Man placed the merciful sheep at His right hand and the unmerciful goats at His left hand. Because their actions toward others had been so totally opposite, how the Son of Man treated the sheep and goats was also totally opposite.

VIII

The greatest spiritual treasure of this parable is the kingdom inherited by those at the Son of Man's right hand. The magnitude of the inheritance is vast in size, eternal in nature, and incomprehensible in human understanding. It is the ultimate and final gift of God to those redeemed by faith in Jesus, yet a divine blessing that many Christians seldom fully consider.

Interestingly, an ancient practice in allocating an ownership interest in one's estate to his heirs was by the casting of lots. Whatever method was used, it was essentially a random drawing that determined each heir's inheritance. That gradually changed to specific designations of property to specified heirs, but the old terminology was retained somewhat. The portion given to an individual heir was his "allotment" of the estate.

Thus, when you consider the inheritance of those at the Son of Man's right hand, you must first look at the nature of the estate and, secondly, the portion of the estate being allotted to those redeemed by faith in Jesus.

The Bible describes the estate as a heavenly kingdom without a specified beginning and having no end. It is as old as God and will exist forever, even as God will. The writer of Proverbs, which is a book of divine wisdom, personifies wisdom by saying, "I have been established from everlasting. From the beginning, before there was ever an earth." The Gospel of John refers to the nature of Jesus as "the Word," and states that "In the beginning was the Word, and the Word was with God and the Word was God. All things were made through Him, and without Him nothing was made that was made...and the Word became flesh and dwelt among us and we beheld His glory. "

Thus, the Son of Man promises those faithful followers at His right hand, whom He refers to as "you blessed of My Father," that they will inherit a kingdom prepared for them "from the foundation of the world."

What will be the size of the portion allotted to them as their inheritance? It won't be just a portion; it will be all of it. The Apostle Paul stated in his letter to the Christians in Rome that we are a "joint heir" with Jesus to all the blessings of the heavenly realm.

In order to better understand our inheritance, one must realize two great truths about Christianity: God reveals Himself in the Bible as Creator God and Redeemer God. His ultimate purpose as creator was the creation of a perfect, pure, heavenly paradise inhabited by the angels and by those redeemed by Jesus, our blessed Redeemer. As the Son of God and the Son of Man (fully God and fully Man), this kingdom belongs to Him—and to those to whom He gives His kingdom as their allotted inheritance and as a gift of grace.

The concepts of Christianity, such as spiritual rebirth, redemption, and sanctification, are not just religious phraseology. Considered in personal terms, they are the essential steps in making you an heir to the kingdom. If you are reborn spiritually and recreated in Jesus' image and likeness, and if you share His life jointly with Him through His new covenant, then you will also jointly share His kingdom with Him. His heavenly kingdom was made for Him and for those spiritually re-created in His image to be like Him. The writer of I John specifically states that, "...when He is revealed, we shall be like Him." The most amazing truth that you can personally fathom is that God created the kingdom of heaven to be jointly shared by Jesus and you!

How much of His kingdom does he then allocate as an inheritance to those at the Son of Man's right hand? All of it! A joint-heir inherits all of the heavenly estate, as do other joint-heirs.

Heaven is not a subdivision with each heir receiving a few square feet. Every redeemed heir sitting at the Son of Man's right hand is an eternal co-owner through inheritance, along with Jesus, to all of the heavenly kingdom that God specially created before He laid the foundation of the world. If you are sitting at the right hand of the Son of Man, you won't inherit just a little portion of heaven, you will inherit all of it, and it will be your guaranteed possession for all of eternity.

Just as the life and expression of merciful obedience by the goats at His left hand was different, so, too, will their eternal fate be different. They have no inheritance or reward. Instead, the goats are sent away into everlasting punishment.

A separate study could be made about the Biblical description of this punishment. Suffice it to say, the fate of the rebellious goats will be exactly opposite to that of the sheep, and it can only be described as a nightmarish, hellish fate, one that any wise and prudent person would want to avoid.

Parable of the Sheepgate

Religion has always been manipulated by man. The word of God has often been misinterpreted and misrepresented for both personal and political reasons, and even the merciful teachings of Jesus can become verbal missiles of malice when launched by a misguided malcontent. Jesus devoted Himself to inserting a new understanding of mercy and redeeming love into ancient religious principles that had been turned into callous, cold legalism. He was opposed at every turn by respected religious leaders who considered their interpretation of God's word as final. Divine truth twisted by the mind of a religious zealot is seldom a good thing.

Surprisingly, this is a parable about spiritual discernment and the individual ability to distinguish between fact and fallacy, between true Christian doctrine and religious demagoguery, and between a true preacher and prophet of God and an opportunistic charlatan. It is not always easy, for their robe of presumed righteousness is often very similar, and each offers a strong argument that he speaks for God. However, there are key differences: One is right and the other is wrong; one wears the mantel of a true prophet and the other is a false-prophet wolf disguised as a harmless sheep; and one's voice leads to Jesus and the other's voice most often leads to themselves.

Discernment of truth is a spiritual gift given to Jesus' faithful servants and disciples. Interestingly, this parable surprisingly sets forth an unusual challenge, because it essentially requires each of us to learn how to think like a sheep, and most Christians never give themselves that test of discipleship.

As you read this parable, consider a fascinating truth. If you visualize the common sheepfold as the whole of contemporary Christianity, the central question of the parable is not how the various flocks of sheep got into the common sheepfold, but rather who will lead them out to pasture each day where they can be nourished and mature. Visualize a large group of sheep in a common enclosure, and each morning they hear the voices of different shepherds calling out to them and asking them to follow his leadership. Thus, you must learn to place yourself in the midst of the bleating sheepfold and hear all the different voices enticingly calling out to you and offering to lead you along the path they've chosen for you.

But, if you learn to think like a sheep, you will know that in the midst of this cacophony of competing voices, only one is the voice of your Good Shepherd—the one you are willing to follow. The ability to think like a sheep and to hear His call to you, while ignoring all the rest, will change your life and the thoughts of your heart about your Christian commitment and your individual discipleship.

II

A parable is a literary method of comparing two parallel truths—one physical and the other spiritual—in which the greater spiritual truth is derived from the facts of the physical truth. Thus, this parable's physical setting is a common sheepfold in which multiple flocks, led by different shepherds, are gathered together and protected at night. Each morning, the individual flocks are called out of the sheepfold by their shepherd through hearing and responding to their shepherd's voice.

We live in a common sheepfold of religious beliefs and practices made up of multiple denominations, traditions, and historic beliefs about the interpretation of God's word. Just as the sheep in the sheepfold look the same, many of these beliefs are strikingly similar.

Jesus described Himself as the door to the sheepfold, and there is a fascinating truth in that description. Just as all the sheep of various flocks recognize the entrance door to the sheepfold, so do various religious beliefs recognize Jesus as "the way, the truth, and the life." They enter into the common sheepfold of contemporary Christianity by a recognition of Jesus as Lord, but their response to the voice of the shepherd they follow can profoundly impact their Christian life and their understanding of the truth of God's word.

Have you ever seriously and thoughtfully listened to the variety of voices calling out to Christians and beckoning them to "follow me"? You can find a revealing cross-section of beliefs by simply listening to television evangelists speaking to millions of Americans each day. There are traditional, mainline Christian leaders, but there are also a multitude of "shepherds" who proclaim a form of Christianity at variance with the true teaching of Jesus. Some stress adherence to a form of Old Testament legalism, some stress a "prosperity gospel" in which faith and finances are joint partners, and there are those who would make Christianity a central plank of belief in a political platform, just to name a few. Christians by the thousands respond to the calls of these various shepherds.

If the physical sheepfold in the parable is a spiritual picture of contemporary Christianity, who are the "thieves and robbers" that Jesus described who would lead the sheep away from the true Shepherd, and how do they succeed? Jesus used the joint phrase "thieves and robbers" to warn His followers about those who would take away spiritual blessings, either covertly or overtly. Thus, He cautioned against laying up treasures on earth where thieves break in and steal, but rather layup treasures in heaven that are beyond their reach.

Maybe that warning gives this parable some additional meaning. "Thieves and robbers" is the description Jesus chose to use to describe the impact on Christians by those who beguile believers into a false belief about Jesus' gospel message. This is often done through misrepresentation, and it can be subtle and disarmingly effective. A robber uses more direct pressure, though not always physical, including intimidation, condemnation, or haranguing someone to the breaking point. If thieves and robbers can try to steal sheep from the sheepfold, then thieves and robbers can also rob you of a true understanding of the gospel of Jesus.

For example, an overtly legalistic view of the gospel will deprive you of a deeper understanding of mercy. A well-known conservative Tennessee preacher was known to say, with regard to the sinful acts of members of his congregation, "Either get right, or get out!" Where in the gospels did Jesus say that? My heart breaks over this approach, because I personally know struggling sinners who had the church door slammed in their face by judgmental Christians, and they never returned. Jesus said the best way to obtain mercy yourself is to show mercy to others. Be careful and don't let some forceful preacher rob you of a deep spiritual experience of mercy by proclaiming a message that Jesus never said.

Media evangelists who equate faith and personal fortune are misleading millions. Jesus specifically stated that "life doesn't consist of the abundance of things possessed." Nowhere in the gospels does Jesus say that you will get wealthy through being His disciple. Yet, countless people are robbed every day by these thieves that try to convince you otherwise. Be careful, for they will deceive you and try to steal your treasures, both on earth and those laid up in heaven for you.

There are robbers all around us who take the teachings of Jesus and attempt to politicize and legalize them, thus forcing others to believe as they do. If you lean in that direction, you should think about this: The devil offered Jesus the kingdoms of the world if Jesus would model Himself after Satan—tell lies, mislead innocent people, promise one thing and do another, intimidate, coerce, and overpower those who do not follow—all the while pretending to be a model Christian. Jesus totally refused to use those tactics, yet millions of Americans idolize and blindly follow so-called Christian political leaders who do. Be careful, and "render to Caesar the things that are Caesar's and to God the things that are God's." Be very cautious in believing anyone who proposes to enforce the love of Christ on others by the power of civil law. You may have a spiritual robber in your midst.

III

Jesus identified three groups of people whose actions threaten the safety and security of the Good Shepherd's flock. As previously described, thieves and robbers would intentionally lead the flock astray. But, the third group—hirelings—is in a separate category. Hirelings are mentioned six times in the Old Testament, but they are described in the New Testament only in this parable.

Although Jesus admirably mentions the work of faithful servants in other parables and passages, He places hirelings in a special class of workers for whom He has no respect.

A hireling indeed performs a task. However, it is important to understand that his only motive is money. He is a mercenary. In whatever work he does, his only goal is to make as much money as he can for the time and service he provides. A hireling has no interest in or commitment to the work he does, and he has no vested interest in its success. He isn't concerned with the people or property involved. His only focus is how much financial gain he can reap from doing this job. When he has finished and is paid, he moves to the next job without any further thought about what he has just done or who paid him. His only real master is money, and his only motive in life is how much he can make.

A hireling shepherd, though he walked like a shepherd, dressed like a shepherd, and talked like a shepherd, had one major personality flaw essential to a shepherd—he did not have a shepherd's heart. He did not personally care one iota about the flock, only payday. He made no personal sacrifice for the flock's benefit and will always protect himself first at any sign of danger.

In truth, Judas is a good example. True, he was one of the disciples, but most of the gospel references to him describe his obsession with how much money he could make serving Christ. He regularly stole offerings given to Jesus, he complained about Mary wastefully anointing Jesus' feet with fragrant, costly oil of spikenard that could have been sold instead (probably so he could have more funds to embezzle), and when he finally realized that Jesus was proclaiming a spiritual kingdom, and not an earthly kingdom in which he could greatly profit, he decided to get as much wealth as he could from being a disciple, and he betrayed Jesus for thirty pieces of silver.

Christianity in America is plagued with hirelings. These are people who have little or no thought about serving Christ at a personal sacrifice, and instead focus on every possible scheme to convert Christianity into cash. I am incensed at the unmitigated gall of these preachers who get sinfully rich off of contributions they beg from donors for their ministry. What God-called servant minister of Christ needs a private jet (or in one man's case, three jets) to take him to different events? Why does a preacher who proclaims the lordship of One who owned nothing and had no place to lay His head need to extravagantly live in a palatial mansion and drive a super expensive luxury car? They couldn't care less about the souls of the people to whom they preach, as long as they can get their greedy fingers into their pocketbooks. They are modern-day cold, merciless, calculating hirelings!

IV

If one is to better understand the negative impact of a hireling on Christian beliefs, it is helpful to consider the concept of money and riches, as described by Jesus in the gospels.

Traditionally, wealth was not only considered a divine blessing, but, more importantly, it was also viewed by Jewish society as an indication of righteous favor with God. Thus, earthly riches were eagerly sought, and the wealthy openly flaunted their riches through extravagant living, including apparel made from expensive purple linen and a sumptuous diet and lifestyle.

This presumption of righteous favor with God lead to a merciless condemnation of the poor by the wealthy upper class, who viewed them as sinners, because if they were righteous and in God's favor, they would not be poor. The parable of the rich man and the beggar, Lazarus, is a classic example. The merciless rich man so detested poor Lazarus that he wouldn't give him the bread scraps from his table, and instead allowed Lazarus to starve to death at his front gate.

In openly parading their wealth as proof of God's favor, these false practitioners of religious perfection often stood on street corners to pray, or openly did charitable deeds, not to please God, but rather to earn the compliments and favor of admiring and envious onlookers. When Jesus commented that it was easier for a camel to pass through the eye of a needle than one of these merciless, self-glorifying rich people to enter the kingdom of heaven, His shocked disciples exclaimed, "If the rich can't be saved, then who can be?"

In stark contrast, Jesus set a standard diametrically opposite to the prevalent attitudes of His day. He owned nothing, wanted no earthly wealth, and emphatically stated that "life does not consist of the abundance of things possessed." Jesus completely changed the concept of riches and righteousness from stressing self-righteous greed to the opposite standard of selfless service to God and others without thought of personal benefit.

Jesus was so committed to such selflessness that He described Himself as a servant of all. Do not let that description easily slip past you. A servant was usually a household slave who owned nothing and had no rights or interests—and basically no life—other than that bestowed on him by his master. For Jesus, that flowed from His Father in heaven. Jesus emptied Himself of personal desires and became completely "self-less" in His service to God.

Therefore, His life became the eternal balance scale between a life that is selfishly focused on one's own interests and desires versus a life that is totally selfless and is focused on service to God and others without one thought of self-enrichment. When the scale tips to the side of selflessness, a devoted servant of Christ is found. When the scale tips to the other extreme of self-glorification and self-righteous boasting, a Christian hireling is weighed out.

A hireling always looks first for a way to advance his own self-interests in his religious service. He is never "self-less" in his Christian work for Jesus. Here is a simple three-pronged hireling test: Carefully and thoughtfully listen to someone's description of their Christian service and ministry. A mental image about them will slowly but surely appear in your thoughts that is painted by their own words. Who does your mind's eye see—Jesus or them? Which personal pronoun rings most frequently in your spiritual ears—He or I? Place their testimony on the balance scale anchored to the gift of discernment given to you by the Holy Spirit. Which way does it tip—selfish or selfless?

If the individual fails one out of three, he may just be a good servant struggling with his ego. If he fails two out of three, listen to your own inner voice of reason and follow your spiritual instinct. If he fails all three, you most likely have a Christian hireling on your hands. Use caution in following him and allowing him to influence and shape your Christian beliefs and values.

V

I invited the singers to our church because their family name was that of an old, well-known gospel quartet. I thought we were getting the original group, and I heavily publicized the event. The night of the concert, the sanctuary was full and people were eager to hear great gospel singing. Much to my surprise, a group arrived that was headed by the original group's cousin who had tapped into the family name just enough to deceive, and yet be legal.

Nevertheless, in front of this large audience, I welcomed them to our church, and I expected them to immediately burst forth with some great old hymn that would set our souls on fire. I was wrong. For nearly twenty-five minutes, this huckster sold tapes of their songs, begged for support for their "ministry," and repeatedly told how people could send them financial contributions "so they could continue to sing praises to Jesus."

The longer he talked and pleaded, the madder I got. From my front row pew, I finally stared directly at him and pulled my finger across my throat as a signal to stop the sales speech. He didn't. He then saw me slide to the front of my seat and prepare to stand. I was about thirty seconds away from standing and telling him to either sing or shut up, pack up, and leave. Seeing my red face, suddenly they broke out in a joyous song about Jesus. This man was a hireling. He wasn't interested in praising Jesus; he was only interested in padding his pocket with the donations of this trusting congregation.

Christianity in America is flooded with individuals, groups, and corporate entities whose primary purpose is to profit from our Christian faith. I applaud the talent of Christian artists. On the other hand, I am troubled by the Christian industry in America that annually makes hundreds of millions of dollars selling Jesus.

We seem to have forgotten the selfless image of our Lord, who gave His life to share the gospel without any thought of personal benefit. The issue is pervasive. I have no problem with a Christian servant being reasonably compensated, but today there are multiple pastors and denominational leaders with six-figure salaries and compensation packages that rival a Wall Street executive. That, too, troubles me.

In this parable, Jesus set forth the ultimate test between the love of the true Good Shepherd for His flock and the self-centered indifference of a hireling. The test is simply one of personal sacrifice for the flock. Consider Jesus' description: The Good Shepherd loves the flock and will lay down His life for them. He doesn't think about Himself, but His thoughts about and commitment to the welfare of His flock are unconditional and uninterrupted, regardless of the circumstances or the danger. The Good Shepherd's love for His sheep is the ultimate example of sacrificial, selfless love.

In contrast, the hireling has no personal concern for the flock, and he thinks only of his individual welfare, safety, and security. Because of his indifference and lack of sacrificial concern, he cannot be trusted to adequately care for any flock placed in his care. If his area of service becomes upsetting to him, he will leave the flock alone and move elsewhere, having no concern for their vulnerability to predators that would prey upon them. In truth, he could not care less, and he will make no personal sacrifice for them.

According to Jesus' description, when the hireling "sees the wolf coming," he will abandon the flock and flee. It does not matter how distant the wolf may be. Even the thought of the slightest danger or threat to his personal safety and security will make the hireling abandon his responsibility to the flock. Ultimately the flock will become confused and scattered by the wolf, caused by the absence of a caring shepherd. I've been in the ministry for forty-seven years, with twenty of those serving as a pastor of a Baptist church, and it's been heartbreaking to see how often this same scenario happens in a local congregation of believers.

The Good Shepherd's devotion to His flock is motivated by love and personal sacrifice, but the hireling has no idea what that means. That test was true in Jesus' day, and it remains true today. We are all in the sheepfold of contemporary Christianity. Why don't we recommit ourselves to listening for the voice of our Good Shepherd calling us out to His nourishing pasture each day and ignore the calls of thieves, robbers, and hirelings who will do nothing but rob us of our true Christian faith, lead us astray, and then abandon us.

The Blessings of a Good Pruning

I pruned Carlos yesterday. It was no fun, but it had to be done. Carlos, by the way, is my scuppernong vine, and Carlos is the variety, not its given name. It is a golden, sweet fruit that is simply delicious.

Scuppernongs are a delightful fruit and are a type of muscadine. Interestingly, native muscadines are normally purple, but this variety was originally somewhat rare, and because of its golden bronze color plus the fact they grew around the Scuppernong River in North Carolina, they got the name "scuppernong" attached to them.

But they have to be pruned to be productive. I am not an expert at this, but fruit grows on new vine growth. Thus, if there is a two-foot-long runner, think of how much nutrition is used in the nonproductive part before getting to the new growth and fruit. If the vine is covered in these runners, one can quickly see how that greatly hurts the production of fruit. So, the vine should be periodically cut back so that water and nutrition are not wasted on old growth that bears no fruit.

It's amazing to me that Jesus used almost the same words to describe how God works in our life to make us more spiritually productive. Referring to Himself as the vine and God as the vinedresser, shortly before His betrayal and arrest, Jesus said, "I am the true vine and My Father is the vinedresser. Every branch in Me that does not bear fruit He takes away; and every branch that bears fruit He prunes, that it may bear more fruit."

There is so much in our life that is not spiritually productive, including old habits, old ideas, and old legalistic views of religion. Faith in Jesus can bring about a profound spiritual change in our life, a totally new understanding of the love, mercy, and grace of God, and a new commitment to our personal responsibility to be faithful as His true witnesses in sharing Christ's life with others. Thus, Jesus said, "Behold, I make all things new."

If it is in the newness of a transformed life in Jesus that we live, then He gives us an amazing capacity to be His productive branches of the vine. "I am the vine, you are the branches. He who abides in Me and I in him, bears much fruit; for without Me you can do nothing," Jesus said. When God removes the old unproductive parts of our life and repentance brings about a fundamental redirection, then it's only logical that our life and work for Christ comes from the new spiritual growth in Jesus. Many people live frustrating spiritual lives because they are trying to make fruit grow from old branches, and it will not happen. Always remember that new growth is the only place where fruit appears.

We should get on our knees before our loving Heavenly Father today and ask Him to give us a good spiritual pruning. When the new growth in Jesus appears, there is no limit to the spiritual fruit that each of us can bear.

Musing at Grandpa's Well

I

Just outside my den door sits a concrete structure that once was Grandpa Voss' well, and the well bucket hangs on the wall alongside. It ceased being used as a water well years ago, and I converted it into a plant stand and patio table. But, oh the memories it holds.

When I was a little boy, I loved drawing water from the well, and I was always told to let the bucket down slowly so it would not muddy the water. I can only imagine how many buckets of water were pulled from the well for the needs of a large family and to water the mules and cows.

I sit by it almost every day, and I often think about my grandmother drawing cooking water and also water to heat in a black washpot over an open fire in order to wash the family clothes—and how a little sandy-haired grandchild was taught to draw water from the well and not muddy the water.

Interestingly, one of Jesus' greatest descriptions of Himself occurred at a water well in Samaria during a conversation with a beleaguered woman who could not believe that He would even talk to her, much less offer her hope and peace that she had never known. I have always considered their conversation to be one of the most beautiful and meaningful passages in the gospels.

So, I want to share some lessons about life and the love of Christ that I've learned while musing at grandpa's well. I hope you will enjoy them.

II

Some of the old country homes of my childhood had a common feature: There was a wide board across the end of the porch that held a large bowl used as a wash basin, a bar of soap, and a small towel that everyone used after washing their face and hands before dinner. There was also a water bucket with a dipper that was commonly used to drink water. No one worried about germs because bread and water took priority.

I often think how vital the water from grandpa's well was to my family's life. Interestingly and emotionally, I remember that one of the first things I was taught as a little boy was how to properly draw water from this well and be sustained by its life-giving nurture. Maybe that is why Jesus so powerfully used water and bread to describe His divine life because they are such simple examples, yet brilliantly effective.

As a master teacher, Jesus used the ancient truths of how God turned bitter desert water into life-sustaining sweet water, and how He made nourishing manna fall from the heavenly sky in the desert wilderness. But, with Jesus, it was no longer ancient stories and religious legend. Rather, in Jesus, the idea of the Bread of Life and the Living Water became ultimate reality.

As it was for the Israelites on their journey to the Promised Land, it is still the same for you and me. The two essentials that will sustain our life on our journey to the kingdom of heaven are the Bread of Life and the Living Water. Jesus declared Himself to be both of those, and thus He spoke of Himself as "the way, the truth, and the life." The older I get and the more I focus on His life, the better I understand why the Apostle Paul considered all his work and accomplishments to be meaningless compared to knowing the fullness of the life of Christ and being found in Him.

As I ponder these last seventy-four years, my spirit is often buoyed by these words from an old hymn: "When He shall come with trumpet sound, oh may I then in Him be found, dressed in His righteousness alone, faultless to stand before the throne." You will be spiritually enriched and nurtured if you will slowly ponder and spiritually absorb those words and their meaning into your life.

Jesus is the Bread of Life and the Living Water. Jesus is the life of God. Jesus is eternal life. The life of Jesus is the one perfect, pure, sinless life God ordained life to be from the beginning of time. He is now, always has been, and always will be in perfect union with His Heavenly Father. Consider for a moment what it means for that life to be given to you as a free, divine act of love and grace.

For all of us, life is getting shorter by the day, and we have no guarantee when it will end. But this I know: When I stand on this earth no more, then I shall stand before God's throne as a new creation in Christ. The record of my sins will be covered over by Jesus' blood; I shall be in unbroken harmony with God through the life of the new covenant in Christ; and I shall be splendidly dressed and radiantly robed in the righteousness of Christ alone, and, despite all my earthly sins, I shall be found faultless. Then, I will know the full meaning of being divinely nurtured by the Bread and Water of Life as I journeyed to my heavenly home.

On that day and in that moment, nothing I have ever said, nothing I have ever written, and no good deed I have ever done will contribute one thing to my salvation. My salvation is solely in the life of Jesus given to me by God's grace through my covenant faith in Him. And because my life will be found faultlessly absorbed into His life, the joy of my eternal life within the kingdom of heaven will burst forth in joyous thanksgiving and boundless celebration. What a day that will be!

Maybe it's just advancing age creeping up on me, but these are some things I think about while quietly sitting beside grandpa's well and musing about life and how much Jesus loves me.

III

I grew up in a home where there was never enough...of anything. Seemingly, there was never enough food to stave off frequent bouts of hunger; there were never enough clothes to stay warm on a cold winter day; there were never enough daylight hours for all the work which made us milk cows into the dark night; and there was never enough money to pay all the bills on time. So, I grew up wondering what life would be like if there was simply enough to not constantly work and worry.

Oddly enough, that worry even extended to concern about water. With a herd of Holstein cows that drank a few hundred gallons of water every day, there was a constant concern about adequate water. I have no idea what we would have done if the water well had run dry. So, when I heard the words to a old hymn inviting me to "come drink from a well that never shall run dry," I struggled to comprehend such a blessing, because in my mind, there was no such thing.

I grew up thinking there was a limit to everything and that sooner or later the supply would be exhausted and there wouldn't be enough, leaving me to experience a hunger and craving for more. That even impacted my understanding of God in my younger years. My parents' divorce when I was a child negatively impacted my life more than people knew. I became convinced that even family members would stop loving me at some point, friends would no longer care, and I'd be alone. That left me with a life-long sense of inferiority and a fear of rejection that has never left me.

Maybe you can better understand that when I began reading and studying the Bible, Jesus' statement to the Samaritan woman about drinking Living Water that would so quench her thirst she would never thirst again took me right to the border of disbelief. Never in my life had I heard of such a thing. Everything I had ever known in life was temporary, limited, transient, and conditional, including human love and friendship. But, the more I pondered His words, the more I entered into a spiritual understanding of God's abundance that I had never known, and it changed me spiritually.

After years of believing that even God would stop loving me for some sin I had committed, I began to understand the nature of boundless, unconditional divine love. It was entirely new to me; I had never in my life experienced love of that magnitude. Regardless of how often I failed, His love for me had no end. It was limitless. The well would never run dry.

I grew up being taught that God was a stern, unyielding figure who would strike me down for my sins. I was more afraid of Him than anything. I guess having an earthly father who would beat me with a hedge limb until I could barely walk didn't help any, but I had no concept of a loving, heavenly Father whose mercy, compassion, and understanding of my human struggles had no limits. That was beyond my comprehension.

And then there was His "amazing grace." When it ceased being just a beautiful hymn, and instead became a banner over my life, I began to more fully understand how, in the words of the hymn, that even ten thousand years from now, it will be as if it had just begun. His grace that took me from a stinking, impoverished dairy farm and used me to share the gospel of Christ with multitudes of people still is hard to understand. There's no human explanation for the divinely appointed turns in the path I've trod that has brought me safe thus far.

Except for God's unmerited grace, there is no way that I could have been blessed with the opportunity to tell the "old, old story of Jesus and His love" for the last forty-seven years. Just more miracles that I ponder.

So, the concept of there being a Bread of Life and a fountain of Living Water that will forever satisfy the hunger and thirst that I have for Jesus' unconditional love is very personal to me. When Jesus said, "Blessed are those who hunger and thirst for righteousness, for they shall be filled," it was as if He spoke those words to me personally.

One of my reasons for writing these devotionals is to let all of you know that I'm not hungry any more, nor am I thirsty. I have forever linked my life in an unbreakable covenant bond to God's eternal Living Water and to the Bread of Life. His name is Jesus, and He has quenched the hunger and thirsting of my soul. I have no need to worry; the supply is boundless, limitless, amazing, and eternal. Finally, there is enough.

IV

Love is what God is; grace is what God does; and mercy is what God feels. Think about this for a moment: The Beatitudes are eight well-known statements of Jesus describing the joy and blessedness of the Christian life, but only mercy is mentioned in them.

There is a reason for that. In reading the gospels, one doesn't find where some desperate soul begged Jesus to love and be gracious to them, but there are about a dozen specific instances where hurting individuals begged Jesus to be merciful to them. That doesn't include the numerous times in which Jesus healed countless sick people, touched and ministered to lepers, and befriended sinners who had been shunned. Of all the divine characteristics of Jesus, His limitless compassion and mercy are evident in both His words and His works.

Have you ever considered that the heart of God's covenant with Israel is premised on mercy? God saw the people's bondage and heard the groaning of their labor, and He was filled with compassion and mercy for them.

In the Bible, mercy is a divine motivator. The ancient language describes God brooding over the plight of His people to such an extent that He can no longer turn a deaf ear to their pleas for help. Sure, He divinely loves them, and He wishes to bless them, but His mercy compels Him to save them. It was in the midst of the overwhelming hopelessness and despair of enslavement and bondage that God sent Moses to deliver the Israelites to a land where He would fulfill all His divine promises to them.

That is just a preliminary picture of what Jesus does for each of us. Mercy and compassion were His motivation for promising the beleaguered Samaritan woman the Bread of Life and the Living Water,

110

if she would believe Him and turn to Him for deliverance from her spiritual bondage.

When I sit by grandpa's well, musing about my spiritual journey, I am brought back by the motivation of memory to a turning point in life. I had publicly professed my faith in Christ, joined the church, and was baptized in the tradition of a Southern Baptist. But my spiritual struggle only intensified. More and more, I felt enslaved by my human emotions and by my past. Not only were there the daily temptations, but I struggled with anger and bitterness over the pain of an abusive childhood—pain that simply would not go away no matter how hard I tried to forget or how fervently I prayed. Memory was like an ever-present slave master lashing my soul with each unforgettable detail.

Countless times I promised God I would be better, and countless times I failed. I had no one to talk to, because I became convinced that no one would understand, and that no one cared. I was alone, saddled with a burden that was emotionally and spiritually breaking me, and walking a path of despair and defeat.

Have you ever looked at all the words to the hymn "Out of My Bondage, Sorrow, and Night"? They describe me at that time. "Out of my bondage, sorrow, and night, Jesus I come to thee...out of my shameful failure and loss...out of myself to dwell in Thy love...out of despair into raptures above...Jesus, I come to Thee."

The words of old hymns are very special to me, especially these: "Just as I am, without one plea, but that Thy blood was shed for me, and that Thou bid 'st me come to Thee, oh Lamb of God I come! I come."

I stopped all the failed promises of spiritual self-improvement. If Jesus can accept me "just as I am," I can, too. I had finally found someone who would listen, someone who cared, and someone with infinite mercy, compassion, and understanding of my human struggle. His name is Jesus.

And so in my pensive, reflective moments musing by grandpa's well, and looking back on life, I, too, have heard this merciful invitation, "Like the woman at the well, I was seeking for things that could not satisfy. And then I heard my Savior speaking, 'Draw from My well that never shall run dry.'" I did, and so can you, my friend.

The Samaritan woman at the well, who was she? Why is her brief encounter with Jesus beside a water well in the heat of the day such a pivotal point in the gospel record of Jesus' life and ministry? What can we learn about ourselves as we learn more about her?

Essentially, the woman at the well was a nobody who became an eternal example of everybody, in many ways. She represents thousands of lonely, dispirited, abused individuals, especially women, who could have taken her place. She was the least likely individual to experience mercy and compassion from anyone, and she knew that.

The magnitude of her despair, emptiness, and worthlessness is difficult to comprehend. In her male-dominated society, she could only view herself as the property of a man, who could treat her unmercifully and easily dump her through the sham of a divorce, leaving her to be viewed as an adulteress. She had known the crushing hurt of that rejection several times, and now she just lived with someone in order to survive, and he used her for his pleasure and as a water-bearing servant.

As a Samaritan, she knew the personal indignity and pain of racial and ethnic hatred, especially from her Jewish neighbors. Nothing destroys self-esteem and hurts worse than knowing you are viewed as little more than a mongrel dog in the eyes of others.

Thus, her life was meaningless, devoid of purpose, hope, and self-worth. She simply existed in an unmerciful world, bracing herself both physically and emotionally for more pain and rejection, and ultimately death.

And then she met Jesus at a water well. He used the symbol of water to paint both a picture of her life and His life. He told her that, just like the water she was drinking, she was thirsting for something higher and holier in life that could not be satisfied through any earthly means. Regardless of how often she drank the water of physical life, she would thirst again, and again, and again.

But, if she drank the Living Water that He offered, she would never thirst again, and there is a divine reason. Physical water is a chemical compound consisting of two parts of hydrogen and one part of oxygen gases that have liquified. The body quickly absorbs this water, and we thirst again. Living Water, however, is spiritual and is composed of the redeeming love, limitless grace, and compassionate mercy of God in equal parts. It does not flow into the stomach to be used and expelled as body waste. Instead, Living Water flows into the heart and is never wasted or expelled. It profoundly changes us and exponentially grows us spiritually into the image and likeness of Christ. Living Water amazingly cleanses our heart of bitterness toward life, prejudice toward others, and the burden of unforgiven sin.

Living Water miraculously makes you feel loved, maybe for the first time in your life; it fills you with a sense of forgiveness and freedom; it restores a sense of self-worth and makes you know that God places value on your life, regardless of how insignificant and inferior you may feel; it gives life a purpose and meaning that cannot be destroyed or diminished by the pressures of life; and it changes the burdens of temporary grief into a life-long quest for the glory of God.

Living Water will fill you with power and purpose you've never known before; it will embolden you, make you courageous, and cause you to unashamedly share the gospel of peace. Living Water will make you a disciple of Jesus and a true, living witness of the power of His love, mercy, and grace. Your impact on the life of others becomes limitless.

Drinking Living Water is like drinking liquid dynamite, for the word dynamite is derived from the ancient word for the spiritual power of the new covenant in Christ. When it ignites within your heart, there is no power on earth that can limit your walk with Jesus, restrain your outreach to others, or silence your testimony for Christ. Living Water will cause you to feel reborn, and you will realize that all the old, burdensome things of life have passed away and all things have become new.

Once you freely drink the Living Water that only Jesus provides, you will discover an amazing truth: It quenches your thirst for anything else, its source is the kingdom of heaven, its supply is endless, its spiritual nurture is transforming, and you have Jesus' personal guarantee that His well of Living Water will never run dry...not even for all the eternal ages to come.

Living Water so changed the life of this Samaritan woman that she became a central figure in the life and ministry of Jesus. It can change you just the same.

I bear witness to you, my friends, that these things are true.

VI

About twenty-five years ago, I read this challenging definition of commitment, composed by an unknown author. I copied and framed it, and it has hung on my study wall since. I have read it many times over the years, and I have prayed that it describes my commitment to share the Living Water of Jesus.

"Commitment"

"I'm a part of the fellowship of the unashamed. I have Holy Spirit power. The dye has been cast. I have stepped over the line. The decision has been made. I am a disciple of His. I won't look back, let up, slow down, back away or be still.

My past is redeemed. My present makes sense. My future is secure. I'm finished and done with low living, sight walking, small planning, smooth knees, colorless dreams, tamed visions, mundane talking, cheap living and dwarfed goals.

I no longer need pre-eminence, prosperity, position, promotions, plaudits or popularity. I don't have to be right, first, tops, recognized, praised, regarded or rewarded. I now live by faith, lean on His presence, walk by patience, lift by prayer and labor by power.

My face is set, my gait is fast, my goal is heaven, my road is narrow, my way is rough, my companions few, my Guide reliable, and my mission clear. I cannot be bought, compromised, detoured, lured away, turned back, deluded or delayed.

I will not flinch in the face of sacrifice, hesitate in the presence of the adversary, negotiate at the table of the enemy, ponder at the pool of popularity, or meander in the maze of mediocrity.

I won't give up, shut up, or let up, until I have stayed up, stored up, prayed up, paid up, and preached up for the cause of Christ. I am a disciple of Jesus. I must go till He comes, give till I drop, preach till all know and work till He stops me. And when He comes for His own, He will have no problems recognizing me—my banner will be clear!" As I sit musing by grandpa's well, I just want to be a faithful servant for the Lord, who tirelessly works and who quinches his thirst for righteousness with Living Water drawn from the eternal well that never shall run dry.

My Favorite Sermon Series

I have preached well over two thousand sermons during twenty years as a pastor and shared hundreds of Wednesday night Bible studies. In the past several years, I've written a couple of books and posted numerous devotionals on Facebook. You might wonder whether I have any favorites out of all these, and the answer is yes.

There are at least four sermons that I think about fairly often because of their impact on me, and I want to share a summation of each one. I hope you are blessed by them.

I

Cows and Cow Trails

If you have seen cows in a pasture, then you've probably seen a cow trail. Cows are creatures of habit, and they often walk across a pasture along a narrow, well-worn path about twelve inches wide. Once a trail is established, the cows will seldom depart from it.

One morning I was trying to feed some grain to six Hereford cows, and I was calling them to follow me as they walked along their narrow trail. They stopped and listened to my call, as if pondering whether to respond, and then dropped their heads and continued down their path of habit.

I stared in disbelief. I was trying to feed them grain, but they contented themselves with dried-out grass because they would not leave their trail. Suddenly, a resounding inner voice spoke to me in the middle of that cow pasture: "There's My church!" As I stood there, these thoughts flooded my mind. Not long after that, I preached a sermon entitled "Cows and Cow Trails."

One of the greatest challenges Jesus faced was getting His followers to move away from religious ritual and experience the fresh anointing of the Holy Spirit that would make them living witnesses of the spiritual power of the new covenant. The Spirit, Jesus said, would take all things that were Christ's and declare it through them, joyously filling them with the good news of the gospel. Jesus promised that Christians would prove they were His disciples through loving God and others as never before and through sharing the gospel in places they never dreamed they'd go.

However, many were locked in the traditions of the elders and refused to consider new truth or to serve God and others in new ways. They adamantly refused to leave the path of religious ritual and instead desired to just keep doing what they had always done. Many Christians today are no different.

A religious cow trail will never take you anywhere that you haven't been before. There are no new experiences in a cow trail, no freshness, no new views or insight into God's word to see and ponder, no vistas to beckon you to a new spiritual adventure and new discipleship, no new vision for service to God or your fellowman, and no clear understanding about your purpose in life as a Christian. A cow trail's only characteristic is repetition—the same thing over and over until it is meaningless habit. If you are to learn one thing about the dynamic moving of the Holy Spirit, you must learn this: The Holy Spirit does not live and work in a religious cow trail!

I can't tell you how many faces I have looked into from the pulpit on Sunday mornings over the years who were bored, lifeless, and uninvolved. The quickest way to sap the vitality out of worship is to make it a meaningless weekly ritual in which your main unspoken desire is for the service to end so you can go home.

There is no green grass in a cow trail. It is dead. Slowly but surely, every step down that path has stomped the life out of it. There is no joy, vitality, and no celebration of everlasting life. The dynamic life of Christ freely given to us and empowered by the limitless power of the Holy Spirit just becomes the weekly ritual of "going to church" for an hour. Being reborn spiritually and becoming a new creature in Christ is not supposed to be the most boring thing you've ever experienced.

You want to know what will pour water on a preacher's fire quicker than anything else? Let him be so full of the power of the Holy Spirit while preaching that he can't get it all said, and yet he looks into the faces of people nodding off and going to sleep, people checking their watches, teenagers passing notes and laughing, and people making faces at the baby or toddler in the pew ahead of them and totally not interested in nor listening to the sermon.

We say that the preacher is anointed by the Spirit and speaks for God, but a lot of folks don't act like it. Just as a little private test, I would occasionally ask a few people after church what the sermon was about (mostly close friends who I knew would not get mad at me). You guessed it: Within minutes after the service, most could not remember what God had spoken to them. Think about that a moment because it's not just frustrated preacher talk. Can a devoted Christian truly listen to a sermon, as if God were speaking to them through the minister, and then ten minutes later can't remember what Holy God said to them?

A cow trail only gets deeper the longer it's followed, and the ruts and scars carved out by habit last for years. It gets so deep until it's virtually impossible to move in a new direction. The Christian doctrine of sanctification is sorely understated today. We are saved at a great price for a great purpose. Through our salvation, we are called out of our attachment to this world and set apart to live as ambassadors for Christ. We are the continuation of His light in the darkness of this world. That is the greatest calling and the most joyous work anyone can experience—but it's work that can't be performed in a cow trail.

I made a decision years ago to be a different kind of preacher. I did my best to make the gospel message the most interesting and fascinating thing that people had heard. I never told little stories to make a point; I didn't tell jokes to make people laugh; and I didn't use three sermon points that all rhymed. I tried as best I could to teach, instruct, inspire, edify, and lead people not only to salvation through faith in Jesus, but to also inspire them to experience the dynamic, joyous, life-transforming power of the gospel so that worship was the most enjoyable and meaningful experience of their week's activities. I tried to make every sermon unique and different so that it was never routine and boring and always contained food for thought that worshippers had not considered before.

I tried my best to make people enjoy coming to church, to be fascinated by what they heard and learned, and yearn to come back and hear more. I don't know whether I succeeded or not, but I certainly tried. And, believe it or not, a good bit of that determination began by standing in a pasture and watching six cows turn down the refreshing nurture I offered them because they simply would not abandon their worn-out trail of habit and by realizing how vividly their actions portrayed a lot of people's Christian worship habits. I was determined not to be that way as a preacher and to inspire others not to fall into that religious rut, also.

Years ago, I made a commitment to Christ to call others to get out of the worn-out trail of human habit and follow Him down new paths of righteousness for His name's sake, thus becoming faithful servants and living witnesses for Him. Only in that way could His joy in serving His heavenly Father find completion in them. Whether in preaching, writing books, or posting weekly devotionals on Facebook, I've tried to make the gospel the best and most joyous news you've ever heard. For forty-seven years, I've tried to avoid the cow trails.

II

The Prayer of Jabez
(1 Chron. 4: 9-10)

Jabez is an unusual and fascinating Old Testament figure. He is mentioned only one time, and yet his prayer has been the source of numerous studies and books. Jabez prayed for four specific things that God granted him because he was "more honorable than his brethren." He asked God to bless him, and he asked for an increase in his territory; he prayed for the hand of God to be with him; and he asked God to keep him from evil so that he would no longer suffer grief and cause pain.

Because of the sincerity of his prayer and his faith, God granted his request, and centuries later Jabez's influence continues to increase. It is truly an amazing prayer. That is all we know about Jabez, except for one crucial factor—why he prayed his prayer.

One can learn much about Jabez by what isn't written, and the unwritten chronicle of his life has profoundly impacted me over the years, as it has touched others. It's apparent that something heartbreaking happened to Jabez in his infancy, or maybe before his was born. It was so traumatic that his mother named him "Jabez," which literally means "he makes sorrowful," because "I bore him in pain."

Think about that for a moment, and his prayer begins to come alive. Was he unwanted? Was it a terribly difficult labor? Could he have been conceived as the result of some awful and painful act? We don't know, but it was so crushing that his mother gave him a name that is best understood as "pain," and that pain haunted Jabez the rest of his life.

But, Jabez's prayer establishes a spiritual principle that can profoundly impact your life, as it has mine: He refused to become a

118

victim of negative circumstances in his life, and instead he steadfastly determined that he would be victorious over the grief that plagued him. The power of Jabez's prayer lies in his desire to turn his grief into God's glory. And God granted his request!

Jabez's prayer is akin to the Apostle Paul praying numerous times for God to remove the "thorn in the flesh" that constantly buffeted his spirit. He never described the nature of the "thorn," but it brought him continuous pain of some kind. God's only response to Paul's prayers for the pain to subside was, "My grace is sufficient for you, for My strength is made perfect in weakness" (2 Cor. 12:7-9). So, what did Paul do? He turned his grief and pain into a glorious life of service to Christ and others.

If you are to understand the impact that the prayer of Jabez has had on me, and if I am to encourage you as much as I desire with this devotional, then I need to bare my heart and soul in a way that I've never shared before. I am convinced that something unpleasant happened to me as a little boy, and I don't know what it was and I probably never will. But the imbedded and suppressed pain has been with me all my life. I once told my mother that I could remember very little about my early childhood, and she quietly replied, "It's best that you can't." But, when a seventy-four-year-old man suddenly experiences vague memory flashbacks that cause him to start crying, the inner pain is real.

I suspect that many of you deal with undescribed pain that shapes your life, too. As a pastor, I've seen it firsthand. A lady came into my office one morning, obviously upset. She was one of the most admired people in the church, had a wonderful family from all appearances, and her husband was financially successful and a respected church member. As soon as I closed my office door, she began weeping uncontrollably and sobbed, "I just can't take it anymore." She continued repeating those words over and over. "I just can't take the pain." What appeared to others as an ideal family was far from it. Some of you may be there with her.

When I left the last church I served as pastor, I thought my ministry of sharing the gospel was over, and the pain and emptiness was at times almost unbearable. But, Jabez became my encouragement, and I was determined to convert my grief into God's glory. Through writing books and sharing these devotionals over the years, I've actually been blessed with the opportunity to share the gospel with more people than I ever did as a pastor, and the ministry dreams I have for the future will expand that territory even more, if I may use Jabez's prayer phrase to describe my further plans.

After forty-seven years in the ministry, I'm convinced that all of us struggle with emotional, physical, or spiritual pain that deeply impacts our life in one way or another. Often, it is known only to us, and often it is subconscious and stems from things we've tried to suppress and forget. But the scars are there.

You have greater control over the situation than you think, but you must make a decision. You can do nothing and continue being a victim and little will change. The pain will just continue to define you and be a thorn in your flesh, as Paul described. Or, you can become a modern-day Jabez and determine to convert your grief into God's glory. You have no idea how many lives can be changed by your courage, determination, and testimony.

When God places His hand on you and begins to increase your life's influence and impact, you will find that your deepest hurt can become a holy event through His touch and that your greatest grief can become His greatest glory in your life. Then you can begin to understand the mystery behind Romans 8:28 that says, "And we know that all things work together for good to those who love God, to those who are called according to His purpose," and you will better realize that "all things" include all the things that have brought you the greatest pain in life. It is one of the greatest truths that you can experience, but God's amazing grace is indeed sufficient to turn your greatest grief into His greatest glory in your life.

III

Give Me This Mountain

Caleb's long wait was over, and the dream and desire he had cherished for over forty years was finally within his grasp, even if his eighty-five-year-old grasp wasn't what it once was. After all those decades of saying "if only," Caleb could at last climb his mountain again.

Caleb had originally been one of a select team sent in to look at the land divinely promised to the Israelites after their flight from Egyptian bondage. Caleb climbed to the top of Mt. Hebron, saw the Promised Land before him, and believed that God would grant it to the wandering Israelites, as He had promised. The others in his group disagreed and feared disaster and certain defeat if they tried to enter, and the faithless people listened to their dire warnings in spite of all that God had done for them.

For the next forty years, the Israelites wandered in the Sinai wilderness until all the unfaithful generation had died. Now, under Joshua's leadership, they were finally going to enter the land. Of the multitude of thousands who left Egypt, only Joshua and Caleb were still alive. The people who did enter were descendants of those who died because of their lack of faith. For all of those aimless years, Caleb no doubt wondered what might have been if only the people had believed him and faithfully entered into God's promise.

When asked what land area he wanted, Caleb replied, "...the Lord has kept me alive...these forty-five years...while Israel wandered in the wilderness; and now, here I am this day, eighty-five years old. As yet I am as strong this day as on the day that Moses sent me. Now therefore, give me this mountain...."

You may be wondering why Caleb's statement touches me so deeply, and I hope you will truly see my answer as not some self-glorifying boast, but rather as a sincere desire to achieve a forty-year-old goal. Allow me to explain: When I was in seminary in 1979, I took a course on the dynamics of preaching, and each student had to preach a sermon to the class and to our professor. My sermon was entitled, "You Didn't Call Me, but I Surely Did Call You," and it was based on Jesus' statement, "You did not choose Me, but I chose you and appointed you that you should go and bear fruit" (John 15:16). After the class ended, my professor took me aside privately and encouraged me: "You have a unique gift and a unique calling. Use it to bear much fruit for the Lord." The idea that, out of His millions of options, the Lord would call me to preach the gospel for Him has for decades been like a racing engine in my soul, for which I long ago lost the switch-key and can't turn it off.

For over forty years, my desire and dream has been to teach and preach the gospel to as many as possible. But during those decades, I've surely spent some time in the lonely, frustrating wilderness, and I've mentally explored every "what if" ministry question that entered my mind.

But the mountain is still before me, and the dream hasn't died. I'm not yet eighty-five years old, as Caleb was, but at seventy-four, it's coming down the road pretty fast.

But, even at my age, I have a view of my mountain that might surprise you. Like Caleb's mountain was for him, I'm looking at my mountain from the west—moving away from my bondage—and my mountain is to the east. I don't look at the tiring sunsets behind me anymore. Instead, I focus on the sunrises ahead of me and the opportunities that each new day affords. The fear of failure has been cast aside, and the shroud of doubt has been left behind in the dusty despair of the wilderness, along with all the discouraging comments of the naysayers.

You must grasp one great truth about Caleb's mountain: The sun never sets behind it. It is situated to the east of your bondage, just as the garden filled with God's promises was located in the "east of Eden," and it promises the hope of a new day with each new sunrise. When you set your mind to climb Caleb's mountain, you must realize that Egypt and the wilderness is behind you, and you're never going back there again!

The key to understanding Caleb's mountain is that it's never too late for an older person to dream. So, here's my mountain that I still want to climb in the autumn years of my life: I've published one book on the Sermon on the Mount, another one on Jesus' parables, and, God willing, hopefully this devotional book will soon be ready, followed by a book on Jesus' miracles. Then, I hope to write a commentary on Galatians regarding freedom from religious law through grace.

I also want to start a YouTube video ministry of teaching and informal-style preaching. There's a lot of preparation yet to do, but I'm headed up that mountain. I may wear out a few walking canes, and I may have to stop fairly often and let my heart stop fluttering, but I'm determined to get to the top. Before I die, I want to know that I have shared the gospel with multiplied thousands of people. I just want to stand on top on my mountain one day and gaze into the Promised Land while holding a proverbial full fruit basket.

If you think about it seriously, there's probably a mountain you still want to climb—something you've dreamed about and yearned to do for Jesus for a long time. You can still do it. It might take some time and extra effort, but with faith in God and in yourself, and through courage and determination, you can lift your eyes to the spiritual heights of your dreams that are before you and say, "Lord, give me this mountain."

IV

Drinking Water Like a Dog
(Judges 7:2-7)

Gideon faced the daunting task of assembling an army capable of battling the mighty Midianites, and Israel's fate depended on the army's ability and God's strength. The criteria that Gideon used to select his army provide a fascinating insight into not only the attitudes of people then, but those same criteria also establish the basis of commitment and ability so needed in the church today. Selecting soldiers for Gideon's army is not some quaint feature of Old Testament history; indeed, few things are more relevant to the success of a much-needed spiritual revival in America today than the ability to "lap water like a dog."

The Lord knew the boastful attitude that victory can generate, and He knew that the Israelites would glorify themselves, rather than glorifying God, if their large army defeated the enemy. Thus, God instructed Gideon to reduce the size of his army to such a small number that whatever victory they experienced would be the Lord's and not their own. So, here is how God instructed Gideon to pare down his army to a divinely blessed and usable fighting force.

Initially, there were at least 32,000 soldiers. Then Gideon said, "Whoever is fearful and afraid...turn and depart at once," and 22,000 left, with 10,000 remaining. There were still too many. Following

God's selection process, Gideon then brought the 10,000 to the water's edge and watched them drink. God told Gideon, "Everyone who laps from the water with his tongue, as a dog laps, you shall set apart "

That sounds like a strange way to select a soldier, but here is the crucial outcome of this test: Only 300 drank water by "putting their hand to their mouth," and the remaining 9,700 got down on their knees to drink. Then the Lord said to Gideon, "By the three hundred men who lapped I will save you, and deliver the Midianites into your hand." All of the others were sent home as unworthy. Why? What can we learn from the way in which 10,000 people drank water centuries ago that could possibly be relevant to our needs today?

First of all, none of the 10,000 knew they were being tested for fitful service to God, and thus their underlying personal attitude was keenly observed and was the decisive qualifier. They were neither commanded nor coached on how to act. Their method of drinking was their own and was inherent, instinctive, and a natural reflection of personal readiness. The description of lapping water like a dog means they dipped their hand into the water and brought it to their mouth— just as a dog's lapping tongue draws water into its mouth.

Their method was cautious, calculated, and defensive. Lowering their hand into the water, they quickly lifted the water up to their mouth, while remaining vigilant and ready to quickly respond to an attack. Thus, even while drinking water, the chosen 300 never took their eyes off of the threat of the enemy, never laid down their weapons, and consistently made commitment to serve their highest priority. Personal comfort and needs were of secondary importance.

The others were opposite. They laid down their weapons, took their eyes off of the enemy, got on their hands and knees, and placed their mouths in the water in order to drink because their personal comfort and needs were of paramount importance to them. With this attitude, and in this position of relaxation, ease, and disinterest in the presence of the enemy, they were totally vulnerable and were useless as good soldiers.

The 300 chosen were much like the servants in Jesus' parable of the wise and faithful servants who dutifully waited for their master's return, even in the midnight hours when personal rest and comfort would have been a natural priority.

Gideon began with 32,000 people all professing to be a willing warrior for God, but in the end, only one percent of them were truly committed to sacrificial service that brought glory to Him. The other ninety-nine percent were either afraid to take a stand or too obsessed with their own needs and desires to be of any value.

America has multiplied millions of professed Christians all loudly clamoring about the need for a spiritual awakening in this country. But if history teaches us anything, that great spiritual victory, should it ever occur, will be through the grace and power of God and the vigilance and selfless dedication of no more than a small percentage of all those Christians—those who instinctively have the spiritual devotion, dedication, and commitment to drink water like a dog. All the rest will either be too fearful to take a stand for Christ or too focused on themselves to make any meaningful difference.

I have wondered about this unusual test of spiritual worthiness many times over the years and applied it to myself. In the heat of the day, with no knowledge that I was being observed and measured for fitfulness as a soldier for the Lord, and while surrounded by the unrelenting pressures, demands, and influence of thousands of others, how would I have drank the water? What about you?

V

The High Cost of a Bad Haircut
(Judges 16:1-31)

The biblical account of Samson is a powerful portrayal of the life of many Christians and many churches today. Samson is best known not only for his great strength but also for his crushing weakness after his hair was cut off. The two are directly related in a surprising way.

Samson was born into the Nazarite vow of total, life-long service to God. Part of this vow required that no razor would ever touch his head, and thus his hair would never be cut. Samson's hair, therefore, was an outward symbol of his inner consecration to God. There was no question about it: When you saw Samson, you immediately knew you were looking at a devout, godly man. As a result of his total commitment to God, Samson was amazingly strong and was a great servant and warrior for God. That is how each of us is supposed to be through the presence of Christ in us and the indwelling

125

of the Holy Spirit. We are not divinely designed to be weak.

But temptation entered Samson's life in the person of seductive Delilah, who was an agent of the enemy. Her sole purpose was to discover the source of Samson's great strength and remove it so that he could be defeated. Samson was victimized by her devilish trickery, and he told Delilah that his hair was the source of his strength (not the hair itself, but rather his total commitment to God that it represented) and if it were cut, "...then my strength will leave me, and I shall become weak like any other man."

What an amazing confession! Samson fully knew that if he compromised his commitment to God, and the outward, visible characteristics of his godly life were removed, he would be powerless to serve, ineffective as a soldier for God, and would be no different than any other powerless person in the face of the enemy.

Through giving in to temptation and satanic seduction, Samson's hair was indeed cut by Delilah, and one of the great tragedies of a destroyed life is captured in scripture in a few words..."But he did not know that the Lord had departed from him."

Think about that a moment. Samson went from being incredibly strong and undefeatable to being weak, vulnerable, and enslaved because of his passion—because he compromised his commitment to God and the outward sign of his inner consecration disappeared. He just became one of the crowd...just another ole boy more attracted to a voluptuous, good-looking woman and all her promises of pleasure than he was to God.

Consider what it means when the Spirit of God leaves you, but you do not know it. Think about all the promises to God that can't be kept by personal strength, all the plans for life that fall through because of our inability, the feeling of failure caused by the loss of resolve, and the spiritual emptiness and hunger brought about by the lack of divine nurture. The Spirit of God has backed away from many Christians and many churches today because of a willful compromise of true commitment, and America is suffering the consequences.

Samson was first captivated by Delilah and then captured by the enemy. The sad part is that Samson knew what would happen to him if he gave in to temptation and his hair was cut, but he did it anyway. As a result, he was blinded by the enemy, enslaved, and forced to walk in circles grinding grain. What a revealing picture of the high cost of a bad haircut. Here was this once-great man of God who, because he compromised his commitment to God, had now lost his sense of vision, his power and his purpose, and he was just stumbling along in meaningless circles at the grindstone of life. What a sad picture of a compromised man!

But Samson repented and promised God that if he had one more chance, he would faithfully serve Him again. As a result, Samson's hair grew back—the outward sign of his inner commitment to God—and what a surprise was in store for his enemies. While on display as a victory trophy of the temporary victory of evil over divine goodness, Samson's godly strength returned, and he pulled down the pillars of the temple of Dagon, destroying more of the enemies of God than he had ever done before in his life.

When his hair grew back, and the outward sign of his inner, spiritual commitment to God was visible in his life, Samson was again a powerful servant of God. You can be, too. Repentance is a powerful experience. It really doesn't matter how weak you have become, how blinded by your passions you may be, how much like the world you have become, or how meaningless you may feel stumbling at the grindstone while walking in circles with no purpose in life, you can still give your life back to God today. Allow the outward signs of a godly character to reappear in you, and you will be amazed at the divine power God will yet unleash in your life. It doesn't matter how scarred you may be from your sinful soiree; God will yet use you to do more for Him in the remaining days of your life than you have ever done before.

The Wisdom of a Country Waitress

I arrived in the small, county-seat town in the heat of high noon, having just enough time for lunch and some refreshing iced tea before being at the courthouse at 1:00 p.m. A small, white restaurant alongside the town's main street caught my attention and I stopped, anticipating some good country cooking. I wasn't disappointed. It was one of those meatloaf, mashed potatoes, green beans, and cornbread kind of lunches that make you loosen your belt a notch when no one is looking.

But, being unfamiliar with the town, when the waitress brought my ticket, I asked her a simple question, "Can you tell me how to get to the courthouse?" "Sure," she quickly replied. "Get back on this main street and go yonder way until you come to the last red light and turn left. It's about three blocks on your left." And, in a typical gesture of southern hospitality, she added reassuringly with a smile, "You can't miss it."

That sounded simple enough, but I couldn't leave well-enough alone, so I asked in a teasing voice, "And how will I know when I have come to the last red light?" Sensing that I must be some smart aleck, out-of-town lawyer trying to act uppity toward this down-home country girl, she ripped the ticket from her little book, slapped it down on the table where she tried to press it into the formica with her middle finger, stared at me a moment, and then with a slight wiggle of her head, she said slowly and flatly, "Because there won't be no more that come after it."

My lawyerly logic told me I had said enough. This country waitress was in no mood to be interrogated further, even though the major question remained unanswered: How far did I have to go before I concluded that the last red light I went through was in fact the last red light? Somewhere down the road, I would have had to say to myself, "I've gone too far. That was the last red light. I should have changed directions when I had an opportunity."

If you think about it, there is profound insight in her answer, and I've thought about the wisdom of this country waitress many times over the years.

God puts emotional and spiritual red lights in our lives for a purpose. There are strategic places and moments along life's pathway where we need to stop, think about where we're going, and maybe change directions. What this waitress said about the importance of these red lights is rather chilling, if you seriously ponder it for a moment: "Because there won't be no more that come after it." Is it possible that we can go in a certain direction, or act in a certain way, for so long that our personality and our course in life becomes permanently set and there are no more opportunities to change?

The Bible says that God "will not always strive with a man" and there comes a time when He will give us over to the journey we have set for ourselves. There will be no more red lights...no more opportunities for real, substantive change.

Can we as individuals become so crusty and antagonistic toward others that we are unable to love our neighbor as ourself...and there are no more red lights?

Can we as a nation focus on this silly, artificial division of our country into red states and blue states until we cease being the "United States"...and there are no more red lights?

Can our attitude toward struggling immigrants and our racial attitudes become so enflamed that we are no longer "one nation under God with liberty and justice for all"...and there are no more red lights?

Can we dismiss the importance of mutual acceptance of others and instead become a rioting land of renegades hurling epithets at one another so that we cease being the hope of humanity and the polar star of human goodness guiding others to a better life...and there are no more red lights?

I pray for the future direction of America...about our moral and spiritual values and our role as the leader of the free world. May God give us wisdom to keep our eyes on Him, our mouth closed except when our opinion will meaningfully touch the lives of others, our ears open to the thoughts of our neighbors, and our hearts tender and caring about the struggles of our fellow man.

If we continue with this insane, political bitterness that seems so prevalent where we think it's cool and funny for a stadium full of Americans to erupt into an obscene chant about political leaders, and we steadfastly refuse to pray for them as God's holy word instructs us, then our beloved America will go through a red light. and there may not be any more that come after it. We will have chosen our course for years to come. May God give us the wisdom needed for this hour.

Old Testament Devotionals to Explain Spiritual Thanksgiving

Does the King Know About My Crooked Feet?
(II Samuel 9:1-11)

King David was the most powerful and revered ruler in Israel's history, and in his younger years, David had a close, covenant friendship with King Saul's son, Jonathan. Reflecting back on his friendship with Jonathan, King David asked if any of Saul's descendants were still alive "that I may show him kindness for Jonathan's sake." The king was informed that indeed there was a living son of Jonathan named Mephibosheth, and David sent for him.

When Mephibosheth received this invitation, he was gripped with fear, and his fear only worsened as the fateful meeting with King David neared, and for good reason. When Mephibosheth was five years old, his nurse accidentally dropped him, severely injuring his feet and leaving him permanently crippled and lame.

The consequence of Mephibosheth's injury is easily overlooked, but it was devastating and resulted in Mephibosheth feeling inferior, rejected, and condemned by others because of his disability. In fact, Mephibosheth's name means "the mouth of shame." One can mentally imagine a trembling Mephibosheth asking himself, upon receiving this momentous invitation, "But, does the king know about my crooked feet?" A brief explanation will help us better understand his fear.

Israel's religious laws stated that only a perfect sacrificial animal could be offered to God. Anything that was blind, lame, or sick was viewed as condemned, and over time this harsh condemnation was extended to people, especially by the judgmental, religious purists who viewed themselves as perfect under the law.

Consider for a moment that Jesus responded to John the Baptist's question regarding whether He was "the Coming One" by saying, "Tell John the blind see, the lame walk, the lepers are cleansed, the deaf hear, the dead are raised, and poor have the gospel preached to them." In Jesus' parable of the great supper, when invited guests refuse to attend, the master instructs his servants to "bring in the poor and the maimed and the lame and the blind," because they would joyously understand the mercy and grace underlying the invitation to dine at the master's table and be filled with praise and thanksgiving. In both examples, the lame are identified as individuals living with hurtful scorn and condemnation.

When Mephibosheth entered into the king's presence, he bowed, and, with no doubt a quivering voice, asked, "What is your servant that you should look upon such a dead dog as I?" Can you sense the feeling of inferiority and self-loathing underlying his question? It is as if he asked the king, "Why would someone like you even look at a crippled wretch like me?" Such total emotional emptiness is difficult to fathom. At that moment, there was nothing in Mephibosheth's life for which he was thankful.

But that was about to dramatically change, because Mephibosheth was going to have dinner with the king, and not only would he be physically filled, but he would also become filled with praise and thanksgiving that would last the rest of his life. King David not only restored to Mephibosheth all the property of King Saul that he had lost, but the king also instructed that crippled Mephibosheth would thereafter dine at the king's table for the rest of his life like one of the king's sons. Can the inherent constraint of words capture the unrestrained joy and gratitude that Mephibosheth experienced dining at the king's table? I think not.

If you want to experience the full meaning of spiritual Thanksgiving, begin by putting yourself in Mephibosheth's twisted sandals and walking his walk. Please believe me when I tell you this: It does not matter how worthless the cruel words of others or the uncontrollable circumstances of life have made you feel. It does not matter how scarred you are by the trials and tragedies of life. It does not matter how low, empty, rejected, and inferior you may feel. It does not matter how frail, sick, lame, or blind you may be. It does not matter how lowly, lost, or lonely you may consider yourself to be. Nor does it matter that you often feel like one big failure in life. Trust me...the King knows all about how emotionally, physically, and spiritually crippled you are. You are just like Mephibosheth: The King knows all about your crooked feet! In fact, there's nothing about you that He doesn't know, and still, He dearly loves you.

So, if you spiritually sense the King of Glory inviting you to dine with Him, by all means accept His invitation and don't let your negative attitudes about yourself cheat you out of this life-transforming blessing! You must realize that the King's mercy and grace far exceed the magnitude of your sin and sorrow and can amazingly change your deepest grief into your greatest gratitude and thanksgiving.

When you dine at the King's table, you will wondrously realize that your life with the King has been restored through your faith in Christ. When you hunger for righteousness, at the King's table you will be forever filled and never hunger again. You eat at the King's table not as a crippled victim of sin, but rather as an adopted child and an heir to the King's heavenly kingdom. At the King's table, you never dine alone. The power and person of the Holy Spirit is within you and comforts you, the angels of heaven surround you and minister to you, the fellowship of the saints bolsters your faith, and you are reminded of Jesus' promise never to leave you or forsake you. Just like crippled Mephibosheth, your place of honor at the King's table will never be taken from you, and your feast of thanksgiving will never cease.

That is why we as Christians can live in His presence with unrestrained thanksgiving and praise that forever changes our view of God, our view of life, and our view of our own self.

II

Celebrating Thanksgiving with Our Last Biscuit
(1 Kings 17:8-16)

We do not know her name. We know only that she lived near the village of Zarephath and that she faced dire circumstances as a starving widow with a hungry, malnourished child to feed. The countryside around her village was parched by a prolonged drought that left people and animals desperate for food and water.

As a widow, she had no one to help her, and she was desperately doing all that she could to keep herself and her child alive. But she had finally exhausted every means of survival she could find, and she became resolved to the fate that she knew was upon her and her child. She had only enough flour to make bread one last time, which would surely be followed by a slow, agonizing death by starvation.

And then the unthinkable happened—she received a request from a stranger that tested her faith more than anything ever had. A man named Elijah, who was a prophet of God, came into her village asking for food and water. When she told him she had only enough flour to make bread one last time, the prophet made her a promise so audacious that it was almost laughable. If she would make him bread with her last flour that she had for her child and herself, God would providentially bless her so abundantly that her supply of oil and flour would never be used up, and she and her starving child would never hunger again. Contrary to all common logic, she believed him, and generations later her oil and flour still have not been used up. They are nourishing you and me through this devotional. Consider that for a moment.

Seriously, what would you have done in her situation? Do we really believe that if we entrust every single thing we have—even our last biscuit—to the providence of God that somehow and in some way the Lord will make a way for us and supply us with the necessities of life? That doesn't mean we sit on our hands and do nothing. As a wise old preacher once said, "God feeds the birds of the air as long as they keep digging for worms."

But, can I really celebrate spiritual Thanksgiving by offering my last biscuit to God for His service? Indeed, I can. Psalm 37:25 promises, "I have been young, and now am old; yet I have not seen the righteous forsaken, nor his descendants begging bread." There is enormous truth in that verse of scripture.

I'm not as old as some of you, but I am older than most of you. I have been blessed with moments of abundance, but I've also endured many moments when I literally did not know where my next meal was coming from. I know the agonizing feeling of an empty wallet, an empty cupboard, and an empty refrigerator. Trust me, this isn't just gratuitous religious rhetoric. I know what it's like when the flour and corn meal sacks are empty and the chickens stop laying and the cow goes dry, and many of you do, too.

But I have never truly gone hungry or missed a meal because I had nothing to eat. I cannot tell you the times throughout my life when, in my moments of physical need, God miraculously provided an answer. I have seen it happen far too many times to think those moments are but mere coincidences. They are in fact providential blessings from the hand of my loving heavenly Father. I am absolutely amazed that, with all that's going on in the world and with the millions

133

of prayers being voiced to Him, God nevertheless keeps a watchful eye on my cabinet. Sometimes it gets sparce, but never empty.

Thanksgiving is best experienced when you thankfully rejoice not so much over the bounty produced by your physical labor, but rather over the divine blessings felt in your heart. It is an amazing experience to celebrate Thanksgiving by offering God your last biscuit, and then to hear His promise echo in your heart and mind, "And my God shall supply all your need according to His riches in glory by Christ Jesus."

That is why we as Christians can "enter into His gates with thanksgiving and into His courts with praise."

III

A Thanksgiving Meal Served by the Birds
(1 Kings 17:1-6)

Elijah may have been a great prophet and faithful servant of God, but it didn't feel like it—not today—not while cowering and hiding, fearful of being killed. He had done what he thought was right, but his stand for divine truth now tested both his faith and his resolve as never before.

King Ahab was an evil man, in fact, he was more sinful and evil than any king before him. He took Jezebel as his wife, who was about as virtuous as a rabid fox. They were an evil, power-hungry, vindictive pair. Rejecting the Lord, Ahab built altars for the worship of the pagan god, Baal, and served him.

Elijah confronted the king and declared as punishment there would be no rain or dew on the land unless he (Elijah) allowed it. The land became parched, and King Ahab became angry. At God's instruction, Elijah fled to a different location for safety.

But Elijah faced a critical problem. How would he survive? With food and water scarce and people starving, what would he eat and drink? Following God's instructions, Elijah journeyed eastward to where the brook Cherith flows into the Jordan River. He could drink water from the stream while it still flowed in the terrible drought, but what about food? God would use ravens to feed him, but how did Elijah know that at the time? Did he hear a divine voice saying, "Don't worry...just wait for the birds," or is there a more personal experience that truly produced a meal of thanksgiving?

Honestly, I think what Elijah experienced was so deeply moving and personal that he spent the rest of his life talking about what happened there. Why? Because there was no one but Elijah and the birds who knew what occurred. He later shared it as his own testimony of faith, and that's how it became recorded in biblical history.

Consider for a moment what likely developed. Ravens are scavengers that will eat just about anything—insects, meat from dead animals, and whatever else they find. But a raven doesn't take a large bite like a hungry man would. So Elijah sat by the brook and a raven dropped a small piece of meat, and Elijah quickly picked it up and ate it. There is no way of knowing how old it was or what it smelled like, and it was uncooked. Then another small bite fell from the sky, and then another and another. Each day, morning and evening, these small pieces of bread and meat of unknown origin fell from the sky out of the mouths of scavenging ravens. Maybe it's just my own interpretation of this event, but I have a feeling that Elijah would later say, "It wasn't the best food I ever had, but it kept me going, and I made it."

Sometimes I think our best memories of a "thanksgiving" meal are not those of a full table surrounded by family and friends, but rather the food that somehow miraculously appeared when we didn't know where our next bite was coming from—those meals ate alone with God that may have only been a mayonnaise sandwich and a glass of water, but it sustained us and kept us going.

Perhaps Thanksgiving Day should be subtitled "I Made It Day." Just like Elijah, it is an opportunity for you to reflect back on the times in your life when God providentially allowed a blessing to "fall from the sky," so to speak, that enabled you to keep going and gives you the great experience of saying, "I don't know how I did it, but by the grace of God, I made it."

That's why we as Christians can "enter into His gates with thanksgiving and into His courts with praise."

IV

What Do We Do With the Leftovers?

Thanksgiving is a uniquely American holiday on which we give thanks to God for His blessings on our nation. The centerpiece of most Thanksgiving observances is a huge, delicious meal with family and friends at which all of the food is seldom eaten. Then comes the big question: What do we do with the leftovers?

Have you ever considered that your spiritual Thanksgiving is the same? Remember the examples I previously shared about celebrating spiritual Thanksgiving? The widow's oil and flour never was all used—she had leftovers. Elijah never ate all that the ravens brought him—he had leftovers. When Mephibosheth ate at King David's table, he couldn't eat it all—he had leftovers. When manna fell from the sky on the wandering Israelites, they had leftovers. When Jesus said, "Blessed are those who hunger and thirst for righteousness, for they shall be filled," He intended for them to have spiritual leftovers that could be shared with others. Jesus said of Himself, "I am the bread of life. He who comes to Me shall never hunger, and he who believes in Me shall never thirst." If your spiritual Thanksgiving centers around His promise, then you will always have leftovers.

Our spiritual Thanksgiving is a daily experience, not an annual observance. We continuously feast in the abundance of God's love, mercy, and grace. When God poured out His redeeming love on you and saved you, there was abundant, limitless love left over. You had leftovers. When His amazing grace made you His adopted child through faith in Christ, He didn't use it all—there is more grace for others. You had leftovers. He didn't use all His mercy to blot out your sin—there were leftovers.

But here is the question you and I must ask ourselves about our spiritual Thanksgiving: What will we do with the leftovers? May I offer a few suggestions?

Share Jesus' redeeming love—the same love He shared with you—with someone you have long ignored. Use the mercy that God poured into your life to be merciful to someone who feels lost, alone, and rejected by others. Take the abundant grace that God bestowed on you and become a source of abundant blessings to some hopeless soul that you may k n o w there's plenty left over that you can share with others.

True spiritual Thanksgiving has a unique way of becoming discipleship. True discipleship has a unique way of becoming faithful stewardship. True spiritual stewardship has a unique way of using all the spiritual blessings and gifts we have been divinely given to share the gospel and bring others into the kingdom of heaven. In doing so, within the kingdom of heaven we shall better understand the words of the old hymn, "Then He'll call us home to heaven, at His table we'll sit down. Christ will gird Himself and serve us with sweet manna all around." That's when we will look around and see all the others that we brought with us, and we will joyously realize what we spiritually did with the leftovers.

The Signs and Wonders of Christmas

I

A Virgin Shall Conceive

"Therefore the Lord Himself will give you a sign: Behold, the virgin shall conceive and bear a Son, and shall call His name 'Immanuel' (God with us)" (Isa. 7:14).

What is the significance of a centuries-old divine promise of reassurance and our experience of the wonder of Christmas? Signs and wonders are fascinating biblical concepts. Signs are physical acts that are so beyond human capability they must be viewed as acts of God, thus leaving one filled with wonder and amazement at God's power.

Jesus' earthly life began with a wondrous, miraculous birth, and there is no other category in which it may be placed. If you truly believe in the virgin birth, then one of the greatest signs and wonders of God in human history impacts your life today more powerfully than you can imagine. I fully know that it contradicts logic, science, and common sense, but that's what makes it a sign and wonder from God.

This promised child, who would be born through this miraculous means, would be called Immanuel, meaning "God with us." Think about the magnitude of that for a moment. At the time of Jesus' birth, the ordinary person had no concept of what God was like. Basically, they feared Him, worshipped Him only through joyless laws and meaningless ritual, and they had no understanding of His love and mercy for them individually.

Through this birth, God promised to change that by becoming a man, dwelling among us, and fully revealing His loving nature to us. But the miracle and wonder of Christmas doesn't end with Jesus' birth. Through His miraculous life, the One in whom God's life is fully revealed will not only dwell with you, but He will dwell in you by faith. Jesus will give His life of love, mercy, and grace to each of you who believe in Him as a free, unmerited gift.

When you accepted Jesus as your Lord and Savior and entered into a covenant of faith with Him, He gave you His life. This miraculous, unexplainable, all-powerful life that God gave mankind as a sign through a virgin birth is now the wondrous, redeemed life of Christian faith. Your life as a Christian is a miracle of God, and nothing less! Your Christian life is so miraculous that God revealed it to the world, and to you, through causing a virgin to conceive and bear a Child. It is that distinct, wondrous, and different from the world. Therefore, your life in Christ should continue to be an ongoing revelation of this sign and wonder to those around you, and your Christian life should be living proof that "God is with us." That is the wonder of Christmas that we are missing by changing the majesty, joy, and wonder of the virgin birth of Jesus into a meaningless expression of "Holiday Greetings."

I know I'm just an old, worn-out preacher who is out of step with current fads and trends, but I refuse to stop saying this. All this glitz and glitter, going in debt to buy gifts, and having Christmas parades complete with horses, four-wheelers, and old fat Santa Claus is not what Christmas is spiritually about. I understand that it's a delight for families and children. But we must never forget that is not the wonder of Christmas!

The wonder of Christmas is that God is with us and in us through the life of Jesus, and we are forever redeemed, restored, made sinless and perfect in God's sight, and graciously given this eternal life that has been with God since before the foundation of the world was laid. For Jesus' sake, rediscover the miracle and wonder of Christmas this year, and celebrate His life and your eternal life!

II

The Blessing of Being Overshadowed

"And the angel answered and said to her, '... the power of the Highest will overshadow you; therefore, also, that Holy One who is to be born will be called the Son of God'" (Luke 1:35).

Mary's conception is one of the greatest miracles in history and one of the greatest signs God has revealed to mankind, and it should fill each of us with unbridled awe and wonder. When the angel of the Lord told Mary she would conceive, the angel gave her a divine message that can change your understanding of the miracle of Christmas, the miracle of Jesus' life, and the miraculous nature of your own redeemed Christian life.

The angelic messenger said, "…the power of the Highest will overshadow you…." The angel's description of power is expressed in a word from which we derive "dynamite." It represents the power behind all other power—the highest known power. But, the concepts of power and overshadowing are interrelated in a fascinating manner.

Understanding the meaning of overshadowing requires you to think back to the Hebrew exodus from Egypt. During that fateful journey, the two great symbols of God's covenant presence were a cloud by day and a pillar of fire at night. But, think about this. A cloud can create a shadow on the ground, symbolizing the same power and presence as the cloud in the sky. Thus, whereas the cloud is distantly visible overhead, the cloud's shadow is visibly present in earthly circumstances and surroundings.

Visualize a large cloud moving overhead on a sunny day and how the cloud's shadow sweeps across you and your surroundings. Imagine for a moment that the shadow is the power of God's Spirit surrounding you and enveloping and overshadowing you. Whereas, the cloud symbol of His presence remains high, holy, and visibly radiant, nevertheless the cloud's shadow moves across your physical circumstances revealing the presence, power, and purpose of the Holy One above. Thus, God overshadows you. (See Acts 5:15 for an interesting example about the power of Peter's shadow.)

God's promise to Mary, delivered by His angelic messenger, might be summarized in this way: "I will overshadow your physical life and your circumstances with My presence, and I will unleash in you the greatest known power to bring about My will and purpose for you. I will overcome every physical barrier in your life to accomplish My will for you. My unlimited power—the power that can create something out of nothing—will explode within you, and nothing on earth will prevent Me from accomplishing My purpose for you. Biological limitations, physical limitations, religious barriers, the requirements of the law mandating that you be stoned to death, the skeptical attitudes of family and friends, and your personal fear about all of this will be blown away when My power overshadows you and transforms your earthly circumstances.

Your conception and this Child's birth will be so amazing and unexplainable there will be no doubt that the 'Holy One who is to be born will be called the Son of God.' This Child's life will be an eternal divine sign that He is the only begotten Son of God, and His life will be filled with such wondrous power people will worship Him with awe, wonder, and unrestrained reverence. For with God, nothing will be impossible." Mary's response was an amazing display of simple faith: "Let it be to me according to your word."

When you entered into a covenant of faith with Jesus, God gave you this same life. God took away your old sinful life, gave you this life born of Mary, and recreated you in the image and likeness of Christ. That's what it means to be born again as a Christian.

Thus, the angelic message spoken to Mary could also be spoken to you, "I will overtake you and possess you as my chosen vessel. There is no barrier, no circumstance, no fear, failure, or past sin that I cannot overcome to fulfill My purpose in your life. I will forgive your sins, redeem and restore you, and I will overshadow you and give you guidance and purpose in life as never before. My power will explode in your life, blasting away every barrier and reason you can think of not to follow Me and allow Me to use you. There will be no doubt in anyone's mind that you are My child and I am your Heavenly Father. Your earthly life will be a sign that all things are possible with God. You shall be a living witness of My truth, and your life and your testimony shall fill others with awe and wonder."

That is the life that God wishes to give you this Christmas. That is what can happen when you experience the blessings of being divinely overshadowed.

III

Good Tidings of Great Joy

Instead of turning on Christmas tree lights, flip on the switch to your light of imagination and see a different meaning of Christmas this year. Imagine that America had experienced no revelation from God since 1622, a silent span of 400 years, just as it had been 400 years in Israel since the last prophet, Malachi, had spoken. Personally, you had heard no dynamic preaching, and you had seen no obvious movement of God's Spirit. Religion and worship were monotonous rituals that you were afraid not to perform, although you found no joy or meaning in them. It was as if God had quietly abandoned you.

Then, suddenly, one night an angel from God amazingly appeared before you, filling the night sky with blinding, radiant light, and filling you with reverential fear and awe that you had never known before. Seeing that you were nearly scared to death, the angel said, "Don't be afraid! I have brought you a message from God that is such good news it will fill your life with joy greater than you can possibly imagine. God has sent His Son into this world to save you and to transform your life beyond your ability to presently understand."

And, as if this one herald angel were not adequate to convey this joyful message, suddenly the entire night sky was filled with angels from horizon to horizon and the night sky was aglow with their heavenly radiance. Angels were everywhere—above you, in front of you and behind you, standing beside you—so close that the aura of their presence enveloped you. There were countless multitudes of angels, all exuberantly joyful and singing and shouting, "Glory to God in the highest and peace, good-will, and joy on Earth among all mankind."

As you stood motionless and entranced, you realized this was real and every sensory nerve in your body was struggling to grasp and mentally record the fullness of this divine message. Every spiritual and emotional fiber of your being was telling you that, despite the amazing and indescribable nature of what you were seeing and hearing, this was not a dream or some strange, celestial vision. This angelic message was real, and the "good news" you heard filled you with such joyous awe that you felt numb and spiritually overwhelmed.

What would you do if that happened to you? Would you share this personal experience? Would you become the living source of this joyous good news in the mundane, dark drudgery of the world around you? Would it change your understanding of Christmas and how you celebrate this special day?

These five words—good tidings of great joy—will cause you to celebrate the meaning of Christmas anew with the angels of heaven.

IV

Don't Be Afraid

Amidst the joy of Christmas, have you ever considered that the very first words of the angelic message proclaiming Jesus' birth declared an end to fear! Honestly, I've never before pondered the depth and magnitude of that and the profound, joyous good news that it heralds.

In the first biblically recorded conversation that God had with Adam, the first statement ever made by a human to God expressed fear. "I was afraid...and I hid myself from You," Adam shamefully stated.

Even though Isaiah, the prophet, admonished God's people not to be fearful, nevertheless the fear of God continues as a theme in the Old Testament. It was believed that one could not look at God and live. His name could never be stated, so over twenty other names for God were employed to describe His nature. There was fear of not obeying the religious law and not properly observing all the feast days and rituals. People were fearful of living under the onerous demands of thousands of religious laws that dictated every aspect of daily life, and they were fearful of death because of the uncertainty of afterlife beliefs.

Even in Jesus' parables about the servants' stewardship over talents and minas given to them, those who failed did so because of their fear of the master—or their fear of God.

But the "good tidings of great joy" declared by the herald angel forever changed that burdensome fear to boundless joy. Amazingly, the core belief of the new covenant in Jesus abolishes fear in a Christian's life. Of great importance, notice that before the herald angel said anything else, he declared, "You no longer have to be afraid of God!"

In further fulfillment of this divine truth, Jesus said, "Don't let your heart be troubled; you believe in God believe also in Me." When the disciples saw Jesus walking on the water in the midst of a storm, they trembled in fear. Jesus reassuringly told them, "Be of good cheer! It is I; do not be afraid." The New Testament declares in I John 4:18, "There is no fear in love; but perfect love casts out fear. " Try as best you can to grasp the magnitude of that: In the midst of the greatest storm you can face, Jesus declared, "Be cheerful and joyous! Do not be afraid!" What an amazing, mind-boggling divine promise!

These good tidings of great joy declare to you that God is not to be seen as some joyless, austere, demanding, unyielding, and remote Being, but rather He is your loving Heavenly Father who wants to share His life and heavenly kingdom with you. You can say His name—you can call Him "Abba"—you can talk to Him about anything and everything in your life.

You don't have to fear living for Him. Through your faith in Christ, you are His new creation—redeemed and sanctified for good works that glorify Him. You are filled with the power of the Holy Spirit that is greater than any force the devil can throw at you. You are not meant to live fearfully, but powerfully and dynamically as a living witness for God in the world.

You no longer have to fear death. Jesus' resurrection destroyed it's claim on you. You are eternally alive in Christ as an adopted child of God, and you have a guaranteed claim to the fullness of your Father's heavenly kingdom as a joint heir with Christ.

Paraphrasing the lyrics to the hymn "Because He Lives," it is due to Jesus' life in you that you can victoriously face not just today, but all of your tomorrows. "Because He lives, all fear is gone."

That truth is the ultimate good news of great joy that we can share as we celebrate His birth.

VI

Why is it Called Good News?

Have you ever wondered why the gospel is called "good news"? Let's consider the historical background for a moment. Life in Israel was dictated by thousands of religious laws that detailed not just worship practices, but how one washed their hands, how they cleaned cups, saucers, pots, and pans, how far they could walk on the Sabbath or dig in the dirt on the Sabbath. The law prevented helping and healing the sick on the Sabbath, but not watering a donkey, and those are just a few examples.

There were volumes of these religious regulations, and they were burdensome and emotionally and spiritually draining. If one violated the law in the slightest manner, he was viewed as religiously unclean by the pious Pharisees, scribes, and other religious leaders and out of favor with God. If one persisted in violating the law, they were shunned and condemned as a sinner and an infidel.

But there was no other known method of worship. Israel was viewed as being yoked to the law the same as an ox would be yoked to a plow or a cart. The legal yoke could never be removed, nor could the legal constraints be loosened in any manner. Reverence for the law, the teachings of the prophets, and the religious and cultural traditions of the elders were more important than a true and sincere personal relationship with God. There was never one moment of life in which one could experience rest and relief from the constant demands of the religious laws of Israel. To even think of any other way of life was heresy.

Jesus used the concept of living life with this heavy, binding, burdensome religious yoke around every person's neck to make a startling statement that could be viewed only as radical, unbelievable good news: "Come to Me, all you who labor and are heavy laden, and I will give you rest. Take My yoke upon you and learn from Me, for I am gentle and lowly in heart, and you will find rest for your souls. For My yoke is easy and My burden is light."

If you are to understand the joyous, good news of the gospel, you must first experience freedom from the fear of never being good enough to please God. You must cast aside your struggle of self-righteous goodness, as if you could work your way to heaven. You must once and for all bring all your burdens to Christ and leave them there—don't just tell Him about them, keep them yoked around your neck, and keep dragging them around everywhere you go. Look at what He promises you: "You will find rest for your soul."

When you place the yoke of Jesus' boundless love, mercy, and grace around your spiritual life, then you will realize the joyous, good news and more fully understand the meaning of good tidings of great joy. One of the great truths about Christmas is that it is not about all the hustle and bustle of the holiday. Rather, it is about finally experiencing the rest and peace of Christ, and that's what makes it a holy day.

VII

Why is it Called Good News? Because a Child is Born

A covenant is an ancient relationship concept between two individuals. It is much like a marriage in that each gives themselves exclusively to the other, including name and possessions, and it is the only biblically described way for an individual to be in a life-transforming relationship with God. It is how God shares His holy, sinless life with man. God's first covenant was based on religious law, but it had a major problem: It was impossible for any person to perfectly keep the law and thus, as the Apostle Paul stated, man could never be righteous with God by keeping the law of the old covenant. In truth, Paul said the law was our spiritual tutor to show us how much we needed the new covenant of grace.

Because God knew that we could not follow the law, centuries ago the old prophets foretold the miraculous, virgin birth of a Child who would do for man what he could not do for himself. This Child would be both perfect man and perfect God. His human life would be a perfect covenant union with God—totally righteous and sinless—but He would then do something so mind-boggling and gracious that it's hard to fully conceive. He would personally enter into an individual covenant with anyone who believed in Him based solely on their faith, and He would give to that faithful individual the fullness of both His righteous life with God and the fullness of His heavenly kingdom. He would jointly share all that He had received from God with anyone who would believe in Him as their Lord and Savior. There were no works of religious law to be done, no ritual to be followed, and no self-effort required—just faith.

Because of this covenant through His life, God would then consider any person who believed to also be equally sinless and perfect in His sight. Through this new covenant, the righteousness of God became available to anyone as a free gift of grace based solely on faith and not self-righteous works of religious law. The magnitude of God's grace in that new covenant through Christ is the most joyous news that any struggling sinner could imagine. The burden and the yoke of the law had been removed by grace.

This amazing gift of salvation rests solely on the life of Jesus, and it is not dependent on one single thing that we do, except believe Him. It is all Him. Listen to what Isaiah, the prophet, said about this Child: "For unto us a Child is born, unto us a Son is given; and the government will be upon His shoulder. And His name will be called Wonderful, Counselor, Mighty God, Everlasting Father, Prince of Peace."

Everything that God desires to do for us is through Him. The governing of every dimension of God's kingdom is on His shoulder, and He governs us in that heavenly kingdom as a wonderful counselor with the wisdom and power of mighty God and with the blessings of our everlasting heavenly Father. The full nature of His relationship with us through the new covenant is heavenly peace that we find through no earthly experience. It is the peace of His own perfect relationship with His Father that He imparts to us as a gift of grace.

Can you imagine receiving the very life of God as a free gift this Christmas? Wouldn't your life explode in joyful praise and thanksgiving? Wouldn't this be good tidings of great joy that would totally transform your celebration of Christmas?

VIII

Amazing Heavenly Joy

Christmas is founded on joy, and not just a little bit of joy, but rather great joy...exceedingly great joy...boundless joy..."mega" joy, to use the Greek concept. In other words, there is no greater joy that one can experience in their relationship with God than the joy God created for you at Christmas.

We often think of joy as an inner personal experience based on circumstances or emotions. But Christmas joy is different because it is a gift from God. Christmas joy is not initially your joy, but rather it is God's joy that He feels in giving you a savior, who is His Son, Jesus.

You probably have never thought about God being happy, joyful, and overflowing with exceedingly great joy. It is joy so great that when the herald angel told the shepherds that Jesus had been born, the sky was filled with a multitude of angels singing joyous praises to God for this gift of His son. They did so not because this was in their angel job description, but because heaven could not contain the joy surrounding the birth of this Child.

Christmas joy is divinely unique because it is God's joy that you enter into and experience through your faith in Jesus. The Bible, in its original language, describes the "good tidings of great joy" as joy that is based on God's grace. It is exceedingly great joy that God freely gives to you that transforms your life.

You are given the opportunity to fully see the joyous heart of God and His great love for you. You can finally understand that God is not some humorless, stern, unyielding judge sitting behind a judgment bench shaking His book of religious laws at you and pointing out every one you have broken. Instead, He is your loving heavenly

Father whose heart rejoices with exceeding joy and gladness at the opportunity to give you His Son as your Savior.

Christmas is about God's love and not about His law, and that's what makes it such amazing good news. You get the opportunity to see the depth of your Father's love for you! Christmas joy is the experience of the prodigal son who expected his father to stone him to death because of his sin, but was astonished to find his father running to meet him, throwing his arms around him and kissing him, and welcoming him home. The prodigal son entered into the joy of his father, and so can you.

Jesus once said, "These things I have spoken to you, that My joy may remain in you, and that your joy may be full." Think closely about that. It is Jesus' joy in us that makes our Christian joy complete. That is the good tidings...the amazing good news of Christmas. You are given the incomprehensible opportunity to experience the joy of God and to make God's joy complete in your life by making His Son your Savior. Can you imagine the joy of the angels of heaven when you do?

That's why it is called good tidings of great joy.

IX

Casting a God-Spell

The Gospel of Luke fascinatingly describes the good news of Jesus' birth using a word that changes your purpose in life. Good "tidings" is the basis of our word and concept for evangelism.

The good news is more than just chit-chat news. It is a declaration so overwhelming that listeners are startled upon hearing it. When God is the source of the news, it creates awe and worship and is viewed as a sign and wonder from God. Here's an example: When Jesus finished the Sermon on the Mount, listeners were so amazed and startled that they were mentally and spiritually dazed.

When the Bible was first translated into Old English, the word "spellian" was used to describe this divine, good news. It's the basis of our phrase "spell it out," denoting clarity and power. But the divine news could be so amazing and powerful that it left listeners in a "spell," literally awed and speechless. The best way to understand the magnitude of the news of Jesus' birth is by realizing that it can cast a "god-spell" on those who hear it and believe it. It is from this concept that the word "gospel" (good news) is derived.

Amazingly, the concept goes a step further. In the original language, the news and the life of the one sharing the news are inseparable. Thus, the angels shared it, then Jesus shared it, and then Jesus commissioned you and me to share this amazing news. It is the foundation of personal evangelism: We became evangelists!

Do you want a new purpose and passion in your life this Christmas? The good tidings of great joy with which you have been entrusted have the divine power to literally cast a "god-spell" on others—if you will just faithfully share this good news with them.

X

Christmas Grace

If God were not a God of grace,
then joy would have no name.
For grace is greater than all our sin,
and covers our guilt and shame.
For the gift of His Son is the grace of God,
    and it sets our spirit free.
If God were not a God of grace,
then Jesus would have had no birth.
For grace is the hope of a Savior given
to a sinful and tormented Earth.
For the Virgin Birth is the grace of God,
    and it sets our spirit free.
If God were not a God of grace,
then there would have been no manger.
For grace is the sweetness of Mary's babe,
and God is no longer a stranger.
For the lowly stall is the grace of God,
    and it sets our spirit free.
If God were not a God of grace,
there would be no Savior's love.
For grace is born of a Father's heart
from the peace of heaven above.

For the love of Christ is the grace of God,
      and it sets our spirit free.
If God were not a God of grace,
there would have been no cross,
and man would die for his own sin
and know not gain but loss.
For the cross of Christ is the grace of God,
      and it sets our spirit free.
If God were not a God of grace,
no tomb would have been needed
to hold the Lamb in death's cold grip
until victory was completed.
For the tomb of Christ is the grace of God,
      and it sets our spirit free.
If God were not a God of grace,
the stone would not have rolled,
setting free the Christ in power divine,
so that death should cease its toll.
For the empty tomb is the grace of God,
      and it sets our spirit free.
If God were not a God of grace,
there would be no heavenly home.
For a beautiful mansion awaits us there
next door to the heavenly throne.
For heaven above is the grace of God,
      and it sets our spirit free.
If God were not a God of grace,
then Christmas would have no reason.
For Christmas is the gift of God's own Son,
to be rejoiced in His own season.
For Christmas is the grace of God,
      and it sets our spirit free

I Have Finished the Work

(John 17:4)

I

Jesus stated that doing God's will was both His will and His food. However, prior to His arrest and crucifixion, Jesus referred to the "work" that had been completed by praying with a sense of finality, "I have finished the work which You have given Me to do."

John chapter 17 is one of the most fascinating chapters in the New Testament. Not only does it reveal Jesus' passionate prayer for all Christians, but it also captures the essence of Christianity in Jesus' own words. Examining His statements in light of His declaration that He had accomplished and completed these enumerated tasks of ministry is an amazing study.

The "work" that Jesus accomplished changed the world and established our Christian faith.

II

The work of Jesus is the foundation of His ministry, and understanding the nature of the work is essential in understanding both Christianity as a whole and also our own Christian life. Jesus personally viewed the work that He accomplished as irrefutable proof of His divine nature, His relationship with His heavenly Father, and the fulfillment of God's plan of redemption through Him. Regarding the importance of His works, Jesus said, "...though you do not believe Me, believe the works, that you may know and believe that the Father is in Me, and I in Him" (John 10:38).

The man born blind, who Jesus healed, perfectly expressed this reality to the doubting Pharisees: "If this man were not from God, He could do nothing." It is important to understand that Jesus' work was not labor as we think of work today. The language of the New Testament describes work as a task or an involved effort to which one commits himself that reflects and fully expresses an inner desire and passion. It is not an obligation, but rather an opportunity to reveal one's true nature. Because this work is so personal, one is passionate

151

about perfectly completing the task regardless of the personal sacrifice involved.

Once committed to the effort, the individual will not cease this work until it is fully completed. The work is not drudgery, nor is it done begrudgingly or with hesitation. Instead, work of this nature is often lovingly and graciously done for the benevolent benefit of others without any thought of personal reward, recognition, or remuneration. The nature of the work openly defines both the individual's life and his inner character for all to observe.

With that in mind, John 17:1-26 enumerates no less than seven tasks that may be viewed as Jesus' "I have" statements. Each of these works may be viewed as having been completed and done by Jesus to the fullest extent of His divine ability, and because of His passion and commitment, no aspect of this work remains unfulfilled. Thus, with respect to the meaning and importance of each one, He could say, "I have done this."

If these works are completed, then one must realize that there is nothing more that Jesus could have done to make this work more complete for you. Think of its completed nature in this way: There is the old question, "Is there anything that God can't do?" In reality, the answer is "Yes." The works of Jesus are so complete that God can't add anything more to them! And all those works were lovingly done for you and me and for all other Christians.

III

Much could be written describing God's glory and how we can best understand its meaning. In the Old Testament, glory can mean the magnitude of God's holiness that is so radiant and brilliant that man cannot look upon it and thus fire and light often serve as symbols, such as the pillar of fire at night during the exodus journey.

Doxa is the New Testament word most often translated as "glory," but it has multiple meanings. Interestingly, one significant meaning is the visible radiance of God's divine presence. With that in mind, how can we better understand Jesus' statement that He had glorified God on the earth?

Allow me to share a basic thought about divine glory that might help our understanding: In one sense, God's glory is simply how we are able to see God's presence and know that He is with us, and that leads us to an attitude of praise and worship because of His divine reassurance.

The Bible reveals God's relationship with us as a covenant. That means God must be present in our everyday human experience as Christians because a covenant requires unbroken unity—two lives united in heart, mind, and soul as if they were one. God's covenant promise has always been "You will be My people and I will be Your God, and I will dwell in your midst and be continuously present with you."

But God's kingdom is spiritual and our world is physical, so how can we see Him and know His Spirit is here with us? He does so through His visible glory and through the power of the Holy Spirit. When we consider God's glory, as described in the New Testament, we find Jesus.

One of the names bestowed on Jesus was "Emmanuel," meaning "God with us." When Jesus was born and the herald angel appeared to the startled shepherds, "the glory of the Lord shone around them." The Gospel of John states, "In the beginning was the Word and the Word was with God, and the Word was God...and the Word became flesh and dwelt among us, and we beheld His glory, the glory as of the only begotten of the Father, full of grace and truth." Thus, Jesus spoke of His relationship with God and said, "I and My Father are one." He further declared, "He who has seen Me has seen the Father."

Jesus revealed the glory of God through the truth of His words and the miraculous nature of His works. He could therefore say "...though you do not believe Me, believe the works, that you may know and believe that the Father is in Me, and I in Him." Jesus revealed the true nature of God to us. The Bible states that "For in Him dwells all the fullness of the Godhead bodily." In Him the fullness of God's love, mercy, and grace gloriously radiates for all the world to see.

Indeed, Jesus could say, "I have glorified You on the Earth." But, amazingly, this divine glory then becomes the character of the redeemed church, of which you and I are a part. Describing the nature of the true church, Ephesians 5:27 states that Jesus "might present it to Himself a glorious church...." Thus, when Jesus states, "I in them, and You in Me, that they may be made perfect in one, and that the world may know that You have sent Me" (John 17:23), we can't fathom the divine glory of redeeming love, mercy, and grace that Jesus wants to reveal through our lives to others, if we are willing to be His living witnesses.

My Journey Through the Ten Commandments: A Personal Awakening

I have always been interested in law and how statutory words function as the basis of an orderly society. I suppose that's why I became a lawyer and worked as an attorney for many years. And once I entered the ministry, I became just as fascinated with religious law and its impact on our Christian life, especially my own. The role of religious law in our relationship with God and each other is an interesting study and helps one better understand how Jesus fulfilled its spiritual purpose.

I grew up being taught the Ten Commandments were the basis of a godly nation. But when I seriously looked at the reason God gave these Commandments, I discovered something that was broader and different than just ten laws for social order. In fact, these Commandments are not just the basis for civil law, but rather they are the foundation of a unique ministry divinely given to God's covenant people.

God chose Israel to be a "kingdom of priests and a holy nation" (Exod. 19:6) who He would use to bless all the other nations of the Earth. They were to be His ambassadors to the world in a unique way unlike any other nation—distinct, sanctified, and holy unto Him. The foundation of this priestly ministry was the Ten Commandments, but they were broader than just legal obligations that God commanded the people to do. Rather, they were principles of godly service that Israel was given the exclusive opportunity to experience.

Psalm 119 contains several words that illuminate one's understanding of "commandment." Law, judgments, testimonies, precepts, ordinances, statutes, and commandments are all the same Hebrew concept, and they all reflect the "word" of God (and, yes, you can think about the Word becoming flesh and dwelling among us, as the Gospel of John states). Thus, when God gave Israel the Ten Commandments, "God spoke all these words" (Exod. 20:1).

Rather than just being ten laws for a nation to live by, these Commandments were actually ten spiritual principles and divine precepts reflecting the nature of God—His holy word—that would make Israel a nation of priests and a blessing to all other nations. The first four focused on love for God and the last six focused on love for each other. These ten principles for a priestly nation were based on love and not obligatory law. If kept, no other nation on earth would live and love others like Israel, and they would glorify a loving God to the rest of the world.

But Old Testament history reveals that ancient Israel steadfastly refused to serve God as a nation of priests. It's an amazing biblical truth, but their divine calling was ignored, and the phrase "nation of priests" isn't mentioned again in the Old Testament. In fact, this divine priestly purpose isn't stated again in the Bible until the Apostle Peter, speaking of the New Testament church, wrote, "But you are a chosen generation, a royal priesthood, a holy nation, His own special people..." (1 Peter 2:9).

Instead of humbling themselves to this holy calling, Israel took these ten commandments for priestly service and made them into cold, unyielding religious law. And it wasn't limited to just ten laws. Indeed, by the time of Jesus' ministry, there were thousands of religious laws filling volumes of scrolls defining every aspect of Jewish life.

This vast body of religious law had the opposite effect to God's priestly intent for Israel. The law became the basis for prejudice, condemnation of others, unmerciful treatment of the poor and sick, and an obsessive desire and demand for compliance. For example, when Jesus healed a crippled woman on the Sabbath in violation of the law and observers marveled at the miracle, the synagogue ruler screamed at the amazed people, "There are six days on which men ought to work; therefore come and be healed on them, and not on the Sabbath day" (Luke 13:14). One could lead his donkey to get water or pull an ox out of a ditch on the Sabbath, but merciful healing was strictly forbidden. That's just one of many examples of obsessively forcing the unmerciful law on others.

Jesus specifically said that He did not come to destroy the law, but rather to fulfill it. What did He mean by that? If the purpose of the law was to divinely establish ten principles for living a priestly life for God by loving God and loving others as yourself, then one's understanding of the law had to shift from cold, condemning law to merciful love. The work of Jesus involved changing the interpretation of God's word—His Commandments—from judgmental law to redeeming love. When the gospels reveal how Jesus loved God with all His heart, and He loved others enough to die for them, they reveal the spiritual fulfillment of the Ten Commandments. That is the great distinction between the old covenant of law (the Old Testament) and the new covenant of grace (the New Testament).

When Jesus was asked which was the greatest commandment, He said, "You shall love the Lord your God with all your heart, with all your soul, and with all your mind. That is the first and greatest commandment. And the second is like it: You shall love your neighbor as yourself" (Matt. 22:36-39). Then He added that all the law and prophets hang on these two. Hang describes a peg on which something weighty is hung. If the peg fails, then what it supports crashes down.

His statement summarizes the Ten Commandments into two great commandments. In doing so, He did not mention civil law or social stability. He said pointedly that unless there is love for God and love for our neighbors, all of our religious beliefs come crashing down. And that is what happened. Israel probably had greater reverence for religious ritual, feast days, the law and the prophets, and the traditions of the elders than they had for God. And they certainly did not love others as themselves. In fact, Gentiles (non-Jews) were despised, and the law prohibited any contact and dealings with them.

The Pharisees, the most conservative religious party, prided themselves in keeping the multitude of religious laws and forcing others to obey. However, Jesus called the Pharisees hypocrites for demanding that others keep religious laws they didn't keep themselves. He also labeled them as blind guides for leading followers astray and the spiritual equivalent of a whitewashed tomb—all clean on the outside, but full of death on the inside.

How could the spiritual intent of these commandments—these principles of a loving, priestly life—be carried out and perfected? Jeremiah said it would be through a new covenant that changed God's people spiritually by writing the law on their hearts. Thus, the Book of Hebrews in the New Testament describes Jesus as the mediator of a new covenant, because the old covenant of law did not work. Jesus described the new covenant as being fulfilled through His blood and His life.

It was a life-transforming moment when I realized that the true meaning of the Ten Commandments is not found in the civil law of the nation, but rather in their spiritual fulfillment in me through Jesus' covenant and my faith in Him. It is through His life in me that I experience the spiritual fulfillment of the Commandments' priestly purpose, and I become a living witness to their truthfulness as an "ambassador for Christ" to the world around me, as the New Testament states.

Knowing that Jesus wants to write the spiritual purpose of the Commandments on my heart, and fulfill them in my life through the indwelling of the Holy Spirit empowering the priesthood of the believer in me, is far more important to me than seeing the Commandments chiseled in stone on a slab of granite in the courthouse lobby and gazed at by countless people who neither understand them, believe them, nor keep them.

Good News

Jesus' Parable of the Sower contributed greatly to the evangelical spread of the gospel, the widespread establishment of the New Testament church, and the formulation of the New Testament as we know it today. The genius of the parable is not so much the four kinds of soil in which the seed fell, but rather the joyous attitude of the sower. Everywhere he went, he sowed without concern for the harvest he would receive.

The sower is Jesus' example of a true evangelist. He sowed freely and unconditionally out of unrestrained joy from sharing the word of God. He realized the seed he was sowing—the glorious truth of God's grace—was the greatest truth he could share and the greatest work he could do. He was called to sow the seed: The harvest was in God's hands.

When the Apostle Paul realized that God's grace had freed him from his life-long obsession with righteousness by keeping all the Jewish religious laws and that it was through His faith in Jesus and God's grace that he was saved, he became a different person with a consuming passion to share this great truth wherever he went. He made multiple missionary journeys, visited numerous cities, preached countless sermons, and wrote several letters, which are now the main part of the New Testament, to Christians in various locations.

We say today that he preached the "gospel." But, interestingly, "gospel" is our translation of the original word "euangelion." Essentially, that word means good and positive news or information. It is also the basis of evangelism, and an evangelist is anyone who joyously shares this good news. When it is applied to God, however, it describes news that is so amazing it leaves the hearer amazed and virtually numb.

Think about the herald angel's message to the shepherds. The angel delivered "good tidings of great joy" (good news) that actually left the shepherds filled with awe and fear. Likewise, when Jesus concluded the Sermon on the Mount, the people were "astonished" because nothing like these truths had ever been preached in Israel. The phrase literally means they were so awe-struck it was as if they had been hit on their head.

When "euangelion" was first translated into Old English, the word "spellian" was used to describe this level of divine news. It was news so amazing it actually left hearers dazed, as if they were under some hypnotic spell—speechless and immobilized by what they had heard. Because of its impact, it wasn't long until this amazing divine truth was referred to as a "god-spell" that had fallen on listeners.

Historical evidence of this impact can be seen in New England revivals in the 1700s, known as The Great Awakening, when services would last for hours and extend for days. Thousands of people were spiritually transformed, with prolonged spiritual impact occurring in multiple communities.

We now call it the "gospel," and eventually this title was applied to the first four books of the New Testament, as well as the overall Christian message. But it's original use and meaning referred to the message of powerful divine truth proclaimed by individuals.

So what motivated Paul? There is very little difference in the original meaning of God's message of good news and the messenger who delivered it. Think of God, Jesus, and the Word as essentially all the same. Now, think of Jesus, the Apostle Paul, and his message of faith and grace. They were all connected to the same divine Spirit and the same good news from God.

How, then, is your Christian life impacted by this truth? When you enter into the New Covenant with Jesus, as did the Apostle Paul, Jesus' life becomes your redeemed life, and His message becomes your message and your testimony. You become one with Jesus in His purpose, passion, and power, and the mission and work of the sower becomes your work and mission as you sow the seed of divine truth without concern for the harvest. Your Christian life, your love for God, your ability to love others as you do your own self, your unconditional mercy and kindness, and your boundless love for all people without prejudice, empowered by the Holy Spirit within you, becomes the greatest news people around you could possibly hear and experience.

The influence and impact of your Christian life on others can leave them awed, amazed, and filled with such reverential reality of the spiritually transforming power of God that they fall into a "god-spell." When you joyously share the good news of salvation by grace through faith, your life as a dynamic sower of the seed of divine truth becomes the best news God can share. You become the embodiment of the true and original meaning of the gospel!

When the redeemed church of the Lord Jesus Christ stops talking about the gospel and fussing over interpretations of the gospel and instead becomes the true living gospel empowered by the Holy Spirit, then they will become the light of the world and spiritual revival will sweep across America. It will begin when each of us sets our spiritual priorities right and humbly desires to become God's "good news." There is no higher calling and no greater purpose in life.

Who is My Neighbor?

(Luke 10:29)

I

There are times when I get to play lawyer while reading the New Testament. On two occasions, lawyers posed questions to Jesus, but they weren't like today's lawyers. These were religious legalists who specialized in arguing fine points of religious law, often based on specific definitions.

In the first example, the lawyer asked Jesus, "And who is my neighbor?" and the purpose of his question is entirely different to what we often think. Allow me to explain.

As a consequence of obligations required under Israel's religious law, two broad categories of people were recognized that basically covered the entire population—neighbors and enemies. Word meanings change over time, so neighbors weren't people who lived nearby, as we think of them today, and enemies weren't people trying to hurt you.

One's neighbor was anyone with a common bond, either familial or based on mutual religious beliefs. Basically, it was another person like you with whom you readily associated. Everyone else fell into the enemy category—anyone you didn't like, had nothing in common, and had no desire to be around. Whereas one was required to have strong positive feelings for his neighbor, conversely, he had no legal obligation whatever to care about his enemies.

So, when the lawyer asked Jesus to define "neighbor," he wasn't looking for an opportunity to love others. He did not need a definition of neighbor to do that. He was free to consider anyone as his neighbor if he cared about them.

Instead, he was seeking to specifically define neighbor so that he would then be free to treat all others as his enemies. In other words, the real purpose of his question was to find out who he had to act kindly toward and who he could write off and not care one iota about. And that was very important to this lawyer, because as long as he met his obligation under the religious law to love his neighbor, he could

161

feel religiously good about himself while being filled with contempt for others.

The true law, based on the Ten Commandments, required one to love their neighbor, but it said nothing about hating one's enemies. Interestingly, the law had been modified by religious legalists over the years to allow, if not mandate, hatred of enemies in order to justify their own prejudices and bitter feelings toward others.

This lawyer fell into that category. He viewed anyone who did not keep the religious law as perfectly as he did as his enemy. Thus, with twisted reverse logic, he simply was asking Jesus to help him figure out who his enemies were—not his neighbors—so that he could freely hate them and still feel righteous before God.

Imagine the shock when Jesus said, "You have heard that it was said, 'You shall love your neighbor and hate your enemies.' But I say to you, love your enemies..." (Matt. 5:43-44). Jesus challenged people then, as He does now, to have the same positive concern for the life and welfare of people they never really cared about as much as they do their best friends. That is quite a challenge, but it is how we spiritually grow as a Christian.

II

When the lawyer asked Jesus, "And who is my neighbor?" he didn't know that Jesus' response would go down in history as one of the greatest examples of mercy ever spoken. Instead of answering the lawyer with the specific definition he desired, Jesus told a parable that forced the lawyer to answer his own question in a manner he would never have anticipated.

The parable compared the attitudes and actions of three people: a priest and a Levite, both of whom were highly respected as religious men, and a despised Samaritan. In the narrative, all three encounter a severely wounded traveler who had been robbed and beaten. From a distance, it was hard to tell whether he was dead or alive.

Both the priest and the Levite uncaringly passed by the man as far away as possible. If the traveler was dead, or covered in blood or other body fluids or waste, touching him would have rendered them religiously unclean under the law. Since they were headed to perform temple service, they chose not to take that chance and be delayed by having to cleanse and purify themselves. That is what the religious law required, and they were bound to those requirements.

In structuring the parable, Jesus injected a new dimension into the determination of who is my neighbor—mercy. And He used one of the most despised and detested men of His day to make His point—a Samaritan. Unlike the priest and Levite, the Samaritan was motivated only by compassion and mercy for the wounded man. Through his own effort and at his own expense, he made sure the wounded traveler was properly cared for.

Whereas the two religious ritualists—the priest and Levite—should have treated the wounded man as a neighbor, they instead treated him like their enemy. The Samaritan, who could have seen the wounded man as his enemy, instead treated him as his neighbor.

Jesus asked the lawyer (who would have hated the Samaritan) which of the three was a neighbor to the wounded man. Reluctantly, and probably sheepishly, he quietly responded, "He who showed mercy on him." Jesus then told him, "Go and do likewise."

In order to better understand the spiritual struggle recorded in the four gospels, one must see Jesus' effort to fulfill the spiritual purpose of the religious law versus the unrestrained efforts of the scribes and Pharisees to prevent him from changing their sacred traditions. All Jesus was trying to do was inject love, mercy, and compassion into the condemning coldness of the law and its ritual.

Throughout the gospels, numerous people asked Jesus for help. The plea most often recorded is, "Lord, have mercy on me." Blind and fanatical obedience to the thousands of laws had turned God's covenant, priestly nation into the most prejudicial, judgmental, and condemning people on Earth. The purpose of the New Covenant in Jesus was to change law into love.

None of us can help everybody, but each of us can help somebody. Maybe our own answer to "Who is my neighbor?" is to befriend someone that the religious legalists around you have shunned and condemned and consider an enemy to society. Instead, show them the love and mercy of Jesus, and this person you thought was an enemy just might become the best neighbor you've ever had.

A Friend of Sinners

In addition to neighbor and enemy, which were previously discussed, "friend" is another relationship category mentioned in the gospels that merits study. In today's English, friend is generally an acquaintance with whom we bond with mutual affection. In the time of Jesus' ministry, the word had a somewhat different meaning with great importance to our Christian understanding.

We get a clue about the word's meaning from an unusual source. In William Shakespeare's "Julius Caesar," Mark Antony begins his lament over Caesar's death by saying, "Friends, Romans, and Countrymen, lend me your ears...." The most important group listening to Antony was the "friends of Caesar."

In the New Testament, when Jesus was brought before Pontius Pilate after His arrest, Pilate was at first inclined to release Jesus, saying that he found no fault in Him. But His accusers resorted to a tactic that unnerved Pilate. "If you let this Man go, then you are no friend of Caesar," they shouted. Fear of the consequences of that accusation tipped the scales for Pilate in favor of crucifixion.

To be considered the "friend" of someone in that day and time was the greatest honor and most endearing relationship one could have with another. Philos (friend) describes a level of affection and friendship akin to brotherly love and is about the highest level of emotional bond that can exist between two individuals.

The judgmental scribes and Pharisees used Jesus' friendship with those they condemned and shunned as an allegation against Him. Jesus responded, "The Son of Man came eating and drinking, and they say, 'Look, a glutton and a winebibber, a friend of tax collectors and sinners!...'" (Matt. 11:19). That is an amazing statement, actually.

Jesus' greatest bond of love and affection was not with the high and mighty, but instead with those that the religious purists considered to be the scum of the Earth. Jesus' love for sinners is not just a theological concept. He truly loved them as His dearest and best friends, and He openly and freely associated with them and enjoyed fellowship meals with them. That gives us a better understanding of the verse that says, "There is a friend that sticks closer than a brother" (Prov. 18:24).

So, the next time you sing the old hymn, "What a Friend We Have in Jesus," pause for a moment and ponder the amazing depth of Jesus' love and friendship with sinners.

Seventy Times Seven

"If You Do That One More Time, You'll Be Sorry." Honestly, how many times in your life have you said this, or something similar? How about, "I've lost count of how often he's done this." Or maybe, "How many times do I have to tell you to stop doing that?" It is simply part of our human makeup to keep a mental tab on the sins of others and how they hurt and offend us, and we all have done so.

Simon Peter once asked Jesus a question reflecting this tabulating tendency, and he was floored by the answer he received. "Lord, how often shall my brother sin against me, and I forgive him? Up to seven times?" (Matt. 18:21-22). It was a question premised on religious legalism because revenge took over after the seventh time, and the freedom to get revenge while still feeling righteous was the motive of the question.

Jesus' answer established a standard for forgiveness that we still struggle with today: "I do not say to you, up to seven times, but up to seventy times seven," and He didn't mean 490 times. Amazingly, Jesus established a standard of limitless forgiveness that challenges us to the core of our Christian belief and commitment.

The number seven is viewed as a perfect number in biblical interpretation, representing completion and fullness, and it appears 735 times in the Bible. But if forgiving another seven times met a legal definition of fulfilling the obligation to forgive, imagine how "seventy times seven" represents a level that is beyond human capability and instead represents the unlimited forgiveness of God manifested in us by our faith in Christ.

Is unlimited forgiveness a standard so high and seemingly unattainable that we dismiss it without even trying? I'll be honest about it: This is one I struggle with. The "seventy times seven" standard moves me spiritually from legalistic scorekeeping of offenses to a standard of divine mercy and forgiveness where not only do I stop keeping count, but instead I treat the offending person as if it had not happened. I may be able to go the extra mile and turn the other cheek, but forgetting and forgiving some of the hurt I've experienced over the years at the seventy times seven level is honestly challenging for me, and yet I know I must try. And you must try, also, if we are to be faithful servants and true witnesses for Jesus.

II

The Parable of the Unforgiving Servant (Matt. 18:23-35) is one of the most shocking parables Jesus shared. A servant owed an astronomical debt of ten thousand talents to a certain king, who was his master. Estimates of the amount by today's standards vary considerably, depending on the calculation method. For our purpose, let's use the most conservative approach.

If one talent equaled wages for one year (some say one talent equaled several years' wages), then the servant would have had to work 10,000 years to pay the debt. If he made a denarius each day, which was an average day's pay and worth about twenty cents, he would have made $73.00 per year, and the 10,000 talents would have totaled $730,000. But, because of the servant's complete inability to pay this staggering sum, his master mercifully forgave the entire debt.

Unmoved by this magnitude of mercy, the servant then found a fellow servant who owed him 100 denarii, or the modern equivalent of about $20.00. He demanded payment, and then cast the fellow servant into prison because of his inability to pay this small amount. Upon learning about this, the master put the unmerciful servant in prison until he repaid the 10,000 talents, which would have been lifetime imprisonment. This disaster befell him solely because of his unmerciful and unforgiving attitude.

Jesus then said these very important words: "So My heavenly Father also will do to you if each of you, from his heart, does not forgive his brother his trespasses." With the power of three simple words, "from his heart," Jesus transformed the historic concept of forgiveness and moved it from one's mind to his heart. With these words, He changed forgiveness from a mental process to a deeply spiritual experience. With these three words, Jesus changed the rigid law of forgiveness to the blessings flowing from a merciful heart.

There is a profound difference between Peter's question, "Lord, how often shall my brother sin against me and I forgive him? Up to seven times?" and Jesus saying that one must forgive "from his heart." The former is mental and is premised on keeping count of wrongs and "keeping a score" against others. The latter is a spiritual experience flowing from a transformed heart from which mercy and forgiveness flow unchecked and unhindered. The first is religious law; the second is redeeming love. Thoughts of your mind shape your attitudes; thoughts of your heart shape your character.

It is fallacy to think of seventy times seven literally. No one would say to another who had repeatedly offended him, "I have forgiven you 489 times according to my last count. One more time and you've had it." Instead, seventy times seven takes us far beyond our physical and mental limits and spiritually transports us near to the heart of God. There you will discover that you cannot keep track of love, grace, mercy, and forgiveness, for they are infinitely limitless.

Seventy times seven compels us to rejoice in our Master's amazing and boundless forgiveness of our own million-dollar sin debt, and when we do, we don't even think about someone's minor twenty-dollar trespass against us.

III

If seventy times seven is to become a spiritual reality in a Christian's life, then forgiveness must become a compelling spiritual priority. It requires commitment and does not automatically happen. Our mental and emotional makeup is the result of a lifetime of experiences, and applying the seventy times seven standard to the bad experiences, relationships, and memories is a true spiritual challenge.

But you must understand it is a vital part of being spiritually reborn and recreated in the image of Christ and becoming a new creature in Him. When Jesus taught us to pray "...and forgive us our trespasses as we forgive those who trespass against us," He specifically placed our personal experience of God's forgiveness on the same level with our forgiveness of others. Forgiveness then becomes an opportunity to more fully experience one of the greatest blessings of our Christian life.

Forgiveness is not emotional pretense, as if one could pretend that hurt never happened. Forgiveness is not psychological denial, as if one could eliminate pain by denying its existence. Forgiveness is not a funeral, as if one could bury past pain so that it never hurt again.

Instead, forgiveness is the dynamic spiritual power of mercy, rooted in redeeming love, to take hurt—even the most grievous, life-changing kind—and place it outside the bond of love and friendship that binds two people together. The pain is not forgotten, nor is it buried, and no one pretends it did not happen. Rather, the power of mercy and redeeming love renders the hurt inconsequential to the relationship and no lasting harm results.

Seventy times seven then shines out from our Christian life as a beacon of merciful hope and encouragement in the troubled lives of others around us. Seventy times seven empowers you to become a missionary of mercy and forgiveness.

IV

Not only did Jesus establish seventy times seven as the standard of forgiveness for Christians, but He also pushed the standard to actions never before considered. In the Sermon on the Mount, Jesus stated, "Therefore if you bring your gift to the altar, and there remember that your brother has something against you, leave your gift there before the altar and go your way. First be reconciled to your brother, and then come and offer your gift" (Matt. 5: 23-24).

The Greek word translated as "against" is challenging. It actually describes movement from a higher to a lower position, and that is very meaningful to the seventy times seven forgiveness command.

You must realize that Jesus isn't describing what someone has done to you, but rather what you have done to them. Thus, if you realize that you have said or done something to another person that has brought them down, made them feel lower, hurt their feelings and made them downcast, made them feel inadequate or inferior as if they were lower than you, and they hold that against you, it is your Christian responsibility to ask for their forgiveness and be reconciled with them.

Far too often we think of forgiveness as applying to what others have done to us and we seldom consider our responsibility to seek forgiveness for things we have done to others. What actions are covered? Any words we have spoken or actions we have taken that has lowered another person's self-esteem and made them feel less significant to you, and they hold that against you. Think of it this way: anything that has happened for which you are responsible that has brought your relationship with another person down a notch or two.

Asking for forgiveness is not an emotional defeat that one is forced into. Conversely, it is a dynamic, powerful, aggressive assertion of one's determination to protect a bond of friendship, preserve a promise, and secure future blessings. It is a powerful, proactive force

169

fortifying a union of friendship, or a relationship of love, that is taxed by indiscretion, unfaithfulness, and untruth and simply is no longer what it has been in the past.

But, the spiritual blessings of forgiveness are amazing. Actively living the seventy times seven standard of forgiveness is how Christians experience the blessedness of being a peacemaker and become known as a son of God (Matt. 5:9).

Living Fearlessly

I

That Awful Sinking Feeling

Fear fascinates me. It always has for some reason. Fear isn't physical, but it can cripple you worse than a debilitating disease or injury. Fear isn't like other emotions over which we have some control. It lives in its own cage from which it unleashes its potent power without warning. It can ruin relationships, cheat us out of life-changing opportunities, and lock us into physical, emotional, and spiritual limitations that deprive us of the fullness of a dynamic and rewarding life.

I have been preaching and teaching the gospel for nearly fifty years, and I've encountered virtually every kind of human emotion. Fear, in my opinion, is the greatest obstacle we face as Christians and the greatest impediment to our spiritual growth.

Meaningful Bible truths are often tucked away in scripture texts and are missed due to our focus on the larger picture. I enjoy mentally exploring those and bringing them to life—somewhat like a "what if" scenario. But that's what life is all about. It's a mixture of personal triumphs and tragedies, and the tragic failures in life often result from fear. The cause of those failures and our lack of spiritual growth are often overlooked, even ignored, but we are nevertheless shaped by them.

Let me give you an example that I've pondered many times. It is the greatest missed opportunity in the history of Christianity, and the opportunity was destroyed by fear. In the midst of a dark, stormy night, Jesus challenged Peter to walk on the water of the Sea of Galilee, just as Jesus was doing. In focusing on his eventual failure, we overlook the amazing truth that Peter did in fact walk on water. In those first tentative steps, Peter accomplished the impossible, and he rose above every physical force that restrained and restricted him. In this brief moment, Peter realized that Jesus could empower him to do anything. Why didn't he keep going? Why didn't he encourage the other disciples to follow? What an amazing, life-transforming victory they would have experienced. That incredible opportunity sank into the stormy sea of doubt because the curse of fear hit him.

Why? How could that have happened? May I suggest an answer not ordinarily considered? First of all, how would the writer know what Peter experienced unless Peter later told him? But Peter's explanation leaves one wondering. "I saw the wind, and I was afraid," he explained.

You must realize that he didn't sink suddenly, which would have been logical, but rather he sank slowly, a little at the time, and he apparently didn't go totally under, only partially. How did he get back to the boat—swim or wade through the water? Even that partial success would have been miraculous.

It was his vision of the wind that gave him the awful sinking feeling that destroyed this opportunity of a lifetime. This sinking feeling wasn't unique just for Peter because it happens to all of us at different times.

There is an interesting relationship in the original language between wind and spirit. The same word is often used to describe both, and Jesus used the wind as an example to explain to Nicodemus the moving of the Holy Spirit. How could Peter see the wind in the dark of night? He couldn't, but he could definitely see what the Holy Spirit could do with him and through him. If he could walk on water, then the Holy Spirit could empower him to do anything, and that thought terrified him. If Jesus could make him walk on water, what else would He empower him to do?

In the greatest moment of his life, Peter looked through the blinders of his physical limitations and not with the vision of divine opportunity. He saw himself only as an uneducated, indecisive fisherman, not as a living expression and extension of divine power in the world. Is it possible that the thought of what God might do in his life scared him into disbelief both in his own ability and in God's power and caused a deep-seated fear about what this might lead to? That is when the sinking feeling really hit him—just as it does for you and me at times.

I've occasionally shared the following thoughts, and they're worth repeating: "Can't never did anything, never tried anything new, never achieved any goals, never created anything to enjoy, never blessed others, never did anything for the Lord, never left anything behind as a testament to his work, and never tasted the fruit of his labor. Can't lived a meaningless life."

Whatever God is leading you to do, rest assured that He will empower you to do it for His glory, even if it means walking on water. Stop looking at your limitations and start looking at divine opportunities, and say to yourself, "Through the power of the Holy Spirit, I can do this!" That is how you learn to live fearlessly and avoid those awful sinking feelings that keep you spiritually pulled down and defeated.

II

I've formed some opinions about fear over the years, based on my own experiences and my observations of others. It might sound simplistic, but fear seems to come in two distinct categories—physical fear and spiritual or emotional fear. Physical fear can be both realistic and logical, such as being fearful of a poisonous snake slithering toward you, or a stranger with a gun.

But spiritual fear falls into a different category. After half-a-century as a minister observing people reacting to God, spiritual fear seems to me to be a failure of faith in both one's self and in God. I didn't say an absence of faith, but a failure of faith that is adequate to fully enable one to totally move into and live in the heavenly realm.

There's no reason to be ashamed about this struggle. It is the most basic challenge of Christian living, and here's why. Christianity involves a fundamental move—the Bible describes it as a change of citizenship—from a physical realm to the spiritual realm of the kingdom of heaven that Jesus said was "at hand." In other words, heaven is not just where we go when we die; rather, it is what we experience as we live. It is a "here and now" experience that never ends that we enter by faith. Most Christians never think of it that way.

There's one big catch. We are physical creatures, with physical desires and dimensions, who are being asked to move into a heavenly realm that has no physical aspect to it—just faith. That transition fills many people with absolute fear, and they just can't do it. We want physical security and stability. We want physical things to clutch, claim, and hold on to for comfort. We are, in many ways, like a child who just doesn't have the courage to take the training wheels off the bicycle and ride freely and joyously.

Yet, it's these very physical crutches that Jesus challenged us to overcome by focusing on laying up treasures in heaven rather than on earth. But it is not easy, and I'm not going to mislead you by telling

173

you that it is. It does not mean that we no longer possess physical things; rather, we no longer let physical things possess us.

When Jesus said that anyone putting their hand to the plow, and then looking back, couldn't fully experience the kingdom of heaven, I think He had this human struggle in mind. Maybe He was just thinking of the Old Testament example of Lott's wife. It is just hard for most people to relegate "things" to a position of secondary importance in life. We tend to put our hand on the plow handle of commitment, and rather than plowing a straight furrow of faith, we start looking back at what we thought brought safety and stability, and our furrow soon becomes awfully crooked and disappointing. There is no joy in failure.

The father of a convulsing child succinctly expressed our own struggle with faith. When Jesus said, "If you can believe, all things are possible to him who believes," the pleading father responded, "Lord, I believe; help my unbelief!" Every Christian believes to some degree, or we wouldn't be Christian. It is the degree of our "unbelief" that makes us keep looking back that we must work on.

The great victory of living fearlessly is experienced by putting your hand on the plow stock of faith and plowing ahead without looking back on what might have been or could have been. The real challenge is focusing only on what can be.

III

The Faithless Failure of the Warrior King

This nameless king intrigues me, not because of his notable success, but rather because of his inglorious failure. He is the central figure of Jesus' parable, and he is forever recorded in biblical history as a perfect example of an amazing victory that was missed because irrational fear destroyed his faith in himself and his faith in God.

Initially, he was bold, courageous, and self-assured. He realized that success would never be achieved by focusing on his limitations, but rather on his abilities and his vision for the future. Thus, fate suddenly placed him in a position to go down in history as a brilliant, strategically thinking warrior who used his limited resources to achieve unparalleled success—until he was defeated by faithless fear.

For whatever reason, he chose to go into battle with another king whose army was much larger than his—twice as large, in fact. But those odds did not initially deter him. He was committed, courageous, and unfazed by any previous setbacks or the possibility of failure.

But he was defeated by something more powerful and sinister than the threat of an opposing enemy. He was defeated within before the battle began. The parable describes the consequences of faithless fear perhaps better than any other New Testament passage.

He became a defeated warrior while the enemy was still a long distance away. He faced no immediate physical threat, but he was destroyed when his courage and faith melted like butter in a hot frying pan. One should grasp the fact that this pivotal battle was not fought over a broad terrain; rather, it was fought within the heart of one man who missed the chance to inspire others by losing a battle with himself.

The parable states that, while the enemy was still a great distance away, this "warrior" king sent messengers to the enemy king asking for terms of peace. He was looking for a peace treaty before he had developed a battle plan, and success became framed in the terms of surrender. Think about what that actually says. His message was basically this: "I regret having attempted this. If you will help me get out of this predicament, you can know it won't happen again." Thus, the great victory that might have been never happened. The only arrow that was shot was hurled by faithless fear, but it hit the warrior king right in his heart. Sometimes the greatest battle that we fight is with our own self.

Each of us will encounter forces that seem greater than we are, and our faith in God and in ourselves will be tested to the breaking point. Victory will not occur if you look for a way out of the test before you even meet the test. Your prayer must not be, "God, get me out of this!" Your prayer must be, "God, lead me through this and grant me victory. Use me to inspire and encourage others facing a similar battle." That is the first step to living fearlessly.

IV

Let Him Down Easy

I have an odd way of studying the Bible. Not only do I look at the meaning of words, but I sometimes try to inject myself mentally and emotionally into a biblical scene and act it out in my mind, as if I were there. I'm not sure if that's role-play, but it can definitely enhance the meaning of a scripture verse.

A good example is Mark 2:1-12 that describes the determined efforts of four men to get a paralyzed friend to Jesus for healing. Thwarted by a large crowd, they ultimately resorted to cutting a hole in the house's roof and lowering him down into Jesus' presence.

What I see is sheer determination. Consider all that was involved. The obvious thing is their love and compassion for their crippled friend. Then, the one who first had the idea had to enlist the help of others. Having carried their friend to the house where Jesus was visiting, they immediately encountered a large crowd of people that prevented their entrance.

Maybe one of them commented, "We didn't come this far to stop now. Let's take him to the roof and lower him down." One of them had to find long ropes to do that, while the others started ripping a hole in the roof. The homeowner must have been aghast, but that didn't deter them.

Homes of that era are often described as having a flat roof made of large sticks and small tree trunks filled with and covered over with dried mud and straw. Can you imagine how difficult it was to rip through all that? Surely, they didn't bring tools for this work, and instead used their bare hands and sticks or rocks to dig through the hard, dry roof.

Now, put yourself in the room with Jesus. As He taught, debris began falling from the ceiling, and the room was filled with a lot of noise from the digging. A hole finally appeared, and then it got bigger and bigger, as these men made it large enough to get a grown man on a blanket through. It would have taken several minutes to do this, while onlookers watched in disbelief.

Here's an interesting thought. Did Jesus continue teaching with ceiling material falling around Him, or did He stop and watch the efforts of these men? He must have been absolutely amazed at their determination.

You know what else is fascinating? After doing all this, they had no guarantee that Jesus would heal their friend when they lowered him down through the hole. They just had faith that He would, and their faith touched Jesus more deeply than they could have imagined. In fact, when Jesus saw their faith, He said to their crippled friend, "Son, your sins are forgiven you."

James, the brother of Jesus, said, "Faith without works is dead." But, not for these four men. Jesus recognized their faith not by what they said, but rather what they did.

Maybe that's what our hurting nation really needs today. If we as Christians really want to demonstrate the spiritual greatness of America, maybe we should just quit talking about it and start digging. What if each of us did something for others that was so out of the ordinary that family and friends would watch our efforts in awe and admiration, even disbelief? What if the gauge of our faith was the measurement of our determination to help others and reveal the love and mercy of Christ to them?

Are you ready and willing to get your hands dirty and your brow sweaty touching the lives of others for the glory of Christ?

Talitha Cumi: Little Girl, Arise

"Then He took the child by the hand and said to her, 'Talitha cumi,' which is translated, 'Little girl, I say to you, arise'" (Mark 5:41).

He was a ruler of the synagogue, Jairus by name, but today just a father with a heart full of pain. He had position and power, blessed with great wealth, but today just a dad with a daughter near death. Finding the Lord Jesus, Jairus began to plead, not a ruler of men, just a father in need.

"Please, Sir," he begged Him, "my daughter is near death, her body is weakened, with hardly a breath. There's no power that can heal her in all of this land, for all that can save her is the touch of your hand. Please, Lord, come with me, and if only you will lay your hand upon her, I know she'll be healed." As they stood with the multitude, there came one who said, "Don't trouble the teacher, your little girl is now dead." Jairus stood helpless, weeping, and sad, not a ruler of people, just a heart-broken dad. When all hope had left him, he started to grieve, hearing only the Lord's whisper, "Jairus, don't worry. Just believe."

Is there hope for the hopeless? Does God really care when the burdens of life are impossible to bear? Does Jesus really listen to your last desperate cry when everyone around you is passing you by? Can you really find comfort with burdens so great? Can you be like Jairus, just a father with faith?

With laughter and scorn, they shook their heads when Jesus told the mourners, "The little girl is not dead." Why call on Jesus, what could He do? Jairus couldn't answer, but somehow, he knew Jesus would not fail him, he knew that from the start, for today he was just a father with faith in his heart.

Some said he was foolish, some said he was mad, but none of that mattered to this heart-broken dad. His faith overcame doubt, and his hope shattered fear, with the assurance of healing as Jesus drew near. To her bedside of death, he brought the dear Lord and cast all his care on the power of His word.

He was a devout man, greatly admired, but today just a father, empty and tired. Burdened by the rituals and rules of man who today sought the touch of God's loving hand. He had often explained God's ways in the world, but today he just asked Him to touch his little girl.

When life's burdens are heavy, and the answers are few, faith gets very personal, just Jesus and you. Rising above the anguish that confounded his plight, Jairus knew in his heart that his actions were right, for all that mattered to this great, godly man was the presence of Jesus and the touch of His hand.

Is it ever too late for God to move and His love reveal and His power prove? Does fate strike a time when it must be said that all hope is gone and your dream is dead? Who ordains the path of a faithful man who steps beyond doubt, takes God by the hand, and lives his life in a heavenly sphere knowing all things are possible if Jesus is near—who thinks it's not foolish to ask Jesus to touch the life of one he loves so much? As Jairus stood beside his little girl's bed, he had to believe that his child was not dead.

For Jairus, it was the life of a precious child, a gift from God treasured only for a while. Yet He beckons the faithful to quietly draw near, and learn from his pain, for the lesson is clear. The power of Jesus is abundantly great and He alone can alter the fate that has left you hopeless and sad, as you look at the loss of all that you had. Whatever the pain, despair, or grief, the grace of God can bring healing and relief. For no greater power is given unto man than the presence of Jesus and the touch of His hand.

Oh, humble soul, please hear this plea, for Christ has only good thoughts for thee. He knows the darkness of your midnight hour and that He alone has the strength and power to transform the pain that you now face into a glorious revelation of His mercy and grace. For into your life He will come this day, as you trust in Him and humbly pray. For He is thy God and He cannot fail, and through His power you will prevail. For you, too, will hear His words that opened her eyes, "Dear child of faith, I say, 'Arise.'"

Talitha cumi, little girl arise. At the touch of His hand, she opened her eyes. Death's grip was broken by power from on high. Talitha cumi, the little girl is alive.

I Discovered America and Myself
on the Radio

Some of my favorite childhood memories involve radio. Long before we had a television, the radio provided our only means of entertainment, news, and a verbal avenue to the world. When mama bought a Trutone radio from J.R. Nance at the Western Auto in Purvis, it became a constant feature in my life, vastly broadening my horizons.

Most radio stations operated with only enough power to reach their general geographical area. This allowed multiple stations to use the same frequency if they were separated far enough not to overlap. However, the federal government assigned an exclusive frequency to several radio stations in different locations and permitted them to broadcast at maximum power. Referred to as "50,000 watt clear channel" stations, many could be heard across much of the United States. In some ways, these radio stations introduced me to America beyond the confines of poverty and the limitations of life in rural Lamar County. I heard about an America over these clear channel airwaves that was unlike anything I knew listening only to Jimmy Swan on WBKH in Hattiesburg.

The nearest 50,000 watt clear channel station was WWL in New Orleans, "with studios in the Roosevelt Hotel." I had never been in a hotel and that sounded so inviting to me, especially at 11:00 p.m. when the announcer said, "And now from the Blue Room, high atop the Roosevelt Hotel in beautiful downtown New Orleans, it's music until dawn with Leon Kellner and his orchestra." I could only imagine what that must be like.

A bit later, WWL began an all-night program for truck drivers with Charlie Douglas, as did WBAP in Fort Worth with Bill Mack. Through them, I listened with fascination at commercials describing large truck stops and restaurants along America's complex interstate highway system. It was a different world compared to driving up bumpy Highway 11 to Hattiesburg in the old '61 Chevy.

I often listened to WLAC in Nashville, and even now I can remember the voice of John R selling baby chicks on the radio. I listened to major league baseball and learned how cold and windy Chicago can be by tuning in WLS. Our little dairy farm didn't compare to the midwest farm life I heard about from early-morning listening to

KMOX in St. Louis and WHO in Des Moines, both of which came in surprisingly clear many mornings about 5:00 or 6:00 a.m. From WFAA in Dallas, I learned about life in that wealthy city, and WBAP made me yearn to attend the Fort Worth Livestock Show and see cattle and horses from storied Texas ranches. I listened to Top 40 songs on KAAY in Little Rock at night and WNOE in New Orleans during the day. WNOE introduced me to lifestyles greatly different from life in Purvis. I had no idea people actually ate wild game, such as bear and buffalo, until I listened to commercials for T. Petteri's restaurant in New Orleans. All I knew about was fried squirrel.

With my radio interest fully tuned (pardon the pun), I obtained a radio license a couple of years after entering Ole Miss, and I worked as a radio announcer through the last year of college and during law school. It was interesting, and I especially enjoyed recording commercials for various businesses around Oxford. Through radio, I discovered a whole different me—quiet, reserved, and withdrawn me loved sitting in front of a microphone talking to thousands of people! My favorite part of the work was the afternoon news, and the introduction is forever etched in my memory: "From the WSUH newsroom, this is the five o'clock edition of the news brought to you by Blaylock's Drugs, on the Square in Oxford...And now, the news." I spoke those words numerous times.

But God had a special purpose for my radio fascination. Radio news uniquely taught me about the mechanics of effective audience communication, and many aspects of my individual preaching style and pulpit mannerisms were learned delivering the afternoon news.

Occasionally, when I'm alone and talking to myself, the memories will start flowing and once again I'm a happy, healthy twenty-two-year-old sitting in front of a microphone in a sound proof booth saying, "You're listening to WSUH, 1420 in Oxford...the home of Ole Miss." Those are fond memories, and I miss it.

There are also the recurring memories of standing behind a pulpit in front of a sanctuary full of worshippers, inviting them to open their Bibles as we share the good news of the gospel of Christ together. Nobody knows how I have also missed delivering that news these last several years.

But I know I can never again do either, and so I write. I gave it my best, and I'm grateful for the opportunity I was given.

In many ways, you are much the same, but with differing gifts. I am convinced that each of you possesses untapped talents and abilities that you' ve never dreamed of. That is the marvelous truth about faith and commitment. Just as He did for me, God can also help you discover an entirely different you that can change your life, if you will let Him.

Memories

Forgetting What Lies Behind

Cold, rainy days are not good for me, and there have been too many lately. They send me into an emotional tailspin from memories of working in the cold rain and mud on an impoverished dairy farm as a young boy with no hope of relief. There is a verse in Philippians about "forgetting what lies behind and pressing on to what lies ahead" that truly challenges me, both spiritually and emotionally. How do you deal with memories that you wish you could forget? One of my biggest emotional and spiritual struggles is how I can put all those memories to rest and focus only on what is ahead. You probably have things in your past that haunt you occasionally, too.

The context of a statement often provides greater clarity to its meaning. The Apostle Paul was confined in a Roman prison, often chained to his guards, and facing more imprisonment or even death. Yet in this harsh environment, he wrote to the Christians at Philippi and urged them to rejoice in their faith.

In his letter, he shared his own determination to serve Christ, regardless of the personal cost, as encouragement to them. Consider the depth of his statement: "Brethren, I do not count myself to have apprehended; but one thing I do, forgetting those things which are behind and reaching forward to those things which are ahead, I press on toward the goal for the prize of the upward call of God in Christ Jesus."

That is an amazing statement that can profoundly impact our own Christian life today. In truth, Paul didn't forget his past, and neither can we. None of us has the mental and emotional power to wipe the history slate clean, as if things in our past never happened. Honestly, it's wasted time and energy to try.

But that isn't exactly what Paul meant. The word he used for "forgetting" means putting something behind you and never going back to it for meaning, motivation, and purpose in your life. Paul continued to remember his Jewish heritage and all that he might have achieved as a respected religious leader (read Philippians 3:5-6). Likewise, he continued to remember all the trials, tribulations, and difficulties he had endured in his Christian ministry (Read II

Corinthians 11:25-30). But Paul had an amazing capacity to not let his past determine his future. He was no longer motivated by sad moments and old memories, but rather by a new and glorious mission to serve Christ.

His statement deeply challenges me, as it should each of you. Each of us carries around a proverbial bag full of memories, some good and some bad. They constantly remind us of the paths we have trod in order to reach our current place in life. Some of those paths were smooth and joyful, and others were rough and severely jolted us.

One of the most challenging aspects of life is coming to grips with the reality that we can never walk those paths again. Yesterday is not where we live! There are times when memories flood my mind and I verbally say to myself, "Don't go there! You've been down that road one time, and once is enough!"

I think the burden of memories may have influenced Jesus to say, "No one, having put his hand to the plow, and looking back, is fit for the kingdom of God." Once Jesus left the carpenter shop at thirty years of age, He never looked back. He put all earthly experiences behind Him and sought only to do the will of His Father.

Paul made a similar commitment. He didn't "forget" his past, as if it never happened. However, his commitment to Christ was so consuming that he put all things in his past behind him, including physical experiences and personal relationships, and instead resolutely focused on the future. In doing that, he experienced an inner peace and joy that enabled him to turn a Roman prison into a mission field and shout for joy while wearing chains.

Is it possible that you and I can experience this kind of renewed purpose and joy also?

Put the Past Behind You: Press Forward

(Phil. 3:13)

When the Apostle Paul wrote a message of joy and encouragement to the Christians at Philippi, he did not let Roman imprisonment and chained bondage deter his priestly purpose of sharing the gospel of Christ. Paul had an amazing, God-given ability to fully live the potential of each moment without allowing anything in his past, either good or bad, to detract him from his future mission and reward.

In many ways, Paul's understanding of life's dynamics presaged the poetic words of Omar Khayyam, "The Moving Finger writes; and, having writ, Moves on: nor all thy Piety nor Wit Shall lure it back to cancel half a Line, Nor all thy Tears wash out a Word of it." The past is not only yesterday; it is also today, just now, the last word you spoke, and the last breath you breathed. Your words and deeds now have a life of their own and there's no way you can call them back and render them meaningless.

Paul's sheer determination and indomitable spirit should inspire every Christian. He refused to let his past alter and diminish his future by living each moment to its fullest potential. When he wrote of "pressing ahead," he used a word that appears in the New Testament only in this verse. It describes extending oneself to the maximum extent by straining and stretching forward. It is the image of a runner who thrusts himself forward at the finish line in order to cross over first. It is also the image of a horse or ox leaning forward in their harness, almost to a stumbling point, in order to pull a heavy load.

When Paul was imprisoned and chained, he did not give up in despair. Instead, he pressed forward by sharing Christ with his guards, turning a horrid Roman prison into a mission field, and, even while straining against his shackles, writing letters of encouragement and doctrinal interpretation that we know today as the New Testament books of Philippians, Ephesians and Colossians. What an amazing use of adversity and an inspiring victory over despair.

Each of us would be spiritually rejuvenated if we applied only a fraction of Paul's determination in our own life. I don't know how long it has taken you to read this devotional, but that moment is now in your past. You can never recover it. But you can do something with the truth and insight I hope you have gained. You can renew your determination to be a living witness for Christ. You can kick off the shackles of Christian complacency and ask the Lord to give you a new mission and a new purpose for Him. You can expand your limits, strain forward, and press ahead in the glorious work of sharing the gospel of Jesus.

A Family's Love for Southern Gospel

I have a life-long love for Southern gospel music. I think it is part of my genetic makeup—as much a part of me as my eye color and appearance. It is a dimension of my family legacy inherited from Grandpa Voss and nurtured by his children and grandchildren. But that doesn't mean I can sing or that I understand music. I couldn't find the Middle C key on a piano even if it were painted red. A music minister once told me, "You can definitely carry a tune: You just have no idea where you are going with it."

But, Grandpa Voss did. About the time he moved here in the 1930s, he began teaching singing schools. These were week-long sessions focusing on singing gospel music, the sound and pitch of each note, and learning to sing in four-part harmony. The instruction methods often involved learning the sound of notes, and I remember trying to understand the difference between do, re, me, fa, sol, la, ti, and do. I never mastered it. But, other family members did.

Grandpa drove his beloved 1936 Chevrolet Sedan all over South Mississippi, teaching singing schools at any church that would invite him. My uncle, James Voss, continued that ministry for many years after grandpa died in 1954. Uncle James and Aunt Sue raised their family here and were friends with numerous gospel singers, often hosting them here.

Grandpa's granddaughters, Jana Keith and Ann Rollins, continue today with significant music ministries of their own. Grandpa may have passed on his preaching gene to me, but the singing gene ornament never got hung on my Christmas tree. I always ended up "making an awful noise unto the Lord." I just love to listen—and join in softly so that no one can hear me.

One of the pieces of furniture in this house is Grandpa Voss' old cabinet model radio with the wooden tuning knobs and the pre-set station buttons. It is the same radio on which he listened to Mr. Roosevelt's fireside chats and, through the news reports of Edward R. Murrow, kept up with the progress of his boys fighting the war. It is also the radio that brought him Southern gospel music.

Every so often I do something that combines modern technology with old memories. It may sound a bit strange, but I take my fancy phone and find a YouTube video of an old gospel singing group from my childhood, and I lay the phone on the radio, as if the radio were playing. Once again, I'm a little boy eating one of Grandma Voss' big cat-head biscuits and listening to The Chuck Wagon Gang. I'm singing, humming, and tapping my little foot to the music right along with grandpa.

One of the old songs that I often think about was called, "Turn Your Radio On." The lyrics speak of a time different from today: "Come and listen in to a radio station where the mighty hosts of heaven sing…Turn your radio on and listen to the music in the air…Turn your radio on and glory share…Turn the lights down low and listen to the master's radio…Get in touch with God, turn your radio on." Grandpa did almost every day. This old house has heard its share of southern gospel music for the past ninety years, and it will continue to be that way.

Somewhere in heaven, Vestal Goodman and the Happy Goodman Family, Naomi Seago and her brothers, the Chuck Wagon Gang, the Speer Family, Jake Hess, J. D. Sumner, Glen Payne, George Yonce, James Blackwood and the Blackwood Brothers, and all the others who shaped my love for southern gospel music are looking down and smiling—and so are Uncle James and Grandpa Voss.

I Am Resolved

Did Jesus make any resolutions? Well, yes and no. He never wrote out a list of resolutions, as we sometime do, but He nevertheless formulated the greatest resolution in Christian history, and He kept it. As the celebration of Passover neared at the end of the third year of His earthly ministry, the Bible records that Jesus "resolutely set His face toward Jerusalem." There is an enormous amount of meaning in that phrase.

One should consider all the thoughts and, yes, earthly temptations that flooded His mind. People swarmed to Him for healing and help, having never experienced the level of mercy and love He showed them. Many, including His disciples, yearned for Him to reveal His messianic power by rebelling against Rome and re-establishing the ancient glory and power of King David's kingdom. The devil tempted Him to feed the people and surrender His divine power to his satanic plan. Jesus could become the most powerful leader in the world, bask in the praise and adulation of the people, and live a long and glorious life if He would follow the devil's blueprint for life. He refused.

That was not His divine purpose, and living a long earthly life was not His plan. He had come to Earth to offer Himself as a sacrifice for sinful man and as a ransom for many, and He was going to Jerusalem in order to be betrayed, condemned, and crucified in the most horrific manner known to man—crucifixion on a cross. It was to this agonizing end and purpose that He committed Himself with firm and unwavering resolve. Think about the level of courage, determination, and commitment to God that He possessed. It leaves me ashamed to even use the word *resolve* to describe the constant vacillation of my spiritual commitment.

But when I do try to think of what I want to accomplish for Christ in my remaining time on this Earth, the words of an old hymn, written by Palmer Hartsough in 1896, keep echoing in my mind, and they strongly express my desire, if only the Holy Spirit will make them the basis of my spiritual resolve: "I am resolved no longer to linger, charmed by the world's delight. Things that are higher, things that are nobler, these have allured my sight." I have wasted so much time, energy, and resources in my life pursuing the worthless things of life.

Oh, how I truly yearn to spend these sunset years seeking only that which is higher and nobler in life, and in the eyes of God.

"I am resolved to go to the Savior, leaving my sin and strife. He is the true one, He is the just one, He hath the words of life." I have had many disappointments in life, and I've been left in tears by the words and actions of people, but I can honestly testify that no one has ever loved me like Jesus does. I want to draw closer to Him.

"I am resolved to follow the Savior, faithful and true each day. Heed what He sayeth, do what He willeth, He is the living way." In the words of Martin Luther King's great speech only hours before he died, "I'm not afraid of any man. I just want to do God's will."

"I am resolved to enter the kingdom, leaving the paths of sin. Friends may oppose me, foes may beset me, still I will enter in." I've experienced some earthly professional success and pastored some good churches, but I've always encountered criticism, crude comments, and hurtful actions and attitudes. But nothing I have ever done or experienced comes close to the experience of preaching and teaching the gospel of Jesus. People can say or think what they want to about me; the kingdom of heaven is my home, and I want to experience it more fully.

"I am resolved, and who will go with me? Come, friends, without delay; taught by the Bible, led by the Spirit, we'll walk the heavenly way." I want to do nothing else in life but share the gospel of Jesus in whatever way I can. I want my remaining work in life to be a meaningful invitation to all who I can reach for Christ to make this amazing, miraculous journey with me.

Don't delay. Give your life to Christ, and go with me!

The Word Became Flesh

I

The lyrics from the old song describe it as "the most wondrous time of the year," and indeed it is. This month-long celebration spanning from Thanksgiving to Christmas is special. It is a unique time of gathering with friends and family, expressing gratitude to God for the blessings He has bestowed on us, exchanging gifts as an expression of love and friendship, and celebrating the birth of Jesus.

This year, however, seems different. Rather than "peace on earth and goodwill toward men," there is instead political ill-will among Americans and economic and social uncertainty. When we gather this year, the emphasis isn't on hanging a Christmas stocking, but rather wearing your Covid mask. Rather than joy and festivity, families are burying friends and loved ones at an astonishing rate as this awful pandemic spreads fear and uncertainty.

Maybe God wants us to turn our thoughts in another direction. Rather than being gripped in fear, can we rediscover His divine, eternal peace? Is there a fresh, new way to experience the joy of the herald angels in the midst of anxiety? Can we experience a personal spiritual transformation that will change our plea of "God, help us" to a celebratory shout of "Glory to God in the Highest!" What if you were able to experience the truth of Christmas this year as you've never spiritually known it before? Wouldn't that truly make this season "the most wondrous time" for you?

Rather than focusing on fear, focus on faith—faith in a loving Heavenly Father who loves you dearly, in spite of all the circumstances around you. Stop grieving over this world, and start giving glory to God for loving you so much that He sent His Son to transform your life into an instrument of His will and a living witness of His divine love to others. With all the political change taking place, be filled with amazement that He has named you as His ambassador to those around. He has appointed you to share His unconditional love, and you can't wrap that in a box or tie a ribbon around it. You can't write your name on a Hallmark card and adequately describe His love. He asks you to live it—openly, joyfully, sincerely, and fearlessly!

Every time you think about Covid, or hear some acrimonious political debate, pause and devote more time to deeply and prayerfully

191

considering what the Bible means when it states that "the Word became flesh" and began to live in your heart and soul. The dwelling place of God is no longer in a stone-cold temple, but rather in the warmth and love of your transformed life. He now lives in you.

You are a new creature in Christ! Christmas isn't about glitter on a tree; Christmas is about the glory of Christ radiating in your life. Christmas isn't about tinsel; it is about your life becoming a living testimonial for His abiding love and grace.

When "the Word becomes flesh" and dwells within you, fear, anxiety, and uncertainty give way to joy, praise, goodness, and a heartfelt desire to share the real joy of Christmas with those around you. Christmas is about God becoming like us, so that He could make us like Him. Isn't that worth celebrating?

II

Ancient Greek philosophy held that nothing physical was perfect, because invariably every created thing had some imperfection, however small it might be. Perfection existed only in thought, ideas, and within the spiritual realm. Thus, Greek philosophers scoffed at the idea that perfect, spiritual God could become physical human flesh and remain perfect, and so they rejected the divine nature of Jesus.

The Jews so revered God they wouldn't even pronounce His name. The idea that a thirty-year-old carpenter from Nazareth was the fullness of God in human flesh was considered a heresy worthy of death. Jesus' statement that He and His Father were "one" could only be the babblings of a demon-possessed mad man, so they said.

But, as Christians, you and I know it's true, and that's what makes the celebration of Christmas so special. The Apostle Paul stated this divine truth thusly, "For in Him dwells all the fullness of the Godhead bodily, and you are complete in Him." Not a portion of God, but all of God!

When He was born, Jesus wasn't just a baby in a manger. He was the fullness of:

Elohim...Creator God
El Shaddai...Lord God Almighty
El Roi...the God who sees me
El Elyon...the Most High God
El Olam...Everlasting God

Yahweh...Lord, Jehovah
Adonai...Lord, Master
Jehovah-Nissi...the Lord My Banner
Jehovah-Raah...the Lord My Shepherd
Jehovah Rapha...the Lord Who Heals
Jehovah Shammah...the Lord is There
Jehovah Tsedkenu...the Lord Our Righteousness
Jehovah Mekoddishkem...the Lord Who Sanctifies You
Jehovah Jireh...the Lord Will Provide
Jehovah Shalom...the Lord is Peace
Jehovah Sabaoth...the Lord of Hosts

In His relationship with His Heavenly Father, Jesus is the Son of God. In terms of the beauty of His life, He is the Rose of Sharon, the Lily of the Valley, and the Bright Morning Star.

In the rule over God's kingdom, He is the Son of David. Through His divine power, He is the Lion of Judah.

In the sacrifice of His life for sinners, He is God's eternal Sacrificial Lamb.

Through His eternal nature, He is the Alpha and Omega, the first and the last, the beginning and the end.

And when He returns, He will be crowned King of Kings and Lord of Lords.

He is Jesus, the fullness of God in bodily form. God incarnate—God in human flesh.

When you enter into a covenant of faith with Jesus as your Lord and Savior, Jesus gives the fullness of His life to you.

Have you ever paused to consider the magnitude of God's peace, providence, and protection that is encompassed in the gift of His everlasting life? I want to challenge you to begin your celebration of Christmas in a unique way. Take a moment and read back over each of the Old Testament names of God and each name and description of Jesus and prayerfully consider what receiving the gift inherent in each name means to you. Christmas is God's gift of this life to you—not your life, but His life.

In your salvation, He takes all the fullness of the life of Christ and superimposes it over your life, thus blotting out your sins so totally that He no longer sees them. He just sees Jesus in you. That's what atonement means—Jesus' life totally covers over your old carnal life in the eyes of God, and He reckons you to be like Jesus, and He adopts you as His child.

You will never receive another gift like this. Isn't the gift of God's eternal life worth celebrating this Christmas?

III

Where does God's Spirit dwell on earth? That's an age-old question that, surprisingly, is at the very heart of Christmas.

I heard thousands of prayers during twenty years as a pastor. What often surprised me was how theologically incorrect some of them were, especially those about God's spiritual presence among us. "Lord, we gather today in your house to worship You," is not correct. God doesn't have a house in which He dwells. "Lord, on this Sabbath day, we come into Your presence to worship You" isn't correct. We do not "come into His presence"; rather, we live in His presence, because as omnipresent God, His Spirit and presence is all around us. God doesn't live in a red-brick church with a steeple on top.

It's surprising how much of an Old Testament concept of God's presence continues in our New Testament understanding of how God dwells among us. In the Old Testament, the presence of God was identified initially with the tabernacle tent and then with the Temple. A special room called the "Holy of Holies" contained the Mercy Seat, and the Spirit of God was believed to hover over the Mercy Seat, thus enabling God to dwell in the midst of His people. The physical tabernacle and the Temple became synonymous with the dwelling place of God, and many people still view the church building in that way, but that isn't correct.

Many years before the birth of Jesus, Jeremiah the prophet spoke of a future time in which, through a new covenant, "I will put my law in their minds, and I will write it on their hearts, and I will be their God, and they shall be My people."

Jesus' birth made Jeremiah's prophesy reality. His birth radically transformed the ancient concept of God's dwelling place on earth, and you will never experience the real meaning of Christmas until this new covenant truth becomes real in your own life.

The Gospel of John states that the Word—the essence of God's nature—became human flesh and dwelt among us. The dwelling place of God moved from a stone-cold Old Testament tabernacle into

194

the loving hearts of those in a new-life covenant with Jesus. Revelation 21:3 states, "And I heard a loud voice from heaven saying, 'Behold, the tabernacle of God is with men, and He shall dwell with them, and they shall be His people. God Himself will be with them and be their God.'"

The great gift of His presence is something many Christians never pause to consider at Christmas. Because of your faith in Jesus, you don't go into His presence: rather, His presence is within you through the indwelling of the Holy Spirit. You don't go to "the Lord's house" to worship Him, you are the Lord's house! Christians don't go to a church once a week to spend an hour in God's presence. Instead, Christians are the church, and God's presence is continuously within them.

Through the new covenant with Jesus, your life becomes the tabernacle of the Holy Spirit. Your life becomes the dwelling place of the Spirit of God on earth, and through how you live and how you reveal Christ's love to others, you bear living proof, as His witness, that the Spirit of God indeed dwells among us. Isn't that worth celebrating this Christmas?

IV

Light is an ancient symbol of God. It isn't the light radiated by the sun, moon, or stars, but rather a heavenly light of divine origin that powerfully appears and shatters the darkness of life around us. It is light that is mysterious, majestic, and glorious, leaving us in awe and worshipful adoration of God. Throughout the Bible, the Light of God reassures us of His presence, illuminates our path, and guides us to Him.

The ancients referred to it as the Shekinah Glory of God. In the exodus of God's people from captivity and slavery, this light gloriously appeared as a pillar of fire in the night sky, ever reminding His people "I am with you." It became symbolized by the Menorah, the seven-candle golden lampstand in the tabernacle and Temple, constantly giving light that never ceased glowing. It was incorporated in Jewish theology when the Psalmist wrote, "Your word is a lamp to my feet and a light to my path."

The Shekinah Glory of God became a living reality when Jesus was born. The shepherds were stunned not only by the herald angel's announcement, but also by the glory of the Lord that shone all around them.

195

Not many Christians have ever paused long enough in the festivities of Christmas to contemplate the amazing gift of the Shekinah Glory of God given to us. Jesus said, "I am the light of the world," and indeed the Gospel of John states that "we beheld His glory."

But Jesus gave this glory to His disciples when He said to them, "You are the light of the world." It is one of the most amazing concepts in the New Testament. Through the new covenant that all Christians have with Jesus, His life enters into our life. He gives the ancient Shekinah Glory of God to His redeemed Bride, the Church, so that the glory of His life mysteriously and majestically radiates in her and through her in the darkness of the world, thus making her His glorious Bride.

Christmas is the gift of God becoming flesh and dwelling with us and in us—Emmanuel "God with us." But it is also the gift of the glory of His life radiating in our earthly life as a Christian. The Shekinah Glory of God is no longer a pillar of fire in the night sky, or a golden lampstand in a stone Temple, but rather it is the Light of the World given to us by Jesus and fueled by the power of the Holy Spirit.

Through your covenant of faith with Jesus, He has made you the Light of God illuminating the path to God for others. If someone said to you, "The glory of Christ radiates in your life every day, and people around you see Him in you," wouldn't that be a glorious gift worth humbly celebrating?

Overcoming Disappointment

It was the summer of 1980, and I was emotionally, spiritually, and financially exhausted. I was two-thirds of the way through earning a Master of Divinity degree from the New Orleans Baptist Theological Seminary, and I had one more academic year to go, but the grind of the weekly drive from Jackson to New Orleans, the academic demands, and the absence of adequate financial resources were taking a toll.

I suddenly became aware of an opportunity that filled me with unexpected hope. The Executive Director of the Mississippi Bar Association (the statewide organization for lawyers) had retired, and applications for a new director were being sought. Honestly, I saw myself as the perfect candidate. I was an attorney and member of the association, I had considerable experience with association management through my prior employment with the Mississippi Hospital Association, and I was familiar with the Bar Association work, especially lobbying in the Mississippi Legislature, which I had done on behalf of hospitals. The proposed salary and benefits were greater than I had ever made.

I submitted my application, thinking this would be an answer to my prayers. My hope was further heightened when I discovered that the interviewing committee consisted of people I knew personally and with whom I had both a personal and professional relationship.

My interview went well, and the committee was impressed with my qualifications. But their only concern was what I would do about finishing my seminary work, and how I would use the degree in the future. I gave them a good, logical answer, and they all seemed satisfied. These were all friends, and they all seemed supportive and understanding.

I soon learned that I and one other individual were the finalists, but he wasn't an attorney. He did work for a much smaller association than I had, so, surely, I was the top candidate, I thought.

I received the phone call late in the afternoon. I immediately recognized the voice of the selection committee chairman, and I was filled with anticipation of hearing the greatest news of my professional career. "John," he began, "I want you to know what an outstanding candidate you were for this position and how impressed we all were with your interview. But we all discussed this at length, and we feel that you are experiencing something deeper and different than the Bar

Association, and the committee thinks that you need to finish your seminary degree and allow the Lord to lead you to what opportunities await you after that. We have voted to hire the other candidate as our new executive director, and we all wish you the very best."

I choked back the lump in my throat long enough to thank him for his call. Then the tears started, and the depressing reality hit that there would be no end to the pressure or the struggle. Now, it would just be worse due to failure. I had no idea what I was going to do. I cried and prayed half of the night, it seemed. I was totally broken and despondent.

Well, you're probably wondering what happened. So, allow me to give you a glimpse at how God works. A few years prior to this, while I was still working for the Mississippi Hospital Association, the owner of a prominent business in Jackson invited me to lunch one day. I was surprised because we weren't really friends, although I did buy clothes at his store when I could afford it. We enjoyed a pleasant lunch, but nothing more happened. I wondered for a while why he invited me.

Not long after my bitter disappointment over the Bar Association job, his name was heavily on my mind, along with this strange feeling that I should go talk to him, which I did. I explained my situation, and I humbly asked him if there was any work I could do at his store on weekends.

He expressed admiration for my seminary efforts and said he would see what he could do. A couple of days later, he called and said he and a friend were giving me $5,000 to help me finish my degree, and I could get the first $2,500 that day and the remainder when I was closer to finishing. What you need to realize is that was the divine purpose of the lunch invitation years prior. The answer to my prayers and my disappointment was already there waiting for me when I needed it.

I later earned my seminary degree and served as a pastor for twenty years, while also doing legal work. I might have been a good executive for the Bar Association, but oh the miracles and the blessings of being an ordained minister for the Lord that I would have missed, including writing this for you today.

Some of you may be struggling with disappointment and despair, even as you read this. Please don't give up. You may feel that you're at the end of your rope, but you're never at the end of your hope, as the old expression goes. Be faithful and patient and give God time to work. He doesn't always FedEx answers to your prayers overnight. Occasionally, it takes time to see them, even those He has answered for you in advance and has them stored up and waiting for you. Sometimes faith is best understood as just quietly and expectantly waiting to see what God did yesterday in order to bless you tomorrow. Always remember that we serve a loving God who turned the cries of disappointment and despair coming from the Cross into the shouts of joy coming from the empty tomb. He can do the same for you.

Whose Blessing is This?

The church was having a summer revival, as most Baptist churches do, and the guest minister was visiting in my home. In the course of our conversation, he asked if I would be interested in three suits that had been given to him at a previous church, but did not fit him, and I accepted.

They fit me comfortably, and I was glad to have them. Later, when I put one of them on to attend the church service, I felt something in the coat's inside vest pocket, which was an envelope containing four $100 bills. I shouted for joy and thanked God for the surprise blessing.

But I slowly began to realize this wasn't my blessing. Whoever put the money in the coat pocket didn't intend it for me. So, that night before church, I told the minister who had given me the coat what I had found and that the money belonged to him.

Like me, he was very happy and thanked God for the blessing. But, after some moments of reflection, he said it wasn't his blessing. Rather, it was mine because he had given me the coat with no knowledge the money was in the pocket. I disagreed, saying that since I was not the original recipient of the gift, the money wasn't intended for me.

So, whose blessing was this? What is your opinion?

During the opening moments of the service that evening, I lightheartedly explained the dilemma to the congregation and asked for a vote on whether I should keep the money or the visiting minister. In the midst of this friendly chatter, the church treasurer stood up, walked to the offering table, and picked up an offering plate. She held the plate in front of me and said, "Put it here and that answers the question." My memory of her wise action has remained over all these years. It was as if she were saying, "The answer is not whether this is your blessing or his blessing. The greater answer is it's everyone's blessing."

I'm not an advocate of shotgun, fishing net prayers that cover a broad area with no particular focus in mind. It's like a man I knew who regularly prayed for God to forgive "our many sins and shortcomings." I couldn't help but wonder what the difference was between them. Was a shortcoming less offensive to God than a full-blown sin? I never figured it out.

The same is true for prayers for divine blessings. I fully believe in praying for specific needs or for specific people. But, what about broad prayer requests such as "bless all who are traveling today," or "bless the sick and afflicted"? What are we really asking God to do for them? Whose blessing will it be?

When we pray, "God, please bless America," what are we asking Him to do? Do we want God to just bless and empower our own view of how things should be, or do we want Him to bless all Americans the same, even those with whom we differ?

Maybe we should retreat from our limited view of God's love for all of us and His unlimited power to bless. Instead of this incessant bickering over who is right or wrong politically, maybe we should just fall on our knees and thank God for the freedom to vote. As I stood in line waiting to vote recently, I had a long, pleasant conversation with a black couple. In all this Trump vs. Biden gobbledygook, you should never lose sight of the fact that only a few years ago, right here in our area, the Ku Klux Klan would have threatened them with death for exercising that blessing. If you doubt that, just ask the family of Vernon Dahmer in Hattiesburg. The KKK burned his home and store because he wanted the blessing of voting, and he died for seeking that blessing.

Maybe we should fall on our knees this morning and thank God for the freedom of speech and expression—this God-given right to express our opinions and to vocally endorse and support whomever we choose. Maybe most of you have forgotten, or never even knew about, the diabolical actions of the old Mississippi Sovereignty Commission, whose official state-supported work was to spy on citizens of our state and to suppress the freedom of speech and association of those with whom they disagreed. In the view of the Sovereignty Commission, God's blessings were only white in color. Maybe you have forgotten all about those days, but I haven't. It wouldn't surprise me if my name was in their old rusty Rolodex as a young, outspoken college student.

What if we all thanked God for the freedom to vote, the freedom to assemble together, the freedom of speech, and the freedom to openly express our opinions without the fear of recrimination? If we really prayed for God to bless America, wouldn't the fact that the greatest number of people in American history exercised the freedom to vote be a greater blessing than whether He blessed one viewpoint more than another?

If we pray for God to bless America, then perhaps we should also be ready to thank Him for equally blessing all Americans with these precious freedoms. God doesn't just bless red states or blue states or Democrats or Republicans or church-going conservative, evangelical Christians. His blessings on America are not color coded.

When I ask God to bless America, it is not my right and privilege of citizenship to ask Him to show favoritism. When I ask God to bless the America I love, may I never ask, "Whose blessing is this?" The freedom to experience the blessings of America is a divine blessing for everyone! It is just a much bigger and more glorious picture of the coat money going into the offering plate.

Why Did They Follow Him?

The gospel accounts of Jesus calling His disciples is a fascinating study of human response and motivation. Have you ever seriously wondered why they followed Him, and most of them did so immediately? We now place the disciples on a spiritual pedestal of respect and admiration, but they were the opposite when called by Christ. Some were ordinary fishermen, one was a despised tax collector for the Roman Empire, and another was a radical, troublemaking political zealot. There was nothing at all special about them.

Many Christians think that they left their daily work and routine out of a deep spiritual commitment to help Jesus spread the gospel. Perhaps, on closer examination, we would find that their motive was far more personal, motivated by human purposes, prejudices, and even greed.

Probably all of them believed that the anticipated Messiah would transform their life and the nation of Israel. Through His divine power, along with military and political force, the Messiah would usher in the long-awaited Golden Age of peace and prosperity. If Jesus was the Messiah, here was the opportunity of a lifetime to have a high-ranking personal role.

So why did they follow? Actually, the gospels give some enlightening clues. Simon the Zealot wanted to revolt against Rome and brutally inflict revenge on every Roman soldier. Judas set his eyes on the treasury and the riches that would be generated, because he soon began stealing the offerings given to Jesus. Many of the other disciples regularly discussed and debated what roles each of them would occupy and which of them would be greatest in the new messianic kingdom. The mother of two disciples actually came to Jesus, asking that her sons be allowed to sit at His right side and left side as He ruled over the kingdom. Just prior to Jesus ascending to heaven, the disciples asked Him, "Will You at this time restore the kingdom to Israel?" Only Peter actually expressed an understanding that Jesus was truly the Son of God, but after Jesus' crucifixion, Peter despondently said, "I'm going back to fishing."

The gospels do not record that any of the disciples initially committed their life to Christ out of an abundance of love for Him. It wasn't their love and compassion for their fellow-man, their concern for the poor and needy, their willingness to befriend sinners, or their zeal to share the gospel of peace. The disciples initially followed Jesus because of a personal motivation to impose their beliefs on others by force through the power of God and human law and in order to maximize their own personal ambition and status. It was only later, when the Holy Spirit changed their understanding and infused them with true spiritual power from God, that they became the devoted disciples who we respect today.

I love my country and I love the church, and after all these years, I still choke up describing my call to be a preacher and teacher of the gospel. But there is one issue that deeply concerns me, and that is our erroneous desire to use Christianity and the gospel of Christ to advance human desires, personal agendas, and political beliefs.

Jesus never did that, and we shouldn't either. In fact, He expressly rejected every temptation of Satan and every plea of His followers to use His power for political purposes or to impose His will on others. One notable Baptist leader commented as his final wish, "Whatever you do, keep the Church and the State separated." Christianity is defined by love for others, and you cannot impose redeeming love on others by collective force—you must personally share it.

We should all be more zealous to share our faith in Christ and help America have a renewed spiritual awakening, but, through the power of the Holy Spirit, we should do it for the right reasons.

A Baptist in a Beer Joint

Mental health professionals know that the phrase "God told me" can be a red flag indicating emotional and mental struggles. A preacher knows that the phrase "God told me" is often the divine inspiration for a meaningful sermon or life-changing action. Sometimes, you can get caught in the middle and wonder if you are totally insane for feeling that God is leading you to do something completely out of the ordinary. The struggle can be real and even frightening.

It happened to me several years ago, and I have always wondered about the outcome. There was a nondescript beer joint called "Bartos" just inside Forrest County that I drove past every day going to work, not the kind of establishment that the pastor of Good Hope Baptist Church would ordinarily enter.

One day, I got this strange feeling that I should stop and go inside. I laughed to myself about it at first. But the feeling persisted and became almost overwhelming. I dreaded going to work knowing the spiritual warfare I would experience going past Bartos. This pressure never subsided. I felt a real sense that God was telling me to do this, and I knew I wouldn't find any peace about it until I obeyed. But, why? What was the purpose, I wondered? I had no idea what I was supposed to say or do once inside.

Finally, I decided to stop. I made up some excuse for a Baptist preacher coming into a beer joint in broad daylight, and I went inside. There was only one customer sitting on a barstool, sipping his beer. I recognized him as a man from Purvis, a couple of years older than me, and I said hello.

I told the bartender that I was a Baptist preacher and wondered if I could come by another time and leave some small Bibles or spiritual tracts, along with my name and number. In case someone was down, depressed, and trying to drink their troubles away, I would like the opportunity to share the hope and salvation of Christ with them. He looked at me totally shocked, but he quickly agreed to my request. The man from Purvis, whom I had spoken to, sat there intently listening, but never said a word.

I left totally relieved that this was over. But I kept thinking about the guy I knew and what he must have thought about this crazy Baptist preacher and my offer to share the love of Christ in Bartos.

Strangely, about two weeks later, he suddenly died, and his death shocked me, because I remembered him sitting there listening to me. After that one visit, I never again had any desire to stop. So, if that was God telling me to stop and go in, and I truly felt it was, what was the reason? Here's what I've hoped the answer is for all these years, and I've never found any other logical reason or explanation.

If, when I die, the guy from Purvis sitting on the barstool meets me inside the portals of glory and thanks me, then I will understand. I just want to hear him say, "I don't know why you did it, but your willingness to come into a beer joint and share Jesus that day changed my life. I didn't want my beer anymore; I wanted what you had—Christ. I never dreamed as I sat there listening to you that I had only a few days to live. Thank you." If that happens, what a joyous moment we will share.

Christianity is not about just going to church. It is about going to people of every kind in the name of Jesus and sharing the gospel of peace and salvation with them, sometimes in places you never dreamed you would enter.

If you ever have one of those "God told me" moments, here's my suggestion to you: Be cautious about overreacting—God will give you adequate time; be sure of your purpose; and be confident in your faith. You might even end up being a Baptist in a beer joint.

But, also be committed enough to believe that even if you get laughed at or rejected, you will have planted a seed of faith that just might mature in ways you never imagined, in places you never imagined, and in lives you never imagined.

The Judgments of the Lord

On March 4, 1865, Abraham Lincoln delivered his second inaugural address, a masterpiece of brevity and meaning. Lincoln discussed the bright hope of freedom for the future and also America's dark past and the curse of slavery.

Lincoln also spoke about healing the nation's wounds and divisions. Someone had asked the president how he would treat defeated Southern rebel citizens, and he replied, "I will treat them as if they never left." He echoed that sentiment in his speech by saying, "with malice toward none and charity for all."

But Lincoln also pondered a deeper spiritual question about how God could answer the fervent prayers of people on both sides who earnestly asked for divine blessings on their efforts to defend and advance their political beliefs. Regardless of the cause of the divisive war, or the prayers of one side or the other, Abraham Lincoln concluded that "the judgments of the Lord are true and righteous altogether."

This noble American experiment of democracy—this "new nation conceived in liberty and dedicated to the proposition that all men are created equal"—would continue, as she does today.

In this recent election, there have been countless prayers for God's help and intervention, and many are filled with despair over their loss. Citizens of the South in 1865 certainly felt that, but they prevailed and grew better, and so can we.

This is not the end of America, as some have despondently stated. We have weathered worse storms in the past and emerged stronger, and through God's grace, we shall continue to do so.

Whether you approve of Joe Biden or not, he often shares the encouraging comments of his grandparents in his youth. His grandfather would say, "Joey, keep the faith." But his grandmother would add, "No, Joey, spread the faith!"

Maybe that's what we all should do. Rather than being dejected and ringing our hands in despair, why don't we spread the faith by extending a helping hand to others? Why don't we spread not only our religious faith, but also our political faith in the inherent goodness of America? Why don't we renew our own commitment to lifting the torch of freedom higher in our own life by caring for others as we do our own self and by striving to guarantee liberty and justice for all?

Abraham Lincoln could not possibly have envisioned the America of today, and neither can we envision the America of tomorrow, but God can, and He does. Maybe God sees an America more glorious in the future than she is today. Lift up your heads and remove the crestfallen look on your faces. By keeping the faith and spreading our faith in Christ and in the God-ordained promise of American democracy, the torch of hope in the world that is the United States of America will not only continue to shine, but it will get even brighter.

The hope of freedom, liberty, justice, and human dignity is not just America's promise to the world, they are God's promise to the world manifested through us. We are His workmen committed to His divine purpose, but we cannot see the full impact of our work on the America of tomorrow. That is in the hands of God. We simply must keep the faith and spread the faith, and we must never forget that "the judgments of the Lord are true and righteous altogether."

Junk

I have a simple theory about life and people: There's not many things that are truly worthless and not many people who are beyond redemption. True, there is a lot of junk lying around and a lot of folks who we dismiss, shun, and turn our little nose up to them. But God doesn't, and neither should we, if we are to be a living witness for Christ in this mad, confused world.

Even you and I slide into the "oh, I'm not worth much" and "oh, I just can't do anything anymore" muddy puddle of self-pity. Just read all the complaints on Facebook for a sample.

Try this instead: Take things that you consider worthless and see what beauty you can create with them. There are features in my yard that would be worthless junk to most people. Nothing but an old cedar log, some pieces of heart pine that's past their prime, some pieces of brown rock thrown away at the side of a field, and even a black tub that once held cow feed. Junk? Absolutely not. The makings of something beautiful instead. It's amazing what a different setting, a new background, a new purpose, and some caring hands can do with junk.

The same is true with people. There are folks all around you that you ignore, cast aside, make fun of, and attach no value to their life. We should be ashamed. We were all like that when the Lord began redeeming us. Reach out to the worst person you know in the name of Jesus and experience the beauty of them becoming a beautiful, best friend. It's a much better path into the kingdom of heaven than complaining.

A Memorial Stone

"Then Samuel took a stone and set it up between Mizpah and Shen, and called its name Ebenezer, saying, 'Thus far the Lord has helped us'" (1 Samuel 7:12).

The struggle had been intense, and Samuel well knew that his success had been a divine blessing. But, in his gratitude, Samuel wanted more than just a mental acknowledgement of God's help. Instead, he wanted something physical and permanent, that would never lessen in importance, to always remind him that his success was really God's work in his life and not his own abilities. Indeed, his victories were just a physical manifestation of the divine power within him.

Samuel took a large stone, set it up as a permanent memorial, and called it "Ebenezer," which basically means "the stone of help," and Samuel said, regarding the meaning of the memorial stone, "Thus far the Lord has helped us." The stone was a constant reminder that he could not convert divine blessings into personal pride and boasting. Without God's help, Samuel wouldn't be where he was, and he knew that.

In 1758, Robert Robinson wrote the beautiful hymn "O Thou Fount of Every Blessing," and the second stanza contains these inspiring words: "Here I raise my Ebenezer, here by Thy great help I've come. And I hope by Thy good pleasure safely to arrive at home." It is one of the classic old hymns.

The lyrics challenge me, because if I were to raise my own Ebenezer, what would it be and where would it be? What memorial could I create that would constantly remind me that "here by Thy great help I've come."

This may surprise you, but several hours have passed since I wrote that last paragraph during which I sought to answer my own question, and, for me, I have. I want to erect a flagpole and place an American flag in the center of this old yard. The house is about one hundred years old, and my family has lived here since 1932. How my grandparents survived the early years and raised a large family was not their own efforts alone, for they truly confessed "here by Thy great help I've come."

I look back on my own life, and the accomplishments with which I've been blessed were not of my own efforts, for I must truly confess "here by thy great help I've come." All that we have been divinely blessed to experience through God's grace is due to living in America, and an American flag in my yard would remind me each day of just how abundantly God has poured out His grace on me.

The flag would remind me daily that I am blessed beyond measure to live freely in a country where a beaten-down, impoverished, one-time high school drop-out can have a chance at a better life and can go on to graduate from the University of Mississippi and then earn two post-graduate degrees.

The flag would remind me daily of the blessings of freely preaching and proclaiming my faith in Christ in a land founded on freedom of religion, as I've done for nearly fifty years, and that the amazing opportunity to touch thousands of lives for Jesus was because "by thy great help I've come."

My own Ebenezer would inspire me to keep on preaching the gospel and fighting as best I can in my old age to make America "one nation under God with liberty and justice for all."

My memorial to God's amazing blessings would inspire and encourage me to further realize that, just as God has blessed me thus far, He will continue to do so because of His great love for me and the grace He has poured out on me. In the words of the old hymn, "...and I hope by Thy good pleasure safely to arrive at home."

Because of my faith in Jesus, the love of my Heavenly Father, and my citizenship in America, everything is going to be okay. On this Memorial Day, I am blessed. In gratitude and recognition that it's been the work of the Lord in my life, here I'll raise my Ebenezer.

There's a Bit of Miss Cora's Gladiolus in Each of Us

Big words are sometimes needed to describe big ideas. Metamorphosis is an example. It is a multi-syllable word describing the multiple stages of change that a living creature experiences as it ascends along the path toward maturity. It is how a nondescript worm slowly but surely becomes an amazingly beautiful butterfly. But this kind of profound change in the very heart and character of the creature doesn't happen overnight. Rather, it takes time and occurs in multiple stages of growth and change. Butterflies are not the work of a magician of nature who taps an ugly, crawling worm and transforms it into a beautiful creature of soaring flight in a cloud of pixie dust. Butterflies are the slow, loving work of a Miracle-maker who changes them inwardly at first, but that change causes an amazing transition into the creature of beauty and grace that He always knew they could be.

The New Testament uses the root word for metamorphosis to describe the spiritual change that occurs in a Christian through a fundamental faith in Jesus empowered by the Holy Spirit. It is how a ne'er-do-well sinner becomes a good and faithful servant of Christ and a living witness to the eternal truth spoken by Jesus. In contrast to the expectation that the Messiah would suddenly cause this spiritual change, Jesus repeatedly said that it was instead the work of the Holy Spirit over time, and He told a beautiful parable about how a farmer sows his seed and then goes on with the business of life. But something unseen, mysterious, and divine occurs as he works and sleeps, and this unseen miraculous transformation describes spiritual growth in a Christian. If a believer is sincere in his faith, he is changing a little each day into a different person to what he has been. Jesus said it was like the planted seed that first appears as a tiny leaf, then the shaft appears, and later the seed head, followed by an abundant harvest. No harvest occurs in a Christian's life without growth and change.

Metamorphosis is, on the one hand, a fascinatingly mysterious process delineating how the creature of the past is slowly transformed into the servant of the future. But there are enormously significant truths about this process that are often missed. The process is premised on potential—inherent, dormant, untapped, undeveloped potential. It is the potential hidden within each of us to be something and someone much different and better than we have been.

Change of this magnitude does not occur because some higher force pulls together elements of personality from hither and yon and creates a new personality for us. Spiritual metamorphosis is based on who you have always been deep within, but never had the courage, conviction, and power to change. Metamorphosis is just you coming out of your self-imposed shell of reticence. It is the flowering of who you always sensed you could be, but were always afraid to become.

Many years ago, I purchased a home that had been previously owned by an elderly lady who loved flowers, and she had multiple flower beds in her beautiful yard. One spring a gladiolus began to mysteriously grow in an area previously devoid of flowering plants. Slowly it grew and bloomed into an unbelievably beautiful flower that defied understanding and explanation. I described this unique flower in another devotional.

I have often pondered the mystery of Miss Cora's gladiolus, because it represents so many of us. How long had it sat dormant in the ground with its beauty and potential completely hidden? What innate stirring within caused it to finally push itself out of its dark, subterranean prison into the newness of light? Miss Cora's gladiolus was always what it finally became. It is a true example of the core meaning of metamorphosis, which is "changing form in keeping with inner reality." Deep within the genetic core of its very nature, it was always a thing of immense beauty that would bless countless people, if it could only change and become what it was destined to be.

Each of us is divinely created by God, and deep within our nature as God's creation is the potential to be so much more than we are. Each of us has within our very heart and soul a greater capacity to love others as Christ loves us, and each of us has a greater capacity to show mercy and compassion to those downtrodden and burdened among us. Every spiritual attribute given to man has not reached its full potential in any of us. There is still room to grow and change into the person that God created us to be.

Consider for a moment the tragedy of remaining as we are—spiritually dormant, emotionally dug-in, and physically determined to remain as we have always been. There is a broken, hurting person somewhere in your future whose life will never be transformed by your unconditional love and friendship, unless you are willing to change and love them as they are and love them where they are. There is a lonely

213

life trudging along aimlessly and hopelessly lost without purpose that awaits your kind words of encouragement, if you are willing to change and show mercy to that person, so that you can better experience God's mercy in your own life. There is hunger and hurting all around that will never be relieved, unless you are willing to change and become a friend with sinners and dine and fellowship with them, even as Jesus did. None of the Christ-like potential in our life will ever emerge and radiantly glorify Jesus unless we are willing to be changed.

There is within each of us a bit of Miss Cora's gladiolus—godly love languishing in the darkness of fear of what others may say about us; mercy shackled by unconcern for hurting humanity; and tolerance and understanding of others trapped in the hardness of prejudice. But that can all change. The great joy of Christian living is feeling spiritual growth occurring within you. Just like Jesus' parable, as you go about the routines of life, you begin to realize that you are slowly changing in your view and opinion of others—you are becoming more compassionate and caring, you have a greater level of love for your neighbor and others around you than you ever experienced before, and it's because you are growing through divinely empowered inner change into the image and likeness of Christ.

You can begin today to experience this joyous growth in your life that changes you into the person that God designed you to be— that good and faithful servant who glorifies Jesus in your life in ways you never thought were possible.

The Powerful, Pondering Prayer
of a Godly Mother

When the shepherds told Mary what the angel had said to them about Jesus, the Gospel of Luke states that Mary "pondered" all these things in her heart. It is an intensely revealing statement.

This was not the first time Mary had been divinely told about the Child she cradled in her arms. Nine months earlier another angel had told her that she would conceive and bear a Son who would be the Son of God. Now, she held Him in her arms and looked into His face. Mary was most likely only an older teenage girl, and her emotions must have been flowing in every possible direction.

The ancient meaning of "ponder" describes more than just deeply thinking about something. The word means to bring scattered things together into a logical collection and to assemble them in a meaningful way. When applied to the human thought process, it means to bring together different thoughts that are flooding one's mind from all different sources and to make meaningful sense out of them.

Consider all that flowed in Mary's mind: her own feelings, hopes, and dreams; the ancient dreams of Israel for a Messiah; the angelic messages about this Child; the demands of the law that she should be stoned to death because she was pregnant and unmarried; the gossip and rumors from family, friends, and those who knew her; and the words and attitude of Joseph. For months, all of these wildly distinct and divergent thoughts had constantly flooded her mind. But now, in this dark, dank, and smelly Bethlehem cattle stall, it all came together and made perfect sense to her as she looked into the face of Jesus, and she found a peace and purpose in her life that she had never known. Surely her pondering led to prayers only a mother could pray for her Child.

On this Mother's Day, I ask you to take a moment and reflect back on all the times your mother and grandmothers pondered over your life and prayed for you.

I can't even imagine the thoughts that each of them must have had about me as they fed me, nurtured me, watched me play, and as they looked into my face as they rocked me to sleep. Tears fill my eyes as I think about these three godly mothers pondering over my life and praying for me. Only the Good Lord knows how deeply and sincerely each of them asked Him to bless me as they held me and lovingly looked into my little-boy face. If there is a Prayer Register in heaven, it must surely be filled with their prayer requests for me as they pondered what I would be and who I would be in life. They are all at home in heaven now, but I humbly hope that many of their prayers have been answered.

The Lord hears billions of prayers each day. But I have a feeling the ones that are most precious to Him are the powerful, pondering prayers of a godly mother for her children.

Overcoming an Attack by a
Spiritual Leaf-Roller

Cannas are one of my favorite plants. Not only are the leaves lush and green, but the orange-yellow flowers are uniquely beautiful. Red cannas are a bit different and have deeper green foliage and large red flowers. They, too, make a beautiful flower bed.

But cannas are unfortunately cursed with a destructive little creature called a "leaf-roller" that will destroy the plant if left unchecked. The leaf-roller egg is laid by a particular kind of moth. Once it hatches into the larvae stage and becomes a small worm, it weaves a silk-thread-looking web along the edge of the maturing canna leaf that binds the leaf together. Once the leaf is bound and can't open, the worm then destroys the plant by eating the inside of the leaf. The web can be cut, and the leaf opened, but it is an ugly, nasty, half-eaten mess.

Leaf-rollers can be controlled with certain sprays and insecticides. But, unless proper treatment is undertaken, your beautiful canna bed will soon be history. Interestingly, you can learn a lot about your Christian life from a lowly leaf-roller worm. Seriously, there are some interesting spiritual truths one can observe in a canna leaf under attack by a leaf-roller.

Consider this: Jesus symbolically compared His relationship with His disciples and the church to a vine and its branches. His life, as the vine, flows out into the branches and leaves, making them productive and fruitful. So, the best strategy Satan has for defeating the work of Christ is reducing the effectiveness and fruitfulness of the branches. How does he do that? By binding them so they can't spread out, blossom, and bear fruit. Satan works just like a leaf-roller.

Jesus asked "...how can one enter a strong man's house and plunder his goods unless he first binds the strong man?" Like the devilish little worm, Satan attempts to bind every Christian in some form so they will not grow spiritually. Once they are bound, he eats away at them inwardly until they are spiritually fruitless and virtually ruined.

Satan will bind you with fear, grief, guilt, uncontrolled temptation, and countless other threads of spiritual disillusion until you have no meaningful Christian life. You may exist like a half-eaten canna leaf, but you won't bear much fruit. He will slowly destroy the core of your commitment to Christ, leaving a half-dead Christian life.

When I find a canna leaf bound by a leaf-roller, I cut the threads the worm has woven. It allows the leaf to finally open and cast out the worm. The leaf will never be what it might have been, but at least it can now live free from bondage.

You must do the same to the spiritual and emotional cords that Satan uses to hold back your Christian life and growth. Jesus can cut you free of the devilish entrapment you are in. You are a redeemed, precious child of God, and you deserve to live freely and fruitfully for the glory of Christ.

Whatever it is that has you spiritually bound and is eating away at you from the inside, today is the day to break free. With Christ's help, cut the cords of disillusionment, despair, and doubt. Spread your spiritual branches and freely and fruitfully live for Jesus.

Thoughts About the Fourth of July

I

Self-Evident Truth

The Declaration of Independence was an unprecedented act of political courage, a life-changing commitment for many, and a profound statement of moral reasoning that undergirds the concepts of personal freedom that we enjoy. The Declaration declared certain truths to be "self-evident," and those truths are at the core of American democracy. However, many Americans do not consider the meaning of "self-evident truth," and they are missing a blessing.

British social order was structured on a system of division and inequality among people, and that was believed to be a God-given concept. Supreme authority was the divine right of the king, but society distinguished between royalty and commoners. The two classes did not often interrelate. A commoner could not become a member of the upper class, except through marriage, and even then, they were not fully accepted.

So, fast-forward to self-evident truths. A self-evident truth needs no further proof or explanation, such as two plus two equals four. It is akin to the legal concept of *res ipsa loquitur*, "the thing speaks for itself."

The Declaration directly repudiates any concept of class distinction and declares the equality of man as a moral, self-evident truth when it states, "We hold these truths to be self-evident, that all men are created equal. " This does not mean that everyone has equal gifts and abilities.

Rather, it is a moral declaration that America will have no system of commoners and royalty; no one in America will bow down to any other; no one in America will bend their knee in deference to another; it would not be illegal in America for a commoner to touch the "king," but instead even the most common of men and women may shake their leader's hand, slap him or her on the back, and cheer them on.

In America, the common man is the focus of democracy, and the government is instituted for the specific purpose of securing common people their God-given rights. In America, the most common man or woman can rise to the heights of their natural gifts and abilities. In America, a common man can become an uncommon man of success and achievement, and no class structure prevents that personal achievement.

The Declaration declares that in America that right of the common man is a self-evident moral truth. Nothing of that magnitude had ever been declared before as a basis of government.

Amazing, isn't it.

II

A Revolutionary Declaration of the Divine Right to Independence

Most Americans today have lost sight of the radical nature of the Declaration of Independence. When it was signed, one could not have imagined a document more contrary to the established political norms of the day. The vast British Empire stretched around the world, and the loyalty of its subjects was enforced by one of the world's greatest armies and navies.

But there was also an underlying religious component that underscores the Declaration. The British king was believed to be God's agent in the creation and rule of this vast empire, thus the long-existing British motto, "God save the King" or "God save the Queen." Ruling over the vast empire was the divine right of the king, conferred upon him by God.

All nations of the empire existed for the empire's eternal good, and all individuals were expected to subject their life, property, personal desires, and individual gifts to the good of the empire and the divine glory of the British sovereign, who possessed God's power and permission to rule. There was no concept of the right of a nation or an individual to be free from this loyalty and obligation.

The Declaration of Independence is therefore a radical assertion that this long-standing and revered concept was totally wrong, and, in fact, the exact opposite was true. The Declaration rejects the idea that loyalty to the empire was a divine obligation and instead asserts that when the personal and nationalistic burdens of loyalty become unbearable, both countries and individuals have a superior divine right given to them by God to be free and independent in order to pursue their own concepts of life, liberty, and happiness. According to the Declaration, they are endowed by God with this right. That right is not given by God to a king, but rather to each citizen. That's why this truth started a revolution.

We casually state the title of the document while forgetting that the Declaration of Independence was in fact a public declaration by colonial representatives of the God-given right to independence rather than loyalty to the crown. Allow me to emphasize this: Nothing in the form of a public declaration could have possibly been more radical and revolutionary in July of 1776. In the view of the British, to publicly support, sign, and defend such a declaration proclaiming the divine right to independence was worthy of death. It deeply saddens me that we have lost sight of this God-given gift of freedom to America.

III

With Firm Reliance on Divine Providence

When young David fought Goliath the giant, he must have felt ill-equipped for the looming battle with his slingshot and five stones, but for the fact that he fought the giant "in the name of the Lord." And, he won.

The signers of the Declaration must have had a similar feeling of inadequacy for the inevitable war for independence facing them. The British army and navy were virtually invincible and were led by seasoned and able-minded commanders. The financial reserves backing British forces were essentially unlimited.

The Continental Army was composed of volunteer, citizen soldiers possessing their own weapons, war supplies were very limited, and finances were strained and supplemented by Benjamin Franklin going to France and begging for help. Commanders were limited and most had little or no combat experience.

Victories were few and far between, and the army spent considerable time evacuating areas and fleeing the British in an attempt to survive rather than attacking them. It is said that George

Washington, as commander, lost more battles than he won. Desertions became significant, morale plunged, and desperation prevailed. George Washington probably prayed more than he planned battle strategy.

The historical evidence is that, despite the courage of citizen soldiers, the Continental Army did not win the war on its on strength, skill, and merit. We had help, and lots of it. In fact, the presence and power of the French navy afforded Washington his final and ultimate victory.

I cannot imagine the courage of the signers of the Declaration pledging their life, their personal fortunes, and their honor to a cause they must have known had little chance of success, except for their firm reliance on the power, purpose, and protection of divine providence. They faithfully believed that God had bestowed in them God-given rights of freedom that He would protect for them. American freedom is a gift from God, and we must never forget that.

So, like David, George Washington took his five stones of faith in God, the courage and commitment of his soldiers, a passionate determination to win, help from others, and a visionary belief in the future of America, and he fought the giant in the name of the Lord. And, he won.

In truth, the victory was God's; we just get to enjoy the blessings of victory. The best way to celebrate the Fourth of July is to thank God for your freedom as an American. It is His endowed gift to you.

IV

The God-Given Endowment of an American Citizen

The Declaration of Independence contains one truly startling statement—among many others. The Declaration holds that there are certain "self-evident truths" within the political and moral universe that require no further affirmation or validation, including specifically that American citizens are "endowed" by God with the rights of life, liberty, and the pursuit of happiness, and that those rights can never be taken from us, because they are "unalienable." That is to say, these rights can never be alienated from us because they are the basis of God's endowment to us as citizens. That is a profoundly amazing statement.

An endowment is a legal structure, usually financial in nature, but in this case political, that is created for the purpose of receiving gifts for the betterment of others and for also ensuring that those gifts are perpetuated into the distant future. The purpose of the endowment is always consistent with the desires of the one who established the endowment. One of the greatest tragedies of our current political landscape is that most American citizens have no idea of the true nature of their God-given endowment.

Let's first think about the nature of this statement in the Declaration. America is the most unique nation in the world because her government is a legal endowment created by God and given to man for the specific purpose of receiving, securing, and perpetuating enumerated rights and freedoms divinely given to us by God. The Declaration declared that "In order to secure these rights, governments are instituted among men."

The fundamental purpose of our government is not to diminish or reduce these God-given rights, but rather to secure them, strengthen them, and perpetuate them into the distant future, and the governmental structure derives all of its authority from the consent of the governed. The responsibility of citizenship is to be involved in the process of government in order to strengthen your God-given endowment as a citizen!

The God-given gifts placed in your endowment as an American citizen for perpetuity are "life, liberty, and the pursuit of happiness." Let's look at each one:

At the time the Declaration was signed, every citizen's life was subject to the control of the English sovereign. The life of every citizen was secondary in importance to the king and to the good of the empire. The ultimate purpose of every life was to secure and perpetuate the rights of the king that were viewed as his divine rights given to him (or to a queen) as God's agent over the empire. Rejecting that concept was worthy of death.

The Declaration declared the opposite: The role of the sovereign is to secure the life and rights of each citizen, and what authority the sovereign exercises in securing those rights is given to him only by the beneficiaries of the endowment—ordinary citizens. The right to the fullness of life is controlled only by such rules as are mutually agreed upon by recipients of the endowment. The recipients of the endowment control the sovereign; the sovereign does not control them. The king and his personal desires for power, prestige, and self-perpetuation is of secondary importance, or of no importance at all.

Each American citizen is endowed by God with the right to a life that is greater in importance than any politician, political party, power strategy, or gerrymandering to grab control of an election process and results. The Bible states, "Stand fast therefore in the liberty wherewith Christ has made us free and be not entangled again with the yoke of bondage." Thus, "if Christ has set you free, then you are free indeed," and that applies to the enjoyment of your endowment as a citizen.

God has also endowed you with liberty. It is the freedom of the human spirit to dream, work, have goals, attain success, and reap the benefits of self-effort that no government can ever take from you. This is your unalienable right as an American, and it was placed in your endowment fund as a citizen by Almighty God. It is His perpetual gift to you. The purpose of your government to is receive, strengthen, and perpetuate your right to live your life according to the rules mutually agreed upon by you and other recipients of the endowment, and not by some arbitrary decision of a political force, power, or tyrant beyond your control. The future of your endowment is in your hands.

The pursuit of happiness is another God-given right forever placed in your political endowment fund as an American. But the concept of happiness meant something a bit different in 1776 than it does today. Former Supreme Court Justice Anthony Kennedy explained it this way:

"While in modern times there is a 'hedonistic component' to the definition of happiness, for the framers of the Declaration of Independence 'happiness' meant that feeling of self-worth and dignity you acquire by contributing to your community and to its civic life....In the context of the Declaration, 'happiness' was about an individual's contribution to society rather than pursuits of self-gratification."

God has forever placed in your personal endowment fund as an American citizen the right to make a difference in the life of your country and the life of others, and to feel good about yourself for making this difference. The Bible states that Jesus "went about doing good" and making life more enjoyable, significant, and meaningful for others. If that was a characteristic of Jesus' life, would it not be logical that God likewise placed that joy and happiness in our individual endowment fund so that we may also be a blessing in the lives of others? You are endowed by God with the right to be a good person, a blessing to others, and a means of perpetuating the blessings of the endowment fund of American citizenship far into the future, even for yet unborn citizens and recipients of the endowment.

The Declaration of Independence declares that you have a God-given right to the goodness of your life, the goodness of your dreams, the goodness of your accomplishments, and the goodness of the legacy that you leave behind through the totality of your life as an American citizen, and no power of government can ever deny, detract, or diminish your opportunity to pursue your own version of happiness. But it is up to you to take advantage of your endowment and experience the fullness of the gift of American citizenship that God has given to you.

If and when the recipients of these God-given rights finally see themselves as equal in the eyes of God, without concern for skin color, ethnic background, gender, or personal desires in life, and celebrate the goodness of each life, then, in the words of "America the Beautiful," God will "crown thy good with brotherhood from sea to shining sea."

On this Fourth of July, may the American endowment of citizenship continue to be a beacon of hope in the world.

Breaking the Law to be Merciful

I

Violating the Ancient Law of Social Distancing

Israel's struggle to contain leprosy was as old as the nation itself. The description of this dreaded disease and the required preventive measures to control its spread are included in the earliest laws of Israel, as set out in several chapters in Leviticus. Leprosy caused severe nerve damage in the extremities, skin ulcers, damage to the respiratory tract, and ultimately significant physical disfigurement. It's believed that leprosy spread from person to person through nasal secretions expelled by coughing and sneezing. There was no known cure at that time.

The personal impact of leprosy was likewise devastating. Lepers were required by law to permanently separate themselves from society, and most lived together in leper colonies. They immediately lost everything, including contact with family and friends. The law required lepers to always distance themselves from others in order to avoid transmission of their disease, and when they did travel, they were required to cover their lips, much like wearing a mask, and cry out "unclean, unclean" so that all others could avoid them (Lev. 13:45).

Most considered leprosy to be a divine judgment, and a leper was not only considered physically unclean and contagious, but he was also considered spiritually unclean and condemned by God. In Jesus' day, one cannot imagine a more horrendous and devastating experience than being a leper.

A leper could never again have any human contact, except with another leper. The requirement of social distancing was a life sentence. Most lepers lived by begging for food, which was either thrown to them or left for them to find. Lepers were treated unmercifully by society and knew no friends. They were avoided at all costs. There was, however, one man who paid little attention to the demands of social distancing. His name was Jesus.

Mercy is a strangely powerful emotion. The greater the depth of one's mercy, the more they are irresistibly compelled to compassionately involve themselves in reducing human misery and suffering. The gospels record several instances where Jesus reacted to the plaintive cry, "Lord, have mercy on me." Without concern for law or custom, He reached out to those around Him who were suffering.

Thus, when one leper called out to Jesus and said, "Lord, if You are willing, You can make me clean," Jesus responded, "I am willing; be cleansed." Jesus wasn't restrained by the law and social custom, and He touched the hurting man and healed him (Matt. 8:1-4).

Further, as Jesus traveled to Jerusalem, He heard the pitiful pleas of ten lepers crying out to Him from the required distance of social separation, "Jesus, Master, have mercy on us." They dared not come closer, but Jesus stopped and talked with them. Moved with compassion, Jesus told all ten to go present themselves to the priest with proof of their healing, and all ten did (Luke 17:11-19).

It is at this point that one of the most grateful men in the Bible briefly takes his place in biblical history. All ten lepers were healed through Jesus' merciful power, but only one returned to say, "Thank You." His story is gripping. Not only was he a leper, but he was also a Samaritan, probably the most despised people in Israel. Not only was he hated and shunned for being a leper and a Samaritan, but even the other Jewish lepers would have hated and shunned him within the leper colony for being a detested Samaritan.

It made no difference to Jesus. Divine mercy does not differentiate by race, creed, or ethnic origin. The mercy of God flows equally over all hurting humanity. There are no barriers and no required distance that you must remain separated from our merciful Lord, regardless of who you are or the circumstances of your life.

One can only wonder about the crushing pain, loneliness, and rejection this man must have felt. The deeper the Lord's mercy touches and changes your life, the more inclined you are to say "Thank you" to Him with tears of gratitude streaming down your face. So, it was with the Samaritan leper.

Many of you are facing circumstances in which you feel separated from the love and mercy of Christ, and I understand that. I've had those moments myself. But, my friend, let me assure you of this life-changing truth: There is no sick room Jesus will not enter; there is no diseased and smelly body He will not touch; there is no darkened dungeon of impending death into which He will not bring the light of hope; there is no rejection, despair, or humiliation that may have been heaped on you but that Jesus will bear your burden with you

227

and give you comfort and rest; and there is no sin that you've ever committed that Jesus will not mercifully put on His own shoulders and take to the cross so that you may know forgiveness.

Jesus will not keep His distance from you, and His merciful touch can transform your life today. If you have never placed your faith in Him as your Lord and Savior, I urge you to do so now and let Him soothe your pain with the balm of His mercy and compassion. Don't worry about social distancing with Jesus; even now He is reaching out to touch you and bring healing to your hurting life.

May God bless you in His name.

II

Jesus' Definition of Essential Services

There's been much discussion lately about what is an essential service that may remain open during this pandemic and what isn't. Interestingly, Jesus dealt with a similar question in a different context many years ago. His definition changed our faith and religious practices forever.

Of all the traditions of ancient Judaism, the religious laws related to the Sabbath were the most detailed and restrictive. No labor was allowed on the Sabbath, and early Jewish law provided harsh punishment for violators, including death. The only exceptions permitted were based on necessary and essential activities or emergencies. For example, one could lead a donkey from its stall in order to get water or one could pull an ox out of a ditch, but little else was deemed necessary.

Even though watering an animal was viewed as essential, caring for and healing a sick, hurting human on the Sabbath was prohibited. Greater mercy was shown to a thirsty donkey than to a thirsty, hurting person. Jesus openly broke this cold-hearted law to reveal the mercy of God.

Jesus was teaching in a synagogue on the Sabbath when a woman, bent down and deformed with a crippling condition that she had endured for eighteen years, slowly walked in. Jesus said to her, "Woman, you are loosed from your infirmity." The priest, sensing the awe sweeping over the people, shouted indignantly that there are six days during the week when someone can be healed, but not on the

Sabbath (Luke 13:10-16). Jesus condemned his hypocrisy, and He bluntly asked the priest if he could loosen his donkey to get water on the Sabbath, could He not also loosen the woman from her infirmity on the Sabbath day?

Don't let the significance of Jesus' words and deed pass you by. In this merciful miracle, Jesus rewrote the law by breaking it, and He now declared that mercy for others and a willingness to heal and help others, even on the Sabbath, were more essential to understanding the merciful nature of God than blind obedience to a cold, impersonal religious law.

Ancient Judaism was not known for mercy. The proud, arrogant Pharisees, scribes, and priests prided themselves in their riches, health, power, and position. They shunned the poor, sick, blind, and crippled as condemned by God and turned a cold shoulder and a deaf ear to their pleas for help. (Think of the rich man who would throw scraps of bread to mongrel dogs but not to a pleading, starving beggar at his front gate.) Only those considered "neighbor" under the word's legal definition received kind treatment. All others were condemned as sinners. The gospels contain numerous accounts of people crying out to Jesus for mercy, because no one else cared.

Obedience to law does not produce joy. There was no spiritual joy in being merciful to those considered condemned by God, but Jesus radically changed that. "Blessed are the merciful, for they shall obtain mercy" established a totally new and spiritually transforming experience in the heart of His disciples regarding sinners and the poor and needy. Never before had anyone personally experienced an outpouring of God's mercy in their own life by showing divine compassion and mercy to others. Jesus described it as a new, blessed, and spiritually joyous experience, and He made mercy a fundamental and essential Christian experience.

Think about mercy in this way: Love is what God freely feels toward you; grace is what God freely gives to you; and mercy is what God freely does for you. Jesus loves you dearly and eternal life is what He gives to you, but every aspect of your salvation—your justification, your redemption, your atonement—is what Christ did for you.

How then do we show mercy to others in a way that glorifies His mercy shown to us? Maybe it's simply being as merciful to others as you would want them to be merciful to you. But I guess I'm just having a memory flashback to my childhood days and the old, wood-frame, Good Hope Baptist Church and the little congregation of country folks singing this old hymn. It's a pretty good description of the individual ministry of mercy: "Rescue the perishing, care for the dying, snatch them in pity from sin and the grave, weep o'er the erring one, lift up the fallen, tell them of Jesus the mighty to save..."

Dear friend, it doesn't matter how worthless, dejected, and rejected you may feel. It doesn't matter what sins you've committed, and it doesn't matter how bent low by the burdens of life you are right now. Please believe me: There are no limits to God's boundless mercy that He is willing to pour into your life if you will only give your life to Christ and allow Jesus to be your personal Lord and Savior. He loves you and He died for you, even while you were still a sinner, in order to save you and give you everlasting life.

Mercy is not only what God has done for you, but it's also what He will enable you to do for others. He will transform your attitude and rid you of prejudice, bitterness, and shunning others who are different from you. Jesus will make you a friend of sinners, just as He is, and He will empower you to mercifully reach out to all others, just as He did for you. It will be a blessed and joyous experience.

Jesus not only defined mercy as an essential Christian service, but He also made mercy an essential dimension of your Christian life. May He bless you as you mercifully reach out in His name to the hurting humanity around you. You have no idea of the blessed joy you will experience.

II

When the Waiting Room is Packed

The Pool of Bethesda was known as a place of healing, and many sick and crippled people came there hoping to find comfort. Legend held that when the angel of the Lord stirred the water, the first person who got into the pool would be healed. People lay around the pool hoping for a miraculous healing, because there was little or no merciful concern for the sick and crippled, and they had no other hope. Maybe I'm too cynical, but I see the Pool of Bethesda differently. It was basically a dumping ground for those no one cared to help. The pool was surrounded by five porches on which lay "a great multitude of sick people, blind, lame, paralyzed, waiting for the moving of the water" (John 5:3). Think about what this actually describes. There were all kinds of diseased, crippled, and sick people of every level of physical strength and mental acuity. It must have been a place that reeked with the smell of vomit and human waste, combined with the odor of unwashed human bodies.

It was likewise a place of unimaginable human despair. These poor, abandoned people constantly stared at the pool water waiting for a ripple to stir across the surface. When that occurred, visualize the sudden physical effort to be first into the water. Imagine the screaming, crying, pleading, pulling, pushing, and cursing that must have occurred each time.

Jesus walked into the packed waiting area by the pool on a Sabbath and saw a man who had suffered from some infirmity for thirty-eight years. Jesus asked him, "Do you want to be made well?" The poor suffering soul stated that he had no one to help him into the water. Ponder for a moment the depth of his despondency. Imagine the number of times he had been pushed aside, trampled, and deeply hurt, both physically and emotionally. No one cared and no one showed him mercy, except Jesus.

It was the Sabbath, and Jesus knew the cold, unmerciful religious law said He could not heal on the Sabbath. He also knew the man, once healed, could not carry his blanket, for that would be working on the Sabbath. But, without hesitation, Jesus broke both laws in order to mercifully heal this broken man.

Jesus said to him, "Rise, take up your bed and walk," and the man was immediately healed. In the face of this amazing, merciful miracle, the religious zealots harshly condemned the newly healed man, who was obviously overcome with unspeakable joy. "It is the Sabbath; it is not lawful for you to carry your bed" they stated emphatically. Such legalistic, unmerciful, spiritual coldness is inconceivable, but it was real in the world in which Jesus lived, and it's real in the world in which we live.

Have you ever had to wait in a packed waiting room for treatment and care? With all the social distancing taking place with this virus pandemic, do you ever feel that there's no one truly willing to compassionately touch you and help you? Do you ever get the depressing feeling that there's no one in a packed waiting room who mercifully cares how you're feeling or how bad you're hurting? So did this crippled man, until Jesus broke the religious law to show him the mercy of God.

Dear friend, please listen to me: You are not a number, your name is not "Next," you are not forgotten by Jesus, and you are not without help, compassion, and mercy. Circumstances in life can sometimes leave us feeling like there is no one who really cares and no one who is truly willing to help us, and so we suffer in silence and quietly pray that somehow we will miraculously be the first in line for the next miracle.

Allow these words from the great old hymn "Only Trust Him" to speak comfort to you:

> "Come every soul by sin oppressed, there's mercy with the
>   Lord,
> and He will surely give you rest by trusting in His word.
> Yes, Jesus is the truth, the way
> that leads you into rest.
> Believe in Him without delay,
> and you are fully blessed."

Jesus knows your every care this day. You are not jammed and crammed into some situation and circumstance that His mercy can't reach. You may have people all around you and still feel alone because there is a hunger and a void in your soul that only Jesus' mercy and love can fill. Trust Him as your Lord and Savior and experience His peace this day. You will never again be able to say, "I have no one to help me," because He will.

May God bless each of you through the love and mercy of Christ.

God's Upward Call

"I press toward the goal for the prize of the upward call of God in Christ Jesus" (Phil. 3:14).

Christians traditionally use the word "called" to describe their commitment to a particular endeavor of faith, such as a minister being called to preach. After nearly fifty years in the ministry, my understanding of this concept has deepened over time.

Being called of God is not limited to His verbalization of your name and His appointment of you to a specific ministry task, but rather it is the manifestation and blessings of God's claim on your life resulting from your covenant relationship with Christ. Obviously, certain individuals feel a special leading toward a particular area of work, I know that I did, but in truth all Christians are called of God.

There are three significant calls on our Christian life resulting from our faith in Jesus. We are called out, called up, and called in through our covenant with Christ. All of these are works of God in our life "in Jesus." That is to say, once we are in a covenant relationship with Christ, the Holy Spirit works to draw us into the closest possible relationship with Jesus so that our life is a spiritual reflection and representation of Him to the world around us. Thus, we become a living witness of the divine truth of His life.

In Christ, our desires and motivation in life are changed, and worldly treasures lose their attraction to us. Christians are different because they are called out of the world. In fact, the New Testament word describing the redeemed church means "the called-out ones." John 15:19 states, "If you were of the world, the world would love its own. Yet because you are not of the world, but I chose you out of the world, therefore the world hates you." You cannot be the light of the world if your light is as dim as the darkness around you.

The Holy Spirit is constantly working to help you set your sight on the kingdom of heaven and not the kingdoms of the earth. Thus, as the Apostle Paul stated, we feel the upward call of God in Christ Jesus, and we press forward toward that goal. Pride, power, politics, and personal glory become meaningless in the role of a faithful servant of Christ.

And in the greatest celestial celebration of all, we shall be called in to rejoice in what The Revelation describes as "the marriage supper of the Lamb." It will be that final, great celebration of the eternal union of Jesus with His perfect, purified Bride, the church. And if you are in Christ, you will be there.

The burdens, loneliness, and despair of this world can be a heavy load some days. Just remember the old interpretation of "It came to pass." If you are in Christ, whatever you are facing this morning has come to pass…it hasn't come to stay. Why? Because in Christ you have been called out, called up, and called in, and your life will never be the same.

So Many People, So Little Food

I love fish. I love fish fried, baked, or grilled. I love catfish, bass, trout, bluegill, and bream, and I am country enough that I eat the crispy tail on a fried bream. But I especially like tilapia baked in butter and lemon juice. Add a baked potato and some broccoli, and you have a delicious meal.

Tilapia has an interesting history. It is an ancient species of fish that was abundant in the Sea of Galilee. Tilapia is often referred to as St. Peter's fish or "Peter's Perch" and was likely the kind of fish referred to in various gospel fishing accounts. Knowing that Jesus dined on tilapia enhances its taste to me.

One of Jesus' major miracles involved feeding five thousand people using five loaves of bread and two fish supplied by the disciples. The miracle indeed validated Jesus' messianic power to feed the hungry, and honestly, many followed Him only for that reason.

Over the course of my ministry, I have followed the traditional interpretation that Jesus fed the multitude of five thousand people. But I had a moment of insight recently that deeply challenged me. Quite frankly, Jesus did not feed the five thousand—the disciples fed them. All that Jesus did was bless the bread and fish, break it into pieces, and empower the disciples to perform their work of discipleship.

Upon realizing the size of the multitude that followed Jesus and the lateness of the afternoon hour, the disciples initially wanted to send the people away to buy food for themselves. But Jesus instructed the disciples to feed them, and they loudly proclaimed the impossibility of doing that, for they had only five loaves of bread and two fish among them.

The amazing nature of the miracle then began to unfold. Sitting the people on the grass, Jesus looked up to heaven and blessed the fish and bread, and then He broke the bread—and obviously the fish—into pieces and gave those small pieces to the disciples to feed the people.

Consider the portions: Two fish divided into twelve portions would be no larger than a spoonful. Five loaves divided into twelve portions would be slightly less than one-half loaf of bread. With that, they were instructed to feed 416 people each (5,000 people divided among twelve disciples). Talk about a challenge!

However, notice something very important. The disciples did not return to Jesus for more, nor did they keep asking Him to bless what little they had. They took the meager means each possessed and went to work. They did not complain, grumble, or question Jesus' will, purpose, and work for them. Through their faithfulness, the disciples took something laughably small and meager and made it into a major miracle.

How did they do it? Did each person get only a small bite of fish and bread, or did the meager portions become a full meal? Was the food immediately and miraculously replaced in the hands of each disciple by an even greater amount the moment he shared it? I don't know. What is apparent though is that, as Jesus blessed the fish and bread, He gave the disciples the means to gloriously and miraculously accomplish their work of discipleship.

They never ran out of the means to do His will. The same remains true for us today.

When the multitude of people had finished eating, the disciples filled twelve baskets with food fragments that remained. Think about that: Each disciple began his work with about one-half loaf of bread and a spoonful of fish. After abundantly feeding over four hundred people, each disciple had a basket full of leftover food.

The word describing "basket" indicates it was a moderate-sized wicker basket used primarily for transporting food. Even so, each disciple fed at least 416 people with a spoonful of fish and one-half loaf of bread and still had hundreds of times more food—likely a thousand times more—than when he began his work. It is truly an amazing miracle and reminds us how often Jesus spoke of the increase of the kingdom of heaven within us, such as the parable of the mustard seed.

Kittie L. Suffield penned these words in the wonderful old hymn "Little Is Much When God Is In It": "Does the place you're called to labor seem so small and little known? It is great if God is in it, and He'll not forget His own. Little is much if God is in it! Labor not for wealth or fame; there's a crown, and you can win it, if you go in Jesus' name."

Some of the greatest work for Christ has been done by faithful disciples with so little it was laughable by worldly standards. But Jesus blessed it and made an impossible mission into a glorious miracle.

He can do the same in your life. It does not matter how small your resources are, how limited your gift is, or how humble and unimpressive your circumstances may be. Just remember, little is much if God is in it! Take whatever you have and ask Jesus to bless it and break it from your earthy grasp so He can use it for His heavenly glory. Go to work and watch a miracle unfold in your life.

Fuzzy, That Ain't Real

I have always loved dogs, and I've had an assortment of them over the years, ranging from registered Boxers and German Shepherds to thrown away mutts rescued from a roadside ditch.

When I was about ten years old, I had a Collie named Fuzzy. He was big, boisterous, and playful, and he had a thick coat of brown hair that was, well, fuzzy. Fuzzy was a good watch dog, and he barked loudly and aggressively at anything he viewed as threatening. But my mama had a cardinal rule: Fuzzy couldn't come in the house.

One day, I was home alone, and in direct defiance of my mother's dog rule, I let Fuzzy come inside. He was lonely by himself, so I reasoned, and what harm could he do anyway? He would just casually venture around inside for a few minutes wagging his tail, and then I'd let him out. Mama would never know. I was wrong.

The poet, Robert Burns, once commented—after he had plowed through a rat's nest and destroyed all the little rodent's hard work—that "the best laid plans of mice and men often go awry." He was so prophetically right, especially about me secretly letting Fuzzy in the house.

All our furniture was hand-me-down junk, and my mother's dresser was this old brown thing with a recessed center that was lower than the drawers on either side. Its most prominent feature was a large, round mirror on the back. It was so old that Mary Todd Lincoln may have put it in a garage sale at one time, but it was all mama had.

Also, at that same time, my mother had started selling Avon cosmetics to make some additional money, and the center of the dresser and the tops of both sides were covered in Avon products, all magnified by the big mirror in the back. Because the mirror sat down inside the recessed center area, it wasn't too high off the floor, in fact just about eye level for a big Collie dog (I bet some of you can see where this is headed, and you're already laughing).

As soon as I let him inside, Fuzzy began trotting from room to room inspecting this new territory. When he went in front of mama's dresser mirror, he suddenly stopped and spun around, having spotted another big, brown Collie dog menacingly looking back at him from the center of the dresser. For the sake of convenience and understanding, let's just call Fuzzy's threatening adversary "Mirror Dog."

Well, Fuzzy wasn't in the mood to get whipped on his home turf, so he instantly shifted all his strength and stamina into attack mode. To his surprise, Mirror Dog did, too. Fuzzy bowed up and let out the most vicious bark and growl and lifted the skin on the sides of his mouth, showing his fangs. Not to be outdone, Mirror Dog did the same.

Well, this was not to be, thought Fuzzy, and he attacked Mirror Dog with all his might. Fuzzy leaped onto the dresser and banged his teeth against the mirror, lashing at his opponent with every dog fighting strategy move he could conceive. Mirror Dog fought back just as aggressively and matched him move for move. Every time the mirror swayed to and fro, it appeared to Fuzzy that Mirror Dog was lunging at him, and that only made him madder. By now, Fuzzy had reared up on his hind legs in the recessed center, fighting Mirror Dog with all his might. Mirror Dog was doing the same.

During this wild canine melee, you can imagine what happened to all the Avon—well, maybe you can't. It wasn't a pretty scene. Avon was everywhere—under mama's bed, out in the living room, and even on the windowsill behind the old tattered roll-up window shade. I'm not sure we ever found all of it.

After a lengthy battle, Fuzzy fought Mirror Dog to a draw. Every combative move that Fuzzy made, Mirror Dog matched him. All the while, I was screaming, "Fuzzy, stop! He ain't real!" But a determined Collie can be like a hard-headed child—he has to learn things for himself. Fuzzy fought Mirror Dog until his tongue was hanging out and he was panting for breath. Mirror Dog was exhausted, too. Finally, some Collie common sense kicked in, and Fuzzy made friends with Mirror Dog, having decided that Mirror Dog knew how to wage war as well as he did. He stopped fighting and gave his new friend a big, slobbery lick on the face, and Mirror Dog licked him back.

There's an old expression about "putting lipstick on a pig" in an effort to make something ugly into something pretty. It may work on a pig but finding new Avon lipstick smeared on a Collie dog did not impress my mama and make this situation look better. The only bright spot was that the scratch marks Fuzzy left on the dresser weren't much different from all the other scratches that were already there, so it was kind of easy to overlook the permanent damage from Fuzzy's epic battle with Mirror Dog. And it took a while, but about an hour after mama got home, my little red rear-end quit hurting so bad, too.

If the truth about each of us were known, I'd say that all of us have our Fuzzy moments occasionally. We can see all kinds of threatening things in the mirror of our mind that keep us from fulfilling our true potential, both as an individual and as a servant of Christ. Fear can bark and growl at you and tell you that you're inadequate, ill-equipped, or incapable of greater service for Christ. Think about how many times over the years the little fear devil in the mirror has made you say, "I can't," "I won't," or "Lord, please don't ask me to do that." You must realize that this demon of self-doubt isn't real! Stop attacking yourself and stop fighting with yourself and God! This may sound like a silly suggestion at first, but I'll bet you'll remember it. Anytime the fear of serving Christ grips you, repeat these words as loudly as you want to say them, "Fuzzy, stop! That ain't real!" Then give yourself a hearty, encouraging pat on the back. It's a lot less sloppy than trying to lick yourself in the mirror like ole Fuzzy did.

Give Us Barabbas

Releasing a condemned prisoner was an annual gesture by the hated Romans designed to show their Jewish subjects they could be merciful, if only once a year. On this occasion, Pontius Pilate gave them the choice between Jesus, a man of unquestioned moral character who had been betrayed and falsely charged, and Barabbas, a known thief, murderer, and insurrectionist. The contrast between the two could not have been more striking.

But, whipped into a riotous frenzy by their leaders, the throngs abandoned reason and yielded to desires of their most base instincts and to the demons lurking in the darkest corners of their hearts. "Give us Barabbas," they yelled. "Give us Barabbas!" "And what about this man, Jesus?" Pilate asked. "Crucify Him!" screamed the maddened multitudes. Kill the Christ and give us the thief. What a testament to the fallen, depraved nature of man!

How can an individual, a society, or a nation make such a catastrophically wrong choice? Why would any rational individual knowingly abandon common moral and religious restraint, and with utter disregard for the obvious consequence of their choice, scream out in mindless defiance, "Give us Barabbas"?

Maybe we saw the answer on January 6th. With visionary eyes, one can see that Barabbas symbolizes more than just one common thief. The malicious cry, "Give us Barabbas," reveals a flawed human character that rejects civility, self-restraint, and respect for others. It reveals a paramount, animalistic desire to destroy, to take by force, to willingly injure and maim others, to defy authority and reject established civil law and social decorum, and a desire to impose one's will on others by brute force.

It was the saddest day in American history, even greater than the death of a president or a national calamitous tragedy. Why? Because it revealed what we can allow ourselves to become. It stripped back the nice facade of orderly citizenship and showed that, with enough anger, prejudice, and contempt for law, average Americans can become a rioting, murderous mob, especially when smoldering passions are stirred by inflammatory words and ignite into burning vengeance and anger. It leaves one wondering, with a sad and broken heart, whether we are really "one nation under God" after all. Actions betray words.

I firmly believe in the freedom of speech and the individual right to voice one's opinions. Peaceful proclamation of political views is a cornerstone of our democracy. Mayhem is not.

The love of Jesus springs from the transformed heart of a Christian and not from the laws of Congress. We must resolve that change in America will come about through our renewed determination to love, respect, and care for others, as we do our own selves, and to dedicate ourselves to support and defend the Constitutional rights of others and provide for the common welfare of all, even those with whom we disagree. Therein lies the moral and civil greatness of America.

Getting Closer to God
Over Lauderdale County

My commuter flight departed Nashville uneventfully in late afternoon. The plane was piloted by two young ladies, which initially surprised me until I reminded myself that they were obviously highly qualified and competent. I took my seat by the window just behind the left wing and engine, and I settled back for a routine flight to Meridian, Mississippi.

However, the routine suddenly changed over north Alabama when I noticed something unusual happening with the engine and wing. A line of oily liquid about three inches wide was forming across the wing's surface running from the left engine to the back of the wing. I quickly realized we had a problem.

Being a commuter plane, the cabin was loosely organized, and the door to the cockpit was open. I got the co-pilot's attention and motioned for her to come look. She did, and then she rapidly returned to the cockpit and closed the door. I knew then this was serious.

Within a few minutes, the pilot announced that she was shutting down the left engine because of a mechanical problem, but she assured us the plane could fly safely with only one engine. So, there I sat watching the oily line get bigger, watching the dead propeller spin slowly in the wind, and hoping the other engine didn't fail also.

As we approached Meridian, things got a bit more tense. The pilot informed us that she had declared an emergency, and we would be following emergency landing procedures. Immediately prior to the actual landing, she said we were to lean forward and put our head close to our knees and cover our head with our hands and arms. Fire and rescue units would be chasing the plane down the runway as soon as it touched down, and all safety and rescue measures would be available to help us. She didn't have to say it—everybody knew what she meant: There was a very real possibility we might crash while landing and explode in flames. The cabin was completely silent, with each passenger absorbed in their private thoughts and prayers.

With some seconds to go before landing, the pilot

emphatically declared, "Lean forward now! Brace! Brace!" Every passenger followed her instructions but one—me. I guess I'm just bullheaded at times, but I figured if I was going to get incinerated, it really didn't matter where I had stuck my head. I wanted to see what was happening outside.

Well, this young pilot demonstrated consummate flying skills, and she flew in just over the pursuing fire trucks and landed ahead of them. Both the plane and the fire equipment were barreling down the runway until we stopped, at which time all the rescue units surrounded the plane, but, thankfully, there was no fire.

As we left the plane, I thanked the pilots and commended them for their flying skill and professionalism. I was later told that a hydraulic line had ruptured, spewing hydraulic fluid over the wing. That's when I really began to wonder about the severity of the problem we had experienced. If the plane had not only lost an engine but also necessary hydraulic pressure, how was the pilot able to safely operate the plane's control systems? Was that the real reason for declaring an emergency? Did she bring this plane in for a perfect landing with controls that weren't adequately responding, but she never told us in order to keep us calm?

I never knew the answer. But I know this: There in the sky over Lauderdale County, when I realized how serious this might be, I spent some time talking to God. What do you say to your Heavenly Father and how do you pray if you seriously think you could die within a few minutes?

Allow me to give you some insight: What had seemed so important earlier in the day became meaningless. You realize more fully that life is a precious gift that you can so quickly and easily lose, and there is no guarantee that the dawn will harken in another tomorrow. At its most basic, life is simply an aggregation of moment-by-moment experiences. The script of life is totally unique, because "The End" can suddenly be written in by the hand of fate without any warning, even when the story is most enjoyable.

You don't have personal enemies anymore, and you're no longer mad at anyone. Petty grievances disappear into thin air over Lauderdale County.

You yearn for one more opportunity to tell family and friends how important they are to you, how much you love them, and you wish you could hug them one last time.

You stop asking God to bless you with more unnecessary stuff, and you just ask Him to have mercy on you and let His grace and power protect you.

When you stare directly at your life's end, you just hope there's one more chance to make a new beginning.

What about you? How would you have prayed in that situation? As for me, I've often wondered how different my life would have been if I had continued talking to God once safely on the ground like I did in the air over Lauderdale County. Just being honest with you....

The Original Fake News

The Jewish religious authorities who plotted the crucifixion of Jesus were merciless in their obsession to prevent the changes advocated by Christ. They carefully planned in advance for possible alternative outcomes to their cold-blooded calculations.

They had heard Jesus say that He would rise from the dead after three days, just as He had raised Lazarus, an inexplicable miracle that initially prompted them to begin seriously plotting Jesus' crucifixion. But what would they do if indeed His tomb was found to be empty after His death and burial? Their answer was simple, yet devious: Say it was fake news and not true. Spread the false narrative that His followers had taken His body in an effort to prove what He had predicted. Make those who claimed the truth of Jesus' victory look foolish and belittle their claim. If hush money needed to be paid, that could be easily arranged. Whatever it took to tarnish Jesus' accomplishment, do it. There were no moral limits to their insidious scheming—just laugh at the truth and scornfully dismiss it as fake news.

The Gospel of Matthew describes their plan, thusly: "When they had assembled with the elders and consulted together, they gave a large sum of money to the soldiers, saying, 'Tell them, 'His disciples came at night and stole Him away while we slept.' And if this comes to the governor's ears, we will appease him and make you secure.' So they took the money and did as they were instructed; and this saying is commonly reported among the Jews until this day" (Matt. 28:12-15).

I'm just a simple country teacher and preacher of the gospel, far from being some biblical or historical scholar. But there is one line in Matthew's account that has always haunted me, "and this saying is commonly reported among the Jews until this day."

How many innocent, trusting lives never knew what the real truth was because they were encouraged by leaders whom they trusted to dismiss what Jesus had accomplished as foolish, fake news. And the scripture states that continues until today. Some lies have unbelievable longevity.

In all of today's uncertainty, I just ask God to give us uncommon wisdom to sift through all the negative news, the preplanned explanations of how the train ran off the tracks in some locales, and the slick prognostications by silver-tongued, political

246

analysts and spin-doctors and find the kernel of truth buried under the mountain of useless chaff.

Pure Religion

Years ago, when social texting became the vogue, a humorous commercial depicted a small group of elderly lady friends chatting. One held up her iPhone, pointed to a grouping of 8x10 pictures on her dining room wall, and gushed, "This is such fun. I've posted all your pictures on my wall." Another lady stared at her in disbelief and said, "That's not what posting pictures to your wall means at all."

Is it possible that we have done the same to our Christian faith? Have we slowly lost the meaning of "pure religion"? A few years ago, several people from this area drove to Jackson and gathered with hundreds of others to hear a well-known evangelical leader pray for America. Upon returning home, they openly boasted about being there. I listened, and I quietly thought that's totally opposite to what Jesus taught about prayer. What if everyone there had gone into a private place, like their closet, and prayed for America, as Jesus instructed, rather than making a public affair of it?

There are many other examples. Jesus never led a week-long revival, nor did He host a Bible Conference filled with high priced speakers suffering from overly inflated egos. Rather, He did the opposite and went out into the masses of hurting people and healed the sick and fed the hungry.

Jesus resisted every temptation of the devil and every plea of man, even His own disciples, to use religious faith for personal power and political gain. Jesus had to borrow a jackass to ride into Jerusalem. Today, we have jackasses trying to borrow Jesus to ride into Washington.

In one of the most instructive verses in the New Testament, James, who was Jesus' half-brother, gives us an admonition about the difference between "pure religion" and religious practices that fall into other categories.

To better understand his point, let's think back a moment. When Joseph married Mary, Jesus' mother, she was most likely a teenage girl, based on marriage traditions of that day. After Jesus was born, Mary had at least six more children with Joseph. They were James (writer of the Book of James), Joses, Judas, and Simon, and at least two unnamed girls (Mark 6:3). Including Jesus, there would have been seven children in the family. Interestingly, there is no further mention of Joseph, the father, after he is described as being at the temple when Jesus was twelve years old.

Did Joseph die leaving widowed Mary to care for seven children without help and support? We don't know, but James gives us an eye-opening clue. In fact, James gives us two or three illustrative clues about Jesus' childhood homelife.

James pointedly condemns gossip. Had he heard all the crude and cruel things that the religious perfectionists said about his mother and his brother, Jesus? You don't need a very vivid imagination to realize what was said in their village about a young pregnant girl who claimed to be carrying the Son of God.

James commends prayer and anointing with oil as a means of healing. Did he view his impoverished mother desperately asking for anointed prayers and healing for her sick children because that was all she had?

But the biggest clue is how James defined religion. No doubt he was familiar with all the holy feast days, the religious sacrifices of animals, and the hypocritical practice of religious and civic leaders openly praying on street corners and publicly doing alms in order to be seen by others and flaunt their religiosity.

But James noticed that few of them ever offered to help his struggling mother and his brothers and sisters, choosing instead to humiliate them with merciless gossip and inuendo. Thus, James took a rather pragmatic approach to the public spectacle of feigned, shallow religion. He stated, "Pure and undefiled religion before God and the Father is this: to visit orphans and widows in their trouble, and to keep oneself unspotted from the world" (James 1:27). Maybe it's time Christians in America studied that statement more closely.

Christianity is about being an humble servant of all, not a power-hungry zealot. It is about loving others instead of shunning them and making them feel unwanted, even in a church. Christianity is about quietly giving yourself to others rather than wanting public knowledge and commendation for every good deed one does.

Like the lady said about the pictures on the wall, maybe all this rah-rah Christianity we are flooded with is not what it's about at all.

What a difference it would make if each of us quietly gave food to a needly individual or family. What if we each bought a few winter clothes for a poor child trying to go to school in worn out rags? What if we quietly slipped a monetary gift to a hurting mom trying to buy food for her kids? What if each Christian in America stopped worrying about going to rallies and posting scripture and instead just helped a widow or an orphaned child in their distress—and never told another person what they had done?

We can shout our religious beliefs to highest heaven, we can gather in mass religious rallies, and we can glue ourselves to the television and agree with every word of some "evangelist," but not one bit of that brings an ounce of relief to some hurting soul, a destitute widow, or a hungry child with pleading eyes.

So, what is "pure and undefiled" religion? We must each decide for ourselves, with the guidance of the Holy Spirit. I know what James' answer would be.

A Leader From the Order of Melchizedek

A couple of days ago, I watched a video of former President Ronald Reagan describing his personal reaction to being shot in an attempted assassination. When asked if he were afraid that he was going to die, he replied, "I was concerned, of course, but I had a little chat with my friend upstairs, and I felt that I would be O.K."

I pondered his comment for several minutes. Here was a professing Christian, arguably the most powerful man in the world, who had been saved from death by the grace of God, and the best description he had of Him was "my friend upstairs."

It made me realize anew that one of the greatest leadership needs we have in America is a president who is wholly unreserved in his personal testimony of faith in Jesus as his Lord. I'm not talking about some vague reference to a friend upstairs, but a powerful, forceful testimony of his personal relationship with Jesus as his Lord and Savior and how his faith shapes and bolsters his daily work.

Maybe Jimmy Carter did that in his many years of teaching a Sunday School class, but such personal faith and witness is sadly lacking in America. If we proclaim ourselves to be a Christian nation and one nation under God, can we not ask our leader to describe his personal relationship with Jesus in an honest, open, and straightforward manner?

In the Old Testament, God's principal functionaries were the prophet, priest, and king. The prophet spoke the words of God, the priest served as God's intermediary with man, and the king ruled over God's earthly kingdom. No one ever performed more than one ministry, except little-known Melchizedek who was both a priest of God Most High and king of Salem (Gen14:18). Interestingly, Hebrews 6:20 describes Jesus as "having become High Priest forever according to the order of Melchizedek," and He alone performed all three. He spoke the truth of God as a prophet, served as God's ultimate Priest, and He rules over the Kingdom of God. Jesus was never hesitant to openly describe His relationship with His Heavenly Father or to describe His unconditional faith in God.

I bet you've sung the old hymn "Jesus Our Blessed Redeemer," and repeated these words many times: "Praise Him! Praise Him! Jesus our blessed redeemer! Heav'nly portals loud with Hosannas ring! Jesus, Savior, reigneth for ever and ever. Crown Him, crown Him! Prophet and Priest and King!"

We face major decisions in deciding who will lead our nation. My prayer is that God will guide us to a leader who is singularly determined to make America one nation under God with liberty and justice for all. May we focus on a leader who unashamedly professes his faith in Jesus and who openly and unreservedly describes his personal, life-transforming relationship with Him. May God give us a righteous leader who speaks the truth of God, who stands as an intermediary between the spiritual needs of America and the grace and mercy of God, and a man who will rule over this nation with divine wisdom and with equal concern and compassion for every person so that all Americans may personally experience the liberty and justice guaranteed to them. If God will guide me to that leader, I will trust him, and I will follow him with confidence.

Whatever Happened to Sam and Ida?

Sometimes I quietly stand in the old barn alongside my yard and imagine what it was like—the earthy smell, the sound of animals eating, the daily ritual of milking a brown Jersey cow into a metal bucket, hoping she wouldn't kick and turn it over.

The heart of it all was Sam and Ida, two faithful mules whose hard work over many years made our family farm. Sam was the larger mule and was easy-going and willing to undertake any task asked of him.

Ida, on the other hand, was a flighty little mare mule with an independent streak who would rather eat grass than pull a plow. Ida didn't take being scolded lightly, and she devised her own means of revenge: lda became known as the flatulating mule. She discovered her built-in gas canister located under her little mare-mule tail, and she would fire a blast at anyone who dared tap her on her rump attempting to make her work harder. Just joking, but you had to be careful not to smoke a Prince Albert when you plowed Ida, or a mule-made-methane flame thrower could erupt.

But, about 1952 progress came to the Voss farm in the form of an International Harvester Super A tractor, and there was no more need for Sam and Ida. An impersonal, cold, mechanical machine took their place, and Sam and Ida were loaded up and hauled away to an unknown fate. My oldest brother loved ole Sam, and he once told me that he went behind the barn and cried when his beloved mule left. The old barn life was never the same. You can't talk to a tractor and feel it's warm head against your chest. A machine doesn't have a heart, but it does make more money, and that's all that seems to matter. I've wondered many times whatever happened to Sam and Ida?

There's a little-known verse in the Bible that comes to mind on this Labor Day. Deuteronomy 25:4 says, "You shall not muzzle an ox while it treads out the grain." In other words, if Sam and Ida wanted to get a bite of corn while they were plowing, let them. It was a just reward for the work they were doing.

Using these mules as examples, if we allow Sam and Ida to be people, we find a similar experience today with American labor. For the sake of corporate profits and the continued upward climb of the Dow-Jones average, Sam and Ida become secondary in importance.

Jobs are shipped out of the country to reduce labor costs, machines take the place of hard-working American laborers, the rights of workers are minimized, pension and retirement funds are threatened, and even Social Security faces an uncertain future.

We are sadly disobeying one of the oldest Biblical concepts of worker reward. More and more, American corporate strategy seeks to "muzzle the ox that treads out the grain." We place less emphasis day-by-day on the struggle of working Americans to earn an adequate income which will provide them with the rewards of their labor. Sam and Ida can be replaced with a machine which will generate more profit.

The proverbial ox that treads out the grain in America—the honest, dependable, hard-working American laborer—is far too often muzzled and hungers for both a better wage and a better life while he grinds out the grain of American economic production.

On this Labor Day, I salute both the work and determination of every American worker and their desire to earn a living and reap the benefits of their labor. God help us if we continue to ignore His ancient word and muzzle the ox that treads out the grain.

To all the arrogant, gloating politicians and to all the corporate leaders consumed with profit margins, may I ask this fundamental Labor Day question? Does anybody in Washington or in corporate leadership really care today about what is happening to Sam and Ida?

MENE, MENE, TEKEL, UPHARSIN

Daniel 5:25

There was no visible body. All he saw was just a hand mysteriously writing an indecipherable message on a wall in front of him, and it both perplexed and terrified King Belshazzar. His wisest assistants could not determine the meaning of "MENE, MENE, TEKEL, UPHARSIN," which the hand had written. At the urging of his wife, Daniel, who was renowned for his wisdom, was asked for his interpretation.

Daniel's translation was not what the king wanted to hear. Belshazzar was an evil ruler who blasphemed God both in his words and in his deeds. In fact, he was hosting a great feast for hundreds of influential guests, where they were irreverently eating and drinking from holy vessels taken from the Temple in Jerusalem and "praising the gods of gold and silver, bronze and iron, wood and stone" when the hand wrote the divine message to him. In this sinful setting of arrogance and opulence, King Belshazzar was about to learn the meaning of "the handwriting on the wall."

Daniel informed the heartless king that he had praised the gods of wealth and pleasure, but "the God who holds your breath in His hand and owns all your ways, you have not glorified." Thus, Daniel somberly informed Belshazzar that "MENE, MENE" meant that God had numbered the days of his kingdom, and it would soon end. "TEKEL" meant that the King's wicked life had been weighed on the scales of divine righteousness and found wanting. UPHARSIN was the reality that all the King's power, wealth, and property would be taken from him and given to others. MENE, MENE, TEKEL, UPHARSIN meant "numbered, numbered, weighed, and divided." The opulent party was over, and so were the glory days of this godless man and his friends.

The biblical writer, Amos, once said that he was not a prophet nor the son of a prophet, and I'm certainly not. But I've said from the beginning of this crisis we face that America now stands in front of a burning bush of biblical proportions, and what we are seeing is a sign and wonder from God. The handwriting is on the wall.

255

For a long time, we have drifted away from the spiritual foundation on which this nation was built. We have become idol worshippers, and American idolatry is rampant. We glorify overpaid athletes, and thousands will pay to watch a meaningless game on Sunday while only a few hundred will attend church.

We worship the golden calf of wealth and envy and admire the wealthy while ignoring the plight of the poor and needy.

We blindly follow the prideful, empty promises of politicians who have made a mockery of humble public service and who regularly practice the dastardly art of lying to and misleading the very ones who elected them to office. It is a sad day in America when you simply cannot believe what any public official in Washington says.

Religion has become a political tool to be manipulated by those in power to sway and mislead the faithful and innocent among us. It doesn't matter how many Bibles you hold in your hand for others to see, the true test that counts is whether the Word of God is alive in your heart. I've never seen a greater display of religious hypocrisy in my life than what I have witnessed these recent years.

These words—MENE, MENE, TEKEL, UPHARSIN—have weighed heavily on my mind these past days. I have no idea how God will work in our midst to reveal the full meaning of this burning bush sign and wonder that we stand before, but I feel that profound change is coming.

The godless, arrogant, cold-hearted, self-glorify attitudes of the worldly kingdoms of power in this country have been divinely numbered, weighed, and divided, and before this is over, some of those kingdoms will fall and be given to others. The handwriting is on the wall.

Dr. Martin Luther King once said, "...the arc of the moral universe is long, but it bends toward justice." So, do not despair dear Christian friends, God is at work in this separating the wheat from the chaff. Have faith in His wisdom and in His ways. When we are standing before His burning bush, then we are standing in His presence on Holy Ground, and how He works in our midst will bring glory to Him and not to us.

The Great "I AM"

When Moses was divinely sent to the captive Israelites in Egypt, God instructed him to tell them that His name was "I AM" (Exod. 3:14). That sounds odd to us today, but it would have been very important to the Israelites, and it is for us, too, when we better understand the name.

There are over twenty names for God in the Old Testament. At that time, Moses had not written the first books of the Bible, and knowledge about God consisted of what one generation orally passed on to the next generation. So, in reality, the people would have seriously asked Moses, "Who is the God who sent you to us?"

The Bible portrays God in two great ways—Creator God and Redeemer God. If you're interested, open your Bible to Genesis 3:22, and you will notice a dash at the end of the verse. That concludes the biblical description of Creator God's work. The remainder of the Bible describes the work of Redeemer God.

Here then is one of the crucial aspects of faith: Can Redeemer God perfectly restore sinful man to the same state of sinless perfection that Creator God gave to him in the Garden of Eden? Can God redeem us and free us from bondage with the same power with which He created us? Can He redeem us so totally, through our faith in Christ, that it will be as if we never sinned at all?

The name "I AM" provides the answer. I AM is derived from the Hebrew verb "to be," and, when looked at in the past, present, and future tense, affirms that God was, is, and shall be the same in His divine nature and power. He is unchanging—the same yesterday, today, and forever. In other words, "I AM" means that God will continuously be all that He repeatedly has been. Throughout all eternity, at any given point, God will always be "I AM."

If we had the opportunity to ask God some questions about the name "I AM," His answers would so astound us we would be filled with an overwhelming sense of spiritual reassurance, comfort, and peace:

"Are you Elohim...Creator God...the God who perfectly made all creation out of nothing?"..."I AM."

"Are you the God who made man in Your image and likeness, breathed the breath of divine life into him, and placed him in the paradise of the Garden of Eden?"..."I AM."

"Are You Redeemer God, who will totally redeem and restore fallen man so that he can again be perfect, pure, and sinless in Your sight?"..."I AM."

"Are You the Father of Jesus?"..."I AM."

"Are you the God who so loves this sinful world that You sent Your only Son to live a perfect human life and to sacrifice His life on the cross as atonement for our sins?"... "I AM."

"Are You the God who will forgive, justify, and sanctify us through our faith in Jesus?" ... "I AM."

"Are you the God who alone possesses the divine power to redeem us as perfectly in Christ as you created us?"..."I AM."

"Are You the God who will always be the same loving, compassionate, and merciful God for all eternity that You have always been in ages past?"..."I AM."

"Are You the God who unconditionally loves me, wants to adopt me as Your very own child, and make me a joint-heir with Jesus to all the riches of Your heavenly kingdom?"..."I AM."

"Are You the God who will always love me, even when it seems that no one else does?" ..."I AM."

Oh, dear friends, why do we so foolishly flail and flounder about assessing our options in life, and then so unwisely attempt to build the foundation of our life on the constantly shifting sand of uncertainty? I have never seen life so unfounded and insecure as it seems to be today.

In the storms of life brought on by uncontrollable disease, economic insecurity, and social uncertainty, are you searching for an anchor for your life and soul which you can hold to until the fear of this dark night gives way to the light of a better tomorrow? If so, would you pause with me for a moment, and in an attitude of prayer, submission, and trust, quietly repeat these words of refrain to a wonderful old gospel hymn?

> "Hold to God's unchanging hand,
> Hold to God's unchanging hand,
> Build your hopes on things eternal,
> Hold to God's unchanging hand."

He is the great "I AM," and He is worthy of our worship and praise.

The Power to Change

One of my favorite New Testament books is Philemon. It is only a brief personal note from Paul to Philemon; it contains no great doctrinal truths; and there really isn't any reason for it to be included in the canon of divinely inspired writings, except for one thing—the profound change it produced. The biblical meaning of Philemon lies not so much in its content, but rather in its subsequent consequence.

Onesimus was a slave who had apparently stolen something from his owner, Philemon. He escaped and came to Paul for help and protection. Rather than aiding in his escape, Paul did something radically different. Earlier, Paul had led Philemon to accept Christ, and he did the same for Onesimus.

Now, Philemon and Onesimus were on a different footing and in a different relationship. They were no longer owner and slave, but now both were Christians, and that changed everything. In his brief note, Paul asked Philemon to accept Onesimus back as a "beloved brother."

Paul's note became viewed as divinely inspired scripture because of what happened next. Since Onesimus was now his brother in Christ, Philemon abandoned all his former feelings toward his slave, accepted him within the bond of Christian love, and encouraged him to grow in his Christian understanding and in his service to Christ.

Does the Book of Philemon detail all this? No, but there is evidence of what happened in other sources. In Paul's letter to the church at Colossae, he refers to Onesimus as "a faithful and beloved brother." Onesimus is later identified by Ignatius of Antioch, an early church father, as bishop of the church at Ephesus. Because of Paul's short letter to Philemon, Onesimus went from being a slave to becoming a Christian brother, and then faithfully serving Christ as bishop of a growing and vital church.

That's why the "Book of Philemon" is in the New Testament. Christian love has the power to change people. If it can transform a slave and his owner into Christian brothers and make them fellow servants of Jesus, it can change anyone, including you and me.

Mississippi is going through a lot of change, and some people's feelings and emotions are on edge. But, in recognition of the power of Christian love to change us, let's ask ourselves a simple "what if" question: If the Apostle Paul could write a brief note this morning to all Christians in Mississippi urging us to put aside our differences and accept each other as beloved brothers and sisters in Christ, would our response cause his note to us to become part of the Bible, if it were still being written?

At Peace in the Good Shepherd's Arms

I gently knocked on the door and quietly entered her room, having been told by the nurse what to expect. Although I was the hospital's staff attorney, on certain occasions I was asked to meet with a patient as a minister if the hospital chaplain were not available or the patient's pastor could not be contacted, and this was one of those moments. She was an elderly, frail, black lady in her final hours of life. She constantly moved around on her bed in obvious discomfort, mumbled incoherently, and seemed unaware of her surroundings. But she had asked for a minister, and I now stood by her bedside.

I had no idea what to say, and I did not know if she could even hear or understand me. I stood there for a moment looking at this helpless woman, sensing her pain and her fear. Suddenly, as if by divine inspiration, I leaned over and touched her forehead and began gently stroking her brow. Her weary eyes slowly focused on my face.

"Do you have a good imagination?" I softly asked. She looked at me, uncertain about my question, and slowly nodded her head. "Good," I said, "because I want to tell you a story from the Bible, and I want you to imagine that this is happening to you right now." She slightly nodded her head in agreement.

Imagine that you are a little lamb, and you are alone, frightened, and do not know what will happen to you. But off in the distance you see someone, and He is coming toward you. You look closer, and you realize that it is your Shepherd—the one you have been following—and He is a Good Shepherd, and He cares for you. He has left all His other sheep just to look for you and bring you home.

I have no idea what she saw in her imagination, but I remember the intense look on her face and the firm tone of her voice. "I see Him," she slowly mumbled. "I sure do…I see Him." As I continued to stroke her brow, she stopped moving around in the bed and seemed to relax and breathe easier.

He sees you now, and He is here with you. He is bending down and picking you up in His arms to take you with Him. Her eyes became fixed and focused, as if looking past me at something distant, and she exclaimed, "I feel His arms. I surely do. He is holding me tight and safe."

Your Shepherd is Jesus, I continued, and He is taking you to a green pasture beside still water, and He is going to personally make

261

sure you are safe and cared for. You have no reason to fear. Your Good Shepherd is holding you.

With supreme serenity, she said, "I see Him, I feel Him with me, holding me in His arms, and I'm not afraid." She lay there motionless, eyes closed, and quietly went to sleep. About four hours later, she died peacefully.

Without knowing what I was doing, the Holy Spirit used me to provide this dear lady with a priceless gift of peace in the final moments of her life. Pain and fear take no consideration of skin color, and neither does the grace and peace of God. In many ways, I was deeply moved spiritually standing beside this elderly black lady's bed, holding her hand, gently rubbing her brow, and praying for her. I experienced a peace maybe even greater than she did.

I attended seminary for three years and listened to many theology professors, many of whom I have forgotten, but God used this suffering saint for a few precious moments to teach me a lesson about ministry that has remained with me for years. A minister is a bridge builder—a go-between—who is called by God and empowered by the Holy Spirit to be an intermediary between God and his fellow man. The life of a minister is devoted to the high and holy purpose of personally bringing God to the people and bringing the people to God, even if one at a time, so that there is a holy meeting that brings to hurting man a sense of divine peace, a peace that the world cannot provide. Through the priesthood of every believer, we are all called to build bridges of faith between man and God. We are all called to be "peacemakers."

Anyone with a divine sense of purpose about being a peacemaker does not look at skin color, age, ethnic background, whether one is rich or poor, or powerful or a pauper. He simply holds to the hand of God with one hand and holds to the hand of a hurting individual with the other and becomes a living bridge through which the love and peace of God passes from heaven to earth.

A peacemaker does not condemn one's past, but offers only the forgiveness of Christ, the promise of a home in heaven, and the assurance of eternal life. He helps blot out the painful vision and memories of earth and opens the eyes of the frail to a new vision of a loving Shepherd. He helps a hurting soul look beyond the fears and frustrations of the present and helps them set their eyes on the things which are above. A peacemaker helps the weak to no longer depend on the waning strength of human frailty, but instead to be safely carried in the strong arms of a loving Shepherd.

A devoted peacemaker is color-blind. A peacemaker faithfully stands in the midst of people of every race, creed, and color, and while holding to the hand of God, extends a compassionate hand of divine help and redeeming love to all he can touch. He is a servant of all, and he takes no thought of either standing beside the bed of an old dying black lady or reaching out to a defiant sinner. A peacemaker does not see skin color. He only sees a soul in need of a Savior; he only sees one scared lamb looking for its Good Shepherd.

That frail lady may not have accomplished much in her life, but just before she died, God used her to minister to me in ways that I have never forgotten. Her ministry to me was as meaningful as was my ministry to her. We both became peacemakers.

Jesus said, "Blessed are the peacemakers, for they shall be called sons of God." There can be no higher spiritual attainment in one's Christian life than knowing that Jesus considers you to be a "son of God." We become peacemakers not by building walls of separation between us and hurling verbal diatribes of racial bitterness, but rather by building bridges of mutual understanding and acceptance. The bridge of divine love and peace is not painted a specific color.

Her journey on this earth is over, but mine isn't. There will be other entries in my journal of life as I continue to spiritually grow as a Christian, but none will be more meaningful than the day an old dying black lady taught me the meaning of being a "peacemaker."

His Answers Will Surprise You

By all accounts, John the Baptist was a unique person and a central figure in the birth of Christianity. Although a cousin of Jesus, the true relationship between John and Jesus is not clearly known. John's main characteristics were the power of his preaching and his demand for repentance, which touched a wide spectrum of people, and his courage to denounce sin, even among those at the highest level of government and power.

That trait got him into trouble and brought about his death. John had denounced the illicit marriage of King Herod to his sister-in-law, and he found himself in prison waiting to be executed. Filled with uncertainty and fear, John sent two messengers to Jesus with a deeply personal question, "Are You the Coming One, or do we look for another?"

"Coming One" was a Jewish messianic title designating the long-awaited messiah who would usher in the Golden Age of Judaism. Notably, the messiah would use his great power to rid Israel of hated Roman domination.

Consider what John really asked Jesus: "If you are the Messiah, are you going to save me or let me be killed? When are you going to rise up in power and transform this land? Are you really the messiah we've been waiting for, or is there another yet to come?"

Jesus' answer, brought back by the messengers, must have totally surprised John the Baptist: "The blind receive their sight and the lame walk; the lepers are cleansed and the deaf hear; the dead are raised up and the poor have the gospel preached to them" (Matt. 11:5).

It was as if Jesus reassured John that his life and ministry had not been in vain. Jesus was indeed the Messiah of Israel, and He had brought new meaning to an ancient religion. Mercy and compassion had become more important than blind obedience to cold, impersonal religious law. There was now a new redeeming love for others, who had been shunned and condemned, that had never been known in Israel.

This new spiritual fulfillment of the ancient religious law would become Christianity, and it would change the world. John the Baptist's consolation was knowing that he was the first person to say, "Repent, for the kingdom of heaven is at hand." It was the fulfillment of a divine truth worth dying for. It may have taken John a few minutes to spiritually digest Jesus' answer, but it would have changed his understanding of his situation and his sacrifice.

After decades as an ordained minister, I'm still surprised by Jesus' answers to my questions. That's part of our spiritual growth process. I'm still striving to love my enemies, to have a deeper understanding of who is my neighbor, and to be more merciful to all so that I can better understand God's mercy shown to me. I'm still learning how to forgive seventy times seven, and I try hard not to judgmentally condemn the speck of sin in someone else's eye when I have a plank of sin in my own eye.

I've preached the gospel to thousands, written two books, and shared these devotionals with unknown numbers of people, and I'm still constantly surprised by Jesus' answers. It's a new experience each time I study His life and read His words, and it will always be that way. I'll never reach the end, nor fully know the depth, of the truth of His answers.

If you, too, are surprised by Jesus' answers to your questions, rejoice, for it means you are growing in your faith. The real challenge is accepting His answers rather than your own. His ways are not our ways, and most often His answers are surprisingly different from our own. But that's one of the spiritual joys of our Christian faith. It is the never-ending process of giving new meaning to an old religion within the circumstances of our own life by following His word.

The more we are surprised by His answers and the more we live by those answers, the more the world is made a little better by the life we live. It's called being a disciple of Jesus, and it's a spiritual experience worth living and dying for.

May God richly bless each of you through Jesus' surprising answers to your deepest questions about life.

A Love of Poetry

Oh, the beauty of these words that flow in my head,
whether sitting at my desk or lying in bed.
The rhyme of poetry, or a verse of prose,
     can waft through my senses like the scent of a rose.
It's been that way since I was a lad,
and poetry has been a passion that I've always had.
Poetry is a gift, not given to all,
     that tugs at my heart like a life-mission call.
It flows from within—impossible to rehearse—
that binds my thoughts to meter and verse.
Poetry is a word stream in my heart, mind, and soul
     that harkens me back to writers of old.
Even the Bible, God's Holy Word,
has the most beautiful poetry that I've ever heard.
King Solomon wrote songs about divine passion and love,
     and the Psalmist used poetry to talk to God up above.
King David was a warrior
with shields and swords,
but his greatest power
     was in the poetry of his words.
Poetry infuses my writing with a smooth, rhythmic flow
and gives me gentle words that set it aglow.
The cadence of words, and their beauty and grace,
     is a method of thought that I totally embrace.
I read Shakespeare's sonnets, all tidy and neat,
that gave me poetic memories I often repeat.
Browning inspired me to count the many ways I can love,
     her words falling like droplets of wisdom from a storehouse
     above.
Did Thoreau's "Mist" rise from Walden's little pond,
or did it drift in slowly from wooded vistas beyond?
I've sat under the sprawling branches of an old chestnut tree,
     as Longfellow taught me more truth than I readily could see.
I floated the Mississippi in both sunshine and rain,
and pondered its muddy depths through the humor of Mark Twain.
Oh, and Annabel Lee—how the heavenly seraphs took her away—
     still tugs at my heart strings to this very day.

I could hear the patriot shouts, chilling and clear,
as I rode away from Boston with a man named Revere.
And on a dark, stormy night behind a locked door,
        I shivered as the raven screeched its haunting "nevermore."
I've thought of "Maud Muller" time and again,
and the loss of life's good things that simply "might have been."
So, when I need relief from life's troublesome load,
        I open my Book of Poems and travel that road.
I've trudged with Robert Service through a blizzard on Dawson Trail,
and he held my rapt attention as he spun his wintry tale.
And through my "frozen lashes" I clearly could see,
        the strange, fiery cremation of old shivering Sam McGee.
And with his other great poem, that I can quote with sheer delight,
Service took me to a crowded barroom on a cold winter night.
I listened to a miner, loaded with gold fresh from the creeks,
        play a haunting piano tune that put tears on my cheeks.
I watched a smoky gunfight,
that I'll not forget too soon,
in a sordid and dingy kind of place
        called the Malamute Saloon.
The brawl involved the miner,
whose name nobody knew,
and the man he called a "hound of hell"
        by the name of Dan McGrew.
The poetic plot has more characters,
though only a curious few,
but my favorite of them was his "light-o'-love,"
        that lady known as Lou.
I could go on for line after line,
sharing these thoughts about rhythm and rhyme.
So let me close with this one final thought,
        if my opinion about poetry you really have sought.
If I have one writing inspiration
that I can't possibly ignore,
it's my love of poetry,
        and not a single thing more.
But, now, I'm just a gray-headed old man,
with not a lot left that I can do,
except tell you of my love for poetry
        in this spring of '22.

www.ingramcontent.com/pod-product-compliance
Lightning Source LLC
Chambersburg PA
CBHW070915120626
46546CB00001B/270